PENGUIN BOOKS

#HAPPY X COOL

Rudolf Beger (75) is a former executive in the oil, chemical, automotive, financial services, and real estate industries, and a former chairman of trendsetting conferences at Management Centre Europe (Brussels) and Zentrum für Unternehmensführung (Zurich) and a speaker at industry conferences (Financial Times, UK Celebrity Speakers, pp). Rudolf wrote standard-setting books on corporate communication (in German, *Gabler Verlag*, 1989), and in English, *Present-Day Corporate Communication*, www.springer.com, 2018); he is also the author of a romantic novel entitled *Dreisam*, published by Fouquet's Literatur-Verlag (out of business), 2003 (currently translated into English for publication). In 2021, Rudolf will complete a highly topical 450-page political thriller entitled *The Lobbyist* on the automotive industry (for publication). Rudolf wrote numerous articles, papers and White Papers on EU industrial policy, and was a writer for German antique magazines. His artistic works were shown in around 40 solo and group exhibitions all over the world. In 2011, he won the first prize for his artistic work by the Monaco State Ministry/UNESCO.

Saraphun (Sara) Wongngernyuang (31), a Thai national, is an enthusiastic lifelong learner about happiness. She has had experience in the practice of Buddhism and Christianity since her youth and continues to learn about the philosophy of happiness. She has been studying and training on happiness at Happy Science for more than seven years. In 2019, she translated the self-help books *Tips for Happiness* and *The Laws of Steel* by Japanese author Ryuho Okawa, IRH Press Publishing, from English to Thai. Sara works in the field of government, community development and culture. She published an academic research paper on the preservation of Western (Portuguese) culture in Thailand entitled *The Virgin Mary in the Encounter of Cultures: Preserving Transcultural Heritage in the Immaculate Conception Community, Bangkok* published in a book entitled *Preserving Transcultural Heritage: Your Way or My Way*, Caleidoscópio, University of Lisbon, Portugal (2018).

#HAPPYxCOOL

HAPPINESS IN RELATIONSHIPS AND AT WORK

RUDOLF BEGER,
SARA WONG

PENGUIN BOOKS
An imprint of Penguin Random House

PENGUIN BOOKS

USA | Canada | UK | Ireland | Australia
New Zealand | India | South Africa | China | Southeast Asia

Penguin Books is part of the Penguin Random House group of companies whose addresses can be found at global.penguinrandomhouse.com

Published by Penguin Random House SEA Pte Ltd
9, Changi South Street 3, Level 08-01,
Singapore 486361

Penguin Random House SEA

First published in Penguin Books by Penguin Random House SEA 2021

10 9 8 7 6 5 4 3 2 1

The views and opinions expressed in this book are the authors' own and the facts are as reported by them which have been verified to the extent possible, and the publishers are not in any way liable for the same.

ISBN 9789814914956

Typeset in Adobe Garamond Pro by Manipal Technologies Limited, Manipal

www.penguin.sg

Millions of people never analyse themselves. Mentally, they are mechanical products of the factory of their environment, preoccupied with breakfast, lunch, and dinner, working and sleeping, and going here and there to be entertained. They don't know what or why they are seeking, nor why they never realize complete happiness and lasting satisfaction. By evading self-analysis, people go on being robots, conditioned by their environment. True self-analysis is the greatest art of progress.

—Paramahansa Yogananda, Indian guru

Contents

1

IN SEARCH OF HAPPINESS

FACTORS INFLUENCING HAPPINESS

BEING HAPPY IS 'COOL'

Happiness is not an old-fashioned, dusty, romantic concept. On the contrary, we argue in this book that by fully recognizing the zeitgeist, or spirit of the time, being cool and freeing your mind are prerequisites to happiness.

Happiness is when you are at peace with yourself and feel that you have arrived where you want to be. Being cool—meaning being yourself without getting conditioned by events and your environment—is an important element for achieving this state of mind.

> The individual has always had to struggle to keep from being overwhelmed by the tribe. If you try it, you will be lonely often, and sometimes frightened. But no price is too high to pay for the privilege of owning yourself.
>
> —Friedrich Nietzsche, 19th-century German philosopher

In fact, we will go one step further to claim, 'Being happy is cool!' Because when you are cool or feel happy, you feel good in your own skin.

Happiness and coolness are both the result of honest self-analysis and the behaviour that results from it. Neither can be bought. They are not commodities available for purchase on supermarket shelves.

This is in contrast to our daily experience in a world that is filled with a relentless onslaught of auspicious advertising, which makes everything seem attainable. It is as if one can buy almost anything! But since happiness cannot be bought, longing for happiness can become a cause for anxiety for an individual. This undesirable consequence is often fostered by factors arising from social compulsions.

HAPPINESS: A SOCIAL OBLIGATION?

Telling an unhappy person to be happy is like telling a short person to be tall.

—Unknown

In 2012, the United Nations General Assembly declared 20 March as International Day of Happiness, recognizing 'the relevance of happiness and well-being as universal goals and aspirations in the lives of human beings around the world'.

This emphasis on happiness as a desirable goal has led to a sort of politicization of happiness with the consequence that society is no longer asking for happiness but instead demanding for it as must-have in life.

This has led to a situation in which success, achievement and happiness are 'necessary' conditions of human life. For many people, it has reached a point where it is no longer a desired objective; instead, it has developed into a social obligation.

In this straitjacket model of 'a social obligation to be happy', failure is not an option. You cannot fail because you must not fail. You are doomed to succeed because it's in your own interest, and it is expected of you to not fail.

> You don't just want to be happy, you want to be happier than the others. This is so difficult because we think the others are happier than they are.
>
> —Charles-Louis de Montesquieu, French author and philosopher

The effort to be happy or, at least, to appear happy, has taken on almost compulsive manic traits. Some critical researchers even state that the notion of happiness has become an obsession—a preoccupation that will not bring you happiness. In their view, the notion of happiness has become a term that is misused for commercial, social, and other purposes with the intention to instrumentalize the consumers.

Telling someone that you're unhappy can frequently provoke unexpected and unpleasant reactions from others. This is particularly the case when your admission is perceived as not being socially acceptable because the society in which you live expects you to be happy.

If you really have the courage to show that you're unhappy, it will most probably be perceived by others as an undesirable confession and 'uncool'. You will promptly be made to feel like someone suffering from a mysterious infectious disease, or find yourself marginalized by society. And even if unjustified, you will somehow also be made to feel guilty.

Example: A married couple with a large group of friends enjoyed being the social hotspot of their city. Their many friends regularly accepted their dinner and party invitations with pleasure. The situation changed abruptly when, after many happy years, the marriage was torn apart by the wife's tragic accidental death. However, the reaction of some of the couple's friends to her death could not have been more different. A small group of friends took care of Bryant, the grieving husband, with the sole desire to help him in his most difficult hours. They came to Bryant's house and cooked for him, invited him to their houses, and let him participate in their social activities. However, the majority of Bryant's friends turned away from him because, in their view, he didn't seem to be 'fun' anymore. The fact that Bryant was unhappy didn't fit into their standard image of an exuberant, carefree social life. Bryant suffered from this situation which added to his unhappiness.

NO 'RIGHT' WAY TO HAPPINESS

In response to this imposed societal obligation to be happy, new-age knowledge and lifestyle gurus have emerged to teach you how to be happy. But there are neither easy formulas nor universal recipes that guarantee a sustainable state of happiness.

On the contrary, the ambiguity and vagueness of the notion of happiness means that it is almost impossible to provide effective advice on happiness. In fact, there is no one right way to attain happiness.

This is one of the reasons why authors don't discuss in detail the many existing scientific theories, studies, statistics, philosophies, psychological analyses, or all-promising esoteric and meditative concepts surrounding the idea of happiness. These psychologically overburdened paths to happiness are not part of the authors' messages.

> In meetings philosophy might work, on the field practicality works.
>
> —Amit Kalantri, contemporary Indian author

However, we prefer to argue pragmatically and offer down-to-earth solutions that will not get lost in abstract discussions, and instead, stay close to everyday reality. We will also provide real-life examples to substantiate our arguments.

Part of this reality is to understand that in life you cannot blindly rely on preconceived opinions and thought patterns in the pursuit of your own happiness. Instead, you will be more successful if you dare to find your own independent, individual path.

> Being happy is a very personal thing and it really has nothing to do with anyone else.
>
> —Unknown

Example: A prominent case in point of the connection between pragmatism and happiness is the self-conception of the US, expressed in its 'Declaration of Independence'.

THE RIGHT TO BE HAPPY

The 'Declaration of Independence' starts with the right of the individual to seek happiness. Its idea went beyond the then prevailing European legacy of 'elite by birth', such as monarchy and nobility, which were pre-structuring society. The new US concept was associated with a 'practical' kind of happiness. It promised freedom in all spheres of life—neither influenced by socialist or monarchist parties, nor by religions or the church. In the US, none of these institutions had a chance of limiting individual freedom or seizing power.

This openness towards an individual's inalienable rights, such as the right to life, liberty, and the pursuit of happiness was based on pure pragmatism, as it did not refer to the rights created by authorities. Instead, it was a reference to the existence of 'natural' moral rights—that is, not coming from the state—under which all individuals could do whatever they deemed fit to fulfil their destiny. These rights, therefore, belonged to the individual as human beings and were considered necessary for living a life of dignity and the development of their personality.

HAPPINESS IS YOUR RESPONSIBILITY

Following the guidance provided by the 'Declaration of Independence', we will focus on what we believe is the best way to approach to your individual pursuit of happiness. Taking into account the fact that it is up to you to determine your own destiny, we will provide tips and tricks that are realistic and achievable. These suggestions should help you reach closer to your goal.

> Action may not always bring happiness, but there is no happiness without action.
>
> —William James,
> 19th-century American philosopher and psychologist

Pragmatism means that you—the one who is seeking happiness—should be interested in those factors which impact your state of happiness and that you are able to influence.

Obviously, to be successful in your pursuit, you must be really serious about becoming happier. There must be a corresponding will, determination, and complete engagement from your side. A half-hearted approach will most likely fail.

> A person who does nothing will enjoy no happiness.
>
> —M. Vatsyayana, *Kama Sutra*

If you just wait for happiness to fall from the sky, you may be disappointed. Your chances of personal happiness will increase when you make serious attempts to seize it yourself.

It's you and what you do, that, for the most part, leads to the conditions for your personal happiness.

People who are happy will usually not compare themselves to, nor seek confirmation from, others. Apart from seeing other people and their behaviour as stimulation or incentive, they know that all people are different and, therefore, any comparison is misleading. You can't be happy if you are dependent on the recognition and attention of others. You will only risk losing control and alienating yourself. You will end up in a dead-end street. Happy people are their own best friends—not enemy. They don't need validation from others.

Unhappy persons, on the other hand, will radiate sadness, negativism and pessimism, and a general lack of joy of life. This is because they tend to blame others or external circumstances for their situation, cling to something (in the past) that they cannot change, surrender to a victim role, and surround themselves with other negative-minded people.

Since you are responsible for your personal happiness, it is best to avoid unhappy people because their bitterness is infectious. They will only steal your positive energy. Instead, keep yourself future-oriented and let go of negativity. Although it's not in your power to influence others or external circumstances, know that you can adapt yourself to changed situations—accept them or find a way of life that doesn't affect your personal happiness. However, acceptance does not mean that you have to accept a victim role, or hand over the reins of your life to others. Instead, you can try to take your fate into your own hands and find the strength to influence and change what happens to you.

HAPPINESS: FEELING OR EMOTION?

If you ask people whether they are happy, their response will most likely reflect their current basic mood. The concept of basic mood can be understood as a bouquet of emotions and feelings that can be influenced to a greater or lesser extent: Influencing emotions is less easy than influencing feelings.

Though strongly related, the words 'feeling' and 'emotion' do not mean the same thing. In fact, they are quite distinct. Part of the difference between emotions and feelings can best be explained by comparing them with two sides of the same coin. One side is emotion, while the other is feeling. And, just as it is with coins, what you notice will depend upon which side of the coin you are looking at.

Emotions are common to us all while feelings reflect only your personal associations to emotions.

It is important to understand that emotions can overwhelm you unwillingly. They are a physical reaction to an external stimulus that comes from your perception of a certain situation—for instance, fear, joy, grief, sadness, shame, disgust, trust, surprise, pride, embarrassment, and anger. They have an effect on your behaviour and influence the choices you make, the actions you take and, and more generally, how you live and interact with others. Unlike feelings, however, emotions cannot be influenced or suppressed easily.

Now, let us look at the other side of the coin—feeling, which is a mental response to your emotions. Anger, for instance, can be a particularly powerful emotion. The feelings developed in response to the stimulus 'anger' can be frustration, agitation, hostility, and, more generally, antagonism towards other people.

Example: You gave a personal loan to a supposedly good friend whom you are close to for more than ten years. You have shared many experiences, enjoyed each other's company and fully trusted one another. When the money was due for repayment, you were taken aback. Unexpectedly, your good friend turned out to be a bad friend as he refused to repay the loan. He knew that you had failed to declare the money to the tax authorities and speculated that this would prevent you from taking legal action. You were disappointed not only by this behaviour, but more so by the fact that you had been so wrong in judging your friend. Furthermore, you felt blackmailed by him, which created a feeling of powerlessness that made you furious.

When you experience a feeling for the first time, you may act like an uninvolved outsider. You look at yourself from the outside as if you were not affected. You may even be surprised by your own behaviour. But with growing experience, when your feelings are 'stored' in your memory, you have the opportunity to choose your responses to your feelings at will.

Example: A new-born baby that is spanked responds instinctively by crying. This is a knee-jerk reflex that it has not learnt from anyone. This will continue until the infant has developed a memory of crying. Only then will it be capable of choosing to cry in response to certain situations. This may also involve the baby using its crying tactically, i.e. to induce a certain behaviour of its parents.

This example demonstrates that your free will is not an illusion. On the contrary, once you have achieved a certain level of maturity, you have an option to choose your response to a given situation and change your psychological state of mind by using your free will.

Some people seem naturally happy and do not need to consciously choose to be happy. However, more and more people are unable to maintain their 'inner balance' and subsequently finding inner peace and serenity. Such people are suffering from inner imbalance and disharmonies, which can lead to fears, evasive behaviour, and unhappiness. This can happen especially when the demands of daily life and social pressures become so important that people no longer strive for a balance between several (competing) areas of life, but instead focus on selected areas, for instance just to be modern and to keep up.

Example: It is not conducive to always just rest and enjoy the day. On the other hand, it is also not conducive to work to the bone every day for a long time until you're physically and mentally exhausted. Many people only start looking after their health when it is too late. Some notice only too late that they have no friends left, perhaps, because they paid too little attention to this important area of social life. Others may find that their families have broken because for a long time they concentrated only on their jobs or intensive leisure activities rather than finding happiness in the family.

> It is not difficult to find people who are ten times as rich at the age of sixty as they were at twenty. But not one of them claims to be ten times as happy.
>
> —George Bernard Shaw, Irish playwright, critic, polemicist, and political activist

The reason for this increasing imbalance, both in postmodern Western societies and mixed, traditional, modern, and postmodern Asian and African societies can also be found in their development into increasingly digitalized, materialistic, short-term, and consumption-oriented societies. People around the globe are struggling to make sense of a world that is characterized by the most rapid changes known to history as evidenced by trends such as artificial intelligence, globalization, genomics, global governance, and virtualization. For many people, the line between adapting and falling off by viewing the world as 'a world of madness' is a very fine one.

The new abundance of electronic advertising possibilities through social media and the online space allows companies to place products in the market more effectively. These mediums allow them to create demand for experiences for which there is no natural demand. Advertising helps companies to not only showcase their products and provide information, but also allows them to sell an attitude to life. But to do this successfully, it must address the innermost wishes and desires of their potential customers—for example, the need for love, the hope for health, and, above all, the desire for happiness. To sell products better, it focuses in particular on people's desire to be happy and gives a promise of happiness. 'Buy yourself happiness' is a phrase only too commonly heard nowadays.

Example: You no longer just buy a tub of yoghurt but an 'oasis of wellness and health'. You no longer just buy a pair of shoes, you buy a 'ticket to a better life' by being popular and respected—*If you wear this or that sneaker, you belong. All you have to do is buy the latest model and you can become a part of the in-group that is admired and respected by everyone.* You no longer buy an ordinary car, but an 'adventure where you can feel the freedom of the wild prairies every day', even in your small town. You don't just buy a steak but an 'original father's day gift'! And who buys a skin cream these days? You buy an 'elixir for eternal youthfulness' formulated after 'years of DNA research' and made with 'silk proteins' and 'diamond dust' that promises 'eternal beauty and youth'.

But neither yoghurt, sneakers, skin cream nor a car or steak can really make people happier. It is rather a danger that those who cannot afford to buy the advertised product will develop feelings of 'not belonging' and become unhappy because of it. As a result, they may adopt a more pessimistic attitude to life, which, in turn, will fuel unhappiness and other negative states of mind.

To escape this trap, it would be helpful if you become more aware of your fundamental right to self-determination and your individual ability to decide what is important and right for you. This follows from the idea that who you are and what you do is crucial for your happiness.

The contents of what you receive as advertising messages are stored independently of your will. But you should not overlook that it is you who has the freedom to choose what information you want to focus on and what you want to reject.

Tip: It's entirely up to you whether you view the world as positive, negative, or absurd. But your state and level of happiness requires a choice. You may find it easier to make such a choice when you think and act in terms of *as if*—that means putting yourself in a position where the constraints preventing you from being happy would not exist.

You act, for instance, 'as if' what you are doing is connected to a fixed goal and only achievable in the way you do it; or you act 'as if' you have completely liberated yourself from all barriers that negatively influence your thoughts and actions, even though in reality, your thoughts and feelings seem to be 'walled in alive'.

Tip: If you have the desire to simply dissolve the heavy, burdensome rock in your mind that symbolizes your mental imprisonment, then use your imagination. Close your eyes and imagine how the petrified feelings and thoughts represented by the rock dissolve and crumble into soft sand. Now, replace the image of the disintegrating rock with your feelings and thoughts. Imagine them crumbling and disintegrating into sand and dust. If, in your imagination, you can connect the image of the disintegrating rock with your feelings and thoughts, then these will also disintegrate into sand and dust. The more you visualize this scene, the easier will the rock crumble, and you will be able to free yourself from the negative feelings it holds.

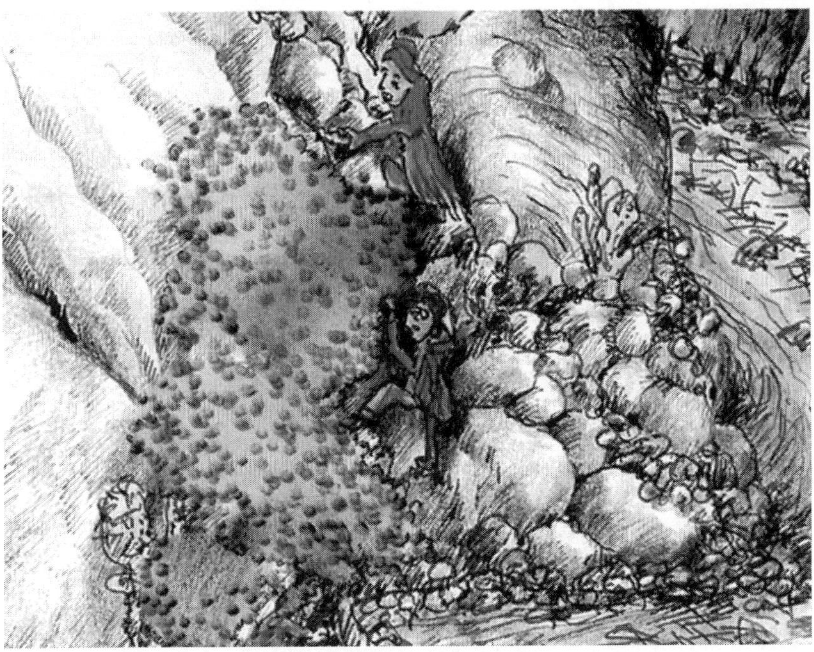

With repeated practice of this exercise, you will gradually develop the ability to exercise control over your mind, and you will be able to choose your response to external stimulants. This will empower you because you will be able to better direct your consciousness.

This will have implications for your state of happiness. Once you decide to become an active player by influencing and shaping the course of your life, you will realize that you should not preoccupy yourself with depressing thoughts, silent suffering, or incessant complaints. On the contrary, you should do what you can to re-adjust and embrace a positive mindset instead.

Example: After initial pride in his new position as an officer, a bright young man named Sergio felt increasingly unhappy. Despite being a zealous worker, Sergio was increasingly demotivated because of a lack of intellectually stimulating work. When looking for possible improvements, Sergio considered many options: resignation, rebellion, submission, and (passive) resistance. In the end, Sergio realized that, instead of lamenting, he should take the initiative and help himself become happy again. Among other self-liberating moves, Sergio made it a habit to write down brief notes every morning on his plans for the day. These notes were his own free-flowing thoughts and daily personal aspirations like learning how to better articulate his thoughts during a company presentation, building up the confidence to speak up more during team meetings, and so on. Sergio's notes were helpful as they served as a set of self-guiding principles for better managing his job. In addition, they helped Sergio to be more pragmatic and realistic. Furthermore, the notes made it easier for Sergio to better focus on what he really wanted to do, rather than surrendering to the expectations of his colleagues. Sergio's growing 'inner freedom' brought him happiness rather than the frustration he had felt before.

HAVING PLEASURE, FEELING GOOD, BEING WELL

At this point, it is important to note that you should not equate feeling good, being well, or experiencing pleasures with a state of happiness. Things that momentarily might make you feel good or enhance your well-being may not necessarily be the same things that make your whole life feel worth living.

Example: It is argued that in today's working and consumer-driven life, people are increasingly losing their roots, their natural life rhythms, and their meaningful value systems. In order to make them less driven by external factors, these so-called feel-good and wellness programmes are offered. They are not only intended to distract people from the stresses of their daily lives, but also to make them happier. What this strategy, however, seems to overlook is that the chance for increased personal happiness cannot be brought about by momentary physical well-being alone but can be achieved only through long-term mental reorientation of an individual. Wellness neither changes the basic situation nor the reason for stress and unhappiness, but only displaces them for a moment.

The same applies to pleasure. When you look around, most people are searching for pleasure. Sometimes, people even mistakenly believe that the pleasures they are experiencing are the same thing as happiness.

Example: Two extreme examples are party drugs and alcohol consumption. Drugs and alcohol provide short-term feelings of happiness which quickly go wrong after the effects of these substances fade away. They deceive the brain. Again, nothing changes the situation. Bad feelings are only suppressed for a short time. Another example is luxury. Admittedly it is exciting to buy a new car, a handbag, a smartphone, or a pair of shoes one after the other. But does it really make you happy? After the purchase, the current feeling of happiness diminishes quickly and the desire for a new search for happiness sets in again. Short-term happiness achieved through consumption must be contrasted with longer-lasting feelings of happiness that cannot be bought with money, such as health, family and friends, experiences, and memories that often bring a smile to our faces years later.

There is nothing wrong with people seeking pleasure but, as illustrated in the previous examples, it should never be confused with happiness. As mentioned, happiness is more than just temporary pleasure or a fleeting moment of contentment. While pleasure may be a by-product of happiness, it does not necessarily cause it. Pleasure is just a feeling of temporary satisfaction and enjoyment.

Therefore, to be truly happy, mere pleasure is not sufficient. Some additional emotional elements such as relationships, accomplishments, meaningfulness, commitments, and engagements are also important. All these add up to lead you to a state of true happiness.

Example: Gambling can be fun and grant momentary happiness. Most people who gamble for money do it for the thrill and pleasure of it. But the satisfaction they get from gambling is always temporary and has nothing to do with lasting happiness. This is especially the case when gambling ceases to be a pleasant distraction and becomes obsessive. In this case, the fleeting satisfaction gives way to addiction. Like other forms of addiction, gambling for money is a lonely and isolating experience that can prevent people from finding their true happiness, which lies in long-term engagements such as relationships and meaningful activities.

All examples provided thus far demonstrate that if you really want to maximize your 'feel-good' and 'well-being' status, then you need more than just positive emotions, feelings, and pleasure.

Studies have shown that people who unilaterally focus on superficial or materialistic pleasures, such as eating and drinking or unrestrained shopping are less happy in the long term.

Example: A lady gourmand who loved and enjoyed food above all else could not sufficiently control her appetite. Eating for her was a pleasure she wouldn't have liked to miss. But in the end, she overindulged in food and drinks and her health was so jeopardized that she had to undergo complicated surgeries. The doctor was worried about her long-term health so forbid her from continuing with her current lifestyle and prescribed an unpleasant diet. As a result, her zest for life was gone, and she felt she could never be happy again.

Unlike true happiness, pleasure is relatively easy to achieve. This is made clear by the fact that you'll find pleasure at the core of most marketing, advertising, and sales promotion activities.

Social media can also play an increasingly negative stimulating role. Their focus on fun, entertainment, and other hedonistic pursuits can influence the social and self-image of the users, notably when they are intensive users. This can lead them to perceive short-term pleasure as more important than the longer-lasting feeling of happiness. This becomes clear through the constant bombardment of 'stories' on Facebook and other social media applications. These features enable people to treat these platforms as a space for 'digital catwalk', where they can let others know just how amazing their lives are.

> Comparison is the root of all unhappiness.
>
> —David Andrew Wiebe, American author

Under this permanent onslaught of new posts, pictures, and messages, it's almost impossible to stop yourself from comparing your life with that of others. Often times, such a comparison is unwarranted but happens automatically and unconsciously. And in many cases, you might come to the conclusion that your life is much more boring than others. Eventually, you might even ask yourself whether you are doing something wrong in your life and may be faced with the decision to either join in common social media activities and catch up with your social media friends or remaining unhappily alone. However, this might be a wrong presumption because in most cases what you see on social media is a false picture or portrayal of the lives of other users. The person you are 'following' may seem happy (and it is possible that they are) but don't forget that you might just be privy to those aspects of their lives that they want you to see—the part that is travelling, posing, socializing, eating, drinking, and partaking in various other entertaining activities.

But unlike what is portrayed by social media, true happiness is much more than just fun activities, self-love, and ego-shows. Happiness is an inner state of mind that cannot necessarily be conveyed by this kind of autobiographical, diary-like string of photos and self-mirroring. The latter is an imperfect picture of a person that tends to be superficial and is more akin to an ego-show.

Example: You are looking for an attractive partner on Tinder. One day, you swipe the photo of a person you feel you are attracted to. Your excitement is solely based on the individual's outer appearance, and you may overlook certain things in the attached self-description that would normally make you sceptical. When you finally meet the person face-to-face, you realize that the electrifying photograph does not correspond to reality in any way. It was the product of professional digital image editing. On social media, you can have a similar experience. The appearance of a person on Facebook is the product of what this person wants you to see. There is always the risk that it has nothing to do with reality.

MANAGING OBSTACLES TO HAPPINESS

> I can't get no satisfaction; I can't get no satisfaction. Cause I try and I try and I try and I try. I can't get no, I can't get no.
>
> —The Rolling Stones

Satisfaction is a state of contentment in which (almost) all essential personal desires have been met. For most people, the main goal in life is personal satisfaction which can also be described using different terms such as subjective well-being. But whatever the term used, they all have more or less the same meaning. Happiness includes satisfaction but in addition refers to the fulfilment of wishes and resulting long-lasting satisfaction. As discussed previously, in order to achieve the state of contentment, psychological well-being is more important than just physical or other superficial experiences. Feelings of physical well-being in isolation don't involve the mind or an intellectual process and, therefore, can't offer sufficient satisfaction on the emotional and behavioural levels to qualify as happiness.

Therefore, what's really important in life is satisfaction *and* happiness.

Example: Louis is a passionate and ambitious sportsman. In his country, he is one of the best in his sport. For many years, he trains every day for the Olympic Games. To succeed, he has to undergo vigorous training, which includes weight training, cardio exercises, jumping ropes, and special calisthenics such as push-ups, crunches, and pull-ups at a rapid pace. But no matter how much pain and hardship he experiences physically, after his training, on the mental level, he is satisfied with what he has achieved. After each training session, Louis knows that he has come a small step closer to his ambitious goal of returning home with an Olympic gold medal. He is satisfied with his level of motivation and the progress he's making with his preparations and happy about getting closer and closer to his big goal.

You can legitimately say that the feeling of happiness is a mere side-effect of a number of constraints that, directly or indirectly, affect your life.

- These constraints, which influence you mentally, can be subjective in nature; for example, projections, judgements, self-fulfilling prophecies, and so on. They can also include some typical elements of a person's personal predisposition, such as shyness, shame, or loneliness.

- Other constraints are objective in nature; for example, ideologies, religious beliefs, consumerism, and sociocultural conditions such as traditions.

Thus, it may be said that you can hardly be happy if your mind is not free of complexes, false projections, self-fulfilling prophecies, false routines, imposed—religious-, ideological-, or traditionally motivated norms and rules, (self-) imposed restrictions, and other internal and external limitations.

> If you want to be happy, then be.
>
> —Leo Tolstoy, 19th-century Russian writer

When your mind is blocked by these kinds of barriers, then it's nearly impossible for you to be who you are and to do what you really want to do.

However, the good news is that you can clear the path to happiness by getting rid of obstacles and barriers that may be in your way, such as outdated traditions, religious restrictions, unjustified shyness, baseless inferiority complexes, and so on.

Contrary to popular belief, the removal of annoying constraints coming from within, and those affecting you from the outside, does not require cloudy theories, philosophies, or psychological treatments. The proposals we make in this book are free of ideology and pragmatic. They can be implemented immediately by anyone with a strong will, determination and perseverance, and without prior knowledge or studies.

Obviously, we cannot promise that it will always be easy, but the goal is grand—the achievement of an inner independence and freedom, which will assist you in liberating yourself from those barriers in your mind that prevent you from living up to your full potential, and from freely deciding who you are, who you want to be, and what you want to do.

FREEDOM OF MIND

When we talk about freedom in this context, we do not mean political freedom such as the freedom to participate in the political process, free voting in legitimate elections, freedom of expression and belief, and so on.

Here, we refer exclusively to the freedom of mind—an amalgamation of personal freedom and independence as the result of an open-minded approach towards psychological liberation. Here, the term 'liberation' refers to the process through which you liberate yourself from the learnings, beliefs, values, opinions, prejudices, judgements, world views, attitudes and standards that you may harbour in your mind because of your interaction with the external world. Each of these has the potential to hold you down to a particular belief and value system to which you might remain bound to for the rest of your life, if not for this exercise. Mental liberation means freedom from all these.

Example: Even if you are politically free, you can still feel restricted in your personal (inner) freedom. This has negative effects on your happiness.

Thus, with regard to happiness, freedom of mind refers to intellectual independence from influences that negatively affect your happiness or your way towards happiness.

> It is the freedom of thought that means happiness.
>
> —Theodor W. Adorno, 20th-century German philosopher

In an ideal situation, you should always have the individual liberty to decide freely about yourselves and the way to achieve personal happiness without feeling constrained by internal and/or external obstacles. But your mind may not be free because of your upbringing, your sociocultural environment, experiences or a possible indoctrination that may have taken place during childhood.

In fact, in a vast majority of cases, people are not even aware that they have been a victim of conditioning behaviour in their early youth, because each individual considers everything that makes up their lives to be normal. Consider the following example on the idea of tradition.

Example: Male, underage children from Orthodox Jewish families can be seen with the outward symbols of their faith from the age of three. These include the traditional black skullcap, black caftan, and side-locks, as well as acceptance of cultural practices such as circumcision. Similarly, Muslim girls must cover their hair and sometimes even their face with a scarf at an early age. Young Catholics from devout families attend confession after their first Holy Communion between the age of 7 and 11. As part of a culture in which elders are particularly revered, Thai children are taught early at school that elders are generally right. This is demonstrated through the traditional proverb, 'When you walk following elders, dogs will not bite you,' which means that elders are knowledgeable and they protect you from bad experiences.

In all the instances mentioned here, the affected children are usually not given a choice with regard to the customs, nor are they allowed to wait until they are older to decide for themselves. Such childhood conditioning may affect the mentality of young people, and this is extremely difficult to reverse.

Sometimes, even without realizing, you can lose your independence of thought to a number of internal (subjective) and external (objective) pressures, constraints, complexes, projections, self-fulfilling prophecies, (self-) imposed restrictions, sociocultural barriers, and traded behavioural patterns.

In many cases, societal norms demanding strict compliance with certain rules and behaviours are totally outdated. Some have lost their original meaning, or can no longer be reasonably justified when brought into connection with contemporary real-life experiences.

Example: In places such as the Middle East, North Africa, South East Asia, Japan, and India, where strong traditional family cultures exist, social pressures are constantly exercised on family members. These family culture constraints are ways through which family elders often control young family members.

Example for objective (external) constraints: Hans, a German national living under the National Socialist regime, fell in love with Esther, a beautiful student at the University of Munich. Though she was from a Jewish family, Hans didn't care. What counted was their unconditional love for each other. After a year, he asked her to marry him and she happily accepted. Some days later, he received a long letter from Esther telling him that she couldn't see him any longer. He immediately took his bike and drove down to her family home to meet her. When he approached the entrance of the house, he saw a big poster hanging at the gate with the words '*JEWS OUT!*' written in big red letters. He rang the doorbell but nobody answered. All blinds were down. A security guard came up to him and ordered him in a harsh tone to leave. Later at home, he read in the papers that a new legislation had been enacted that prohibited by severe penalty Jews to date 'Aryan' Germans, and vice versa. Hans never saw Esther again, and it took him years to be happy once again.

Example for a typical subjective (internal) constraint: Bruno was a shy boy. Already at school his classmates teased him that he blushed when spoken to and stuttered when he was asked for an answer. When Bruno grew older, and after his own endeavours to overcome his shyness failed, he sought the help of a therapist. Though the therapist managed to treat the external symptoms of his shyness such as blushing and stuttering, Bruno remained a shy person who felt uncomfortable in the company of people unknown to him.

You can hardly be happy if your mind is not free of objective (external) and subjective (internal) constraints. Therefore, an important prerequisite for achieving personal happiness is, as a first step, your liberation from any restrictions that stand in the way of your happiness and, as a second step, your individual (inner) freedom.

> Letting go gives us freedom, and freedom is the only condition for happiness. If, in our heart, we still cling to anything—anger, anxiety, or possessions—we cannot be free.
>
> —Thich Nhat Hanh,
> Vietnamese Buddhist monk and peace activist

Freedom is closely connected with knowledge, education, and learning. Only knowledge opens up the possibility of a successful life and happiness.

Example: Lek, a schoolgirl from a very poor background, was a quick learner at school, and it soon became apparent that she was way ahead of her classmates. In her country, however, there were no support programmes for the highly gifted, so Lek's talents were never given a chance to flourish. At a young age, after graduating from school, Lek's family sent her to the city to earn money and contribute to the family's livelihood. Lek submitted without objection to her familial obligations. At first, Lek made her living as a massage therapist. But when she saw that there was little money to be made, she had no choice but to resort to what many of her good-looking colleagues did. Lek became an escort. With this activity, Lek earned enough money, but she was extremely unhappy about her fate. Lek knew that with a proper education or a support programme for the highly gifted, she would have had a totally different career. When an escort-friend told her that she was learning a foreign language in her spare time, with the aim of becoming a translator, Lek decided to do the same to give her life a new perspective.

Happiness is experienced through successful self-realization and recognition by people as being a valued member in a social community. More than that, it is certain that people who keep their curiosity alive by being active and interested in what's going on around them and don't stop learning as they grow older, are more likely to find their own happiness than those who view everything around them with disinterest and ignorance and believe that occasional pleasure equals happiness.

BEING 'COOL'

> Do not take life too seriously. You will never get out of it alive.
>
> —Elbert Hubbard, American author

You will have better chances of success in achieving inner freedom and independence as well as prevailing over limiting factors or constraints in an environment governed by sociocultural norms and/or internal obstacles, if you are approaching the task in a '*cool*' way.

> I saw a guy at a party wearing a leather jacket and I thought: 'That's damned cool.' But then I saw another guy wearing a leather vest and I thought: 'That's not cool.' Then I figured it out: Cool is all about leather sleeves.
>
> —Unknown

It is evident from the abovementioned quote that the term 'cool' needs some explanation before it can be meaningfully used in this book. So, what exactly does it mean to be 'cool'?

Typically, you act 'cool' when you find yourself in a paradoxical situation. A situation is paradoxical when it seems to defy logic by contradicting itself.

Example: A famous paradox expressed in a simple sentence is known as the liar's paradox: *This sentence is a lie.* If the sentence is true, then it is a lie, as it says. Another paradoxical statement illustrates the self-contradictory character of a paradox: *Nobody goes to that restaurant because it's too crowded.* And, yet, the restaurant, in this case, obviously, has many customers—precisely because it is crowded!

If you transfer the principles of this paradox to happiness, you will soon realize that everything that has to do with happiness is almost always paradoxical.

There is most certainly *no one* who doesn't want to be happy. Oftentimes, however, most people stand in their own way (or in the way of others) to happiness. They become their own enemies.

Example: Theresa was a young, attractive single executive who was well admired in office for her hardworking nature and commendable achievements. When Theresa's colleagues asked her why she was still single, Theresa would often respond evasively. Secretly, Theresa knew that she was longing for closeness and a trusted partner. But her mother's strict upbringing was preventing Theresa from opening up to potential partners. The overcautious, anti-male upbringing by her mother was a consequence of the deep aversion to men that Theresa's mother had developed after two incidents from her youth—a rape and her husband's desertion. Though Theresa knew that it was wrong of her mother to raise her in such a way because of her unfortunate personal experiences, she hadn't been able to free herself of her mother's teachings. Theresa continued to stand in the way of her own happiness.

Looking at the history of the notion of 'coolness', being cool is a classic case of resistance to authority. We don't mean this in a revolutionary sense, but rather resistance through alternative means. The origin of coolness goes back to the behaviour of Black African slaves in the US as part of their liberation process. This was influenced by the Black community's inability to control their political and cultural oppression. Typical for this process was not open conflict and violence. Instead, Black African Americans successfully used a creative fusion of *submission* (no open conflict) and *subversion* (creating a new distinctive style of their own), practised as self-control and restraint, in combination with the use of an unusual constellation of creativity, ideas, and actions.

The creative part by African Americans was the introduction of a stylistic concept with features defying White prejudices and supremacist behaviour. Yet, it was without rebellion and without violence. They created a distinct style of their own—a new, almost uncopiable and impenetrable slang, wearing of sunglasses at night, inhabiting a smoky alcohol haze for insulation, jazz, rap, and smoking dope. *To be cool* means that as an African American you would not be 'Uncle-Tom-like' by producing an excessively obedient or servile behaviour vis-à-vis White people or by giving fake smiles to demonstrate that you 'know your place'. Cool, therefore, refers to the ability to be relaxed in one's own style in any environment—even when hostile—as an act of courage and mental strength.

The authors propose to apply cool principles when searching for ways to be happy. If you replace authority—as in the case of Black slave liberation and White slave owners—with the internal and external constraints in your mind, you will find that the concept of coolness is very useful and effective for self-liberation.

As a first step in your search for greater happiness, you must ask yourself whether or not there are any objective (external) and/or subjective (internal or self-imposed) constraints that influence you and stand in the way of your goal.

Example for an objective constraint: After the death of her father, Angela finds that her mother focuses all her attention and care on her. Angela is 28 years old and has no siblings. The mother tries again and again to interfere in her daughter's life without being asked and does not shy away from disapprovingly expressing herself about Angela's private life and her changing partners. Angela is torn between her feelings towards her mother, on the one hand, and her desire for a self-determined life, on the other. She finds it difficult to find a way out of this situation and is unhappy about it.

Example for a subjective constraint: Dorothy has fallen in love with a young man and feels that he is also interested in her. But he is too shy to take the first step. Unfortunately, every time she sees him, she loses her courage because she too suffers from shyness. Instead of looking at him freely and giving him an opportunity to speak to her, she lowers her eyes and pretends not to see him. Last time, when she met him, she was about to tell him how she felt but couldn't. Dorothy is unhappy about the situation.

Tip: Do not get absorbed either by the pressures you may exercise on yourself (subjective constraints) or the constraints that may be imposed on you by external factors such as rigid sociocultural norms in your surrounding environment (objective constraints).

You act cool when you look at yourself dispassionately, as if you were a third party. Create distance so that you are able to look at yourself from a quasi-neutral, detached point of view. This will help you to see your realities much clearly and also stop you from lying to or projecting on yourself. After this analytical step, you come to the constructive part of your cool process towards happiness.

Afro-Americans renounced revolution and violence in their resistance against White supremacy. Instead, they resorted to creative ideas to preserve their dignity and independence. As you know, this was later called 'cool'. By utilizing this successful approach as a model, you should now, in this second phase, look for creative ideas, which, without conflict, promote your efforts for more happiness.

Example: A young woman called Pok grew up in a very tight-knit Thai family. Pok had always followed the family's guidance. Her family expected Pok to marry into a Thai family. However, unexpectedly, Pok fell in love with an ethnic Indian Hindu. Her family opposed their relationship. Even so, Pok continued to stand by her love in the hope that her family would eventually come around. Nonetheless, her family continued to resist, pointing out that they only wanted the best for Pok and were trying to protect her from taking rash actions. Pok had a hard time in defending her decision to marry her love. But instead of fighting or cutting off her relationship with the family, Pok decided to follow a cool approach. In other words, she deliberately detached herself from her emerging negative emotions, avoided conflicts at all costs, and implemented a step-wise plan based on determination, patience, and faith. Pok's idea was to use all conceivable occasions to let her family see how happy she was with her husband. She didn't avoid family gatherings but showed up with her love smilingly, demonstrated compassion for family members, spoiled them with small self-made gifts emphasizing that they were made together with her husband, and offered her husband's and her help in cases where she felt it was needed. Pok was relieved when she saw that, in response to her activities, some members of her family began to show an interest in her husband and started to include him in

their conversations. The real breakthrough came when Pok's first baby was born. Ultimately, also under the influence of the baby's charm, her family accepted the value of their relationship and provided support. Everyone was happy again. Pok's cool strategy had paid off.

This is a perfect example for demonstrating how the concept of coolness can connect with happiness. Pok and her family's unhappiness at her decision to marry outside the community was clearly paradoxical. On the one hand, the parents loved their daughter and wanted the best for her. On the other, by opposing Pok's relationship, they prevented their daughter from being truly happy.

The couple smartly decided to stay cool. Pok convinced her husband to support her by not getting engulfed by emotions. Pok's idea was to stay detached and also prevent her husband from reacting in self-defence or aggression when confronted with a conflict. Instead of adding fuel to the fire by arguing or moving away from Pok's family, the couple chose to relax the existing tensions. As a first step, Pok and her husband acted as if they were not a party to the conflict but just neutral, third-party observers. This helped them to detach themselves emotionally from the situation and enabled them to keep calm. As a second step, Pok tried to de-escalate the situation by carefully and patiently integrating her husband into her family, and by taking measures designed to generate sympathy for him (e.g. handmade gifts). Her husband cooperated patiently and, in the end, they were paving the way into everybody's heart and found happiness by solving their problem in a cool and creative way.

In addition to this example where a 'cool' behaviour restored happiness in the family, it should also be briefly discussed what 'uncool' behaviour can lead to when dealing with happiness.

It's not cool, for instance, when, as part of your pursuit of happiness, you choose one of the two alternatives:

- You submit to total control; for instance, to ideological constraints on your mind. Consider this relationship example here,

  Example: You are a convinced atheist, and you fall in love with a Catholic man. He tells you that you can only marry him when you convert to Catholicism. Initially, you oppose vehemently but then, finally, you give in, because you desperately want to be with this man. But you are not happy with your decision because you know that you and your children will become subject to religious rules that you do not believe in. What you did was against your convictions and free will.

or,

- Total abolition of control; for instance, by wildly revolting against constraints without having developed a Plan B. Consider this workplace example here.

  Example: Paul works in a very successful but conservative company. He worries about the future as markets are undergoing rapid change. Paul makes many suggestions for improvements, such as introduction of more team work, modern 'continuous improvement' principles at the assembly line, and a fair employee reward system. But his superiors, wary of change and the possibility of failure, do not want to modify the existing business model. Paul gets increasingly frustrated. He starts to talk badly about the company's conservatism, his superiors' blindness, and provokes arguments about management decisions at the workplace. His deep-seated frustration also leads him to start criticizing those colleagues who do not share his views and whom he blames for being careerists, opportunists, and conformists. His behaviour results in a hostile and unpleasant working atmosphere. Eventually, Paul is fired because his management is afraid that his critical attitude could endanger the company's performance. When he breaks the bad news to his wife at home, he justifies himself and expresses disappointment that he was misunderstood. After all, all he ever wanted was the best for the company.

In this example, Paul should have developed a Plan B, for instance searching for a new position in a more progressive company.

To be truly cool in dealing with your internal and/or external constraints, you should neither give up, sit back, refuse making efforts, nor accept your fate. That will be uncool. Mere self-pity and lamenting will not make your behaviour cool. Instead, you should free up creative resources inside yourself that lead you to ideas on how to solve your problem in an innovative, non-conflictual way, just like Pok did in the example given previously.

You will be rightly perceived as truly cool when your attainment of inner freedom shows a sense of responsibility. This means taking into account the well-being, needs, and happiness of other people as equally important as your own. However, self-liberalization must not be misunderstood as an invitation to self-centredness or self-isolation. This would not only be uncool but will also lead you to a path that is 'not reasonable' because it involves a risk of being viewed as an unappealing personality who doesn't bother to understand another person's point-of-view or feelings.

Tip: In case, your search for happiness is too bold, straightforward, strictly programmed or overly determined, it will not be cool anymore, and possibly not successful either.

This follows from the fact that 'coolness' is socially constructed and not an inherent feature of a person. 'Coolness' is a perception and you are 'cool' only to the extent that others consider you 'cool'. The more you want to be perceived as 'cool', the more you demonstrate your failure to pursue your own, individual course irrespective of existing norms, beliefs, and other people's expectations. This is considered as a lack of autonomy, which will be viewed as 'uncool' because it requires you following or conceding to the will of others.

Consequently, in the 'culture of cool', winning is cool but being ready to do *anything* to win is not. This statement can also be applied to happiness.

REDEFINING OBSTACLES INTO OPPORTUNITIES

The principles of freedom of mind and coolness discussed here influence and shape mental states and, as a consequence, happiness of people. The resulting behavioural patterns play a major role in people's sense of happiness.

The question is whether you can still be happy when you get affected by external factors which, at first sight, seem like obstacles to happiness because you can neither influence nor control them. A crisis that leads to a time of great difficulty is a good example, such as the Covid pandemic. When Covid was declared a pandemic in March 2020, it dramatically changed the living conditions of people across the world and it is widely assumed that 'happiness' has become one of the many victims of this virus.

Due to the pandemic, your life is now influenced by circumstances never experienced before, such as the constant fear of infection, social distancing, wearing of face masks, lockdowns, curfews, isolation, self-isolation, and work from home.

Example: You may feel overwhelmed when dealing with the stress of the pandemic or when anxiety or depression affects your ability to do your daily routines such as getting to work, partaking in activities you previously enjoyed, and so on.

This has caused a disruption which, at first sight, can be a major impediment to your pursuit of happiness. When you compare your present life to your life before the pandemic, it can be easy to feel bad, upset, and scared.

It is interesting, that the thoughts of fear and restrictions that currently influence the lives of people are not discussed, not even in principle, in most guides on happiness. Therefore, the question whether you can still follow your path to happiness and feel happy during times of crisis, such as the pandemic, will be briefly discussed here.

The answer is clear. Even though the parameters for your happiness may have changed during this crisis, your search for happiness and your happiness can still prevail. In other words, happiness need not become another victim of the pandemic.

Obviously, when you are compelled to voluntary or involuntary isolation at home—borders are closed and normal life is interrupted—it can be difficult to not feel overwhelmed by the situation and the countermeasures to the pandemic. The many changes and the uncertainty the crisis has brought are challenging, and it is not surprising that many people are feeling unhappier than before the pandemic.

THE COVID PANDEMIC AS AN EXAMPLE

The extra time available due the restrictive anti-Covid measures shouldn't upset or threaten you but be taken as an invitation to do something that is a part of the way to more happiness anyway: To reflect on and rediscover yourself.

Before the pandemic, you probably often blamed lack of free time for not being able to think about yourself as most of your time was consumed by your private and professional life. In fact, under non-pandemic conditions, time was a rare commodity. Now there is an opportunity that you might have been waiting for—you have plenty of free, unplanned time. Without the restrictions, you may never even have thought of spending time at home without shopping, meeting people, going to restaurants and events, or partying.

Some people may find it difficult to fill this suddenly available time, but if you are determined to pursue your happiness, *now is the time* to do it. It is predicted that the crisis will continue and that there will probably no quick return to the pre-Covid way of life. In its place, the world will have to gear up to a new normal—also characterized by restrictions. Given the situation, there will be plenty of opportunities to sit back and think about who you are today, what you really want, and what you have to do to feel happier.

> If you can't go outside, go inside.
>
> —Buddha

If you are honest with yourself and, as previously suggested, you take a cool, dispassionate approach, then you will be able to see what social forces, constraints, obligations, and distractions stand in the way of your happiness. You can then work to remove them. This also ties in with the idea discussed in this book of creating freedom of mind by identifying and removing obstacles within yourself that stand in the way of your path to happiness. Having this in mind, it would be wise for you to make productive use of the extra time available because of the crisis. Without this, you would otherwise have had difficulty finding such time in your hectic life.

Example: For three years, Alisa lived alone with her thirteen-year-old son Johan. Her husband separated from her three years ago when he learned that she had had an affair with his best friend. Since then, Alisa has been tormented by her guilty conscience as she blamed herself for the separation and for her son growing up without a father. She compensated her feelings of guilt with an overly protective upbringing of her son. Every day, she took Johan to school, picked him up, drove him to piano practice, then to maths tutoring, and twice a week to basketball practice. When he went to meets friends, she took him there and picked him up as well. 'I feel like a slave', Alisa thought to herself once while waiting for Johan in the car because he was late. For a short time, Alisa had a love affair with a man who soon left when he realized that Alisa was not free, but only lived for her son and constantly blamed herself for something or other. Alisa's self-imposed routine was abruptly interrupted, when a curfew was imposed in response to the Covid pandemic. Suddenly, Alisa had time to reflect on herself and her situation. After much thinking, Alisa came to the conclusion that she had to do something to become happy again. She identified her sense of guilt and the compensatory activities she had engaged in as the source of her unhappiness and decided to change for a new start. As a result, she felt more relaxed about her affair which had caused all the trouble, gave

Johan more freedom to do what he wanted, and soon after fell in love with someone she had met by accident.

When we talk about the exceptional times caused by the pandemic, we should also mention its death toll. Normally, people don't like to talk about death and push this issue aside. But due to the routine publication of the deplorable numbers of daily fatalities, the pandemic has brought death to the forefront of our mind. Almost every day, we are rudely reminded of the finite nature of our lives and that no one is safe from the virus. You should use this new awareness as a motivation to find all possible ways to make your life as happy as possible. Therefore, you should not get upset about the virus, but pause, think, and be prompted to use the time of isolation to further pursue your path to happiness.

The fact that you are forced to spend more time at home and see less people, doesn't affect your ability to think. But it positively affects the amount of time available to you to think. In addition, and unlike in the pre-pandemic situation, your mind will neither be occupied by daily routines nor clouded by all kinds of distracting thoughts. Instead, your mind will be free to think about your happiness and the barriers you need to remove to make progress.

When thinking about yourself and your happiness, staying positive would be helpful for you and those close to you. As mentioned, the daily consumption of reports about the pandemic in the media and the many references to illnesses and death can be depressing. A way to disconnect from the bombardment of negative news can be to reduce your news consumption and instead focus on short overviews of the situation.

Example: Ian sings 'Happy Birthday' twice while washing his hands. He is super informed about Covid, as he is glued to the TV screen all day long watching new reports about the pandemic. When he talks with his family and friends, his only subject for conversation seems to be his fear of the second, and, possibly, the third wave of Covid, which the experts are expecting. His family calls him the 'prophet of doom and gloom' and suffers from his pessimism.

Tip: Read, watch and spend time on topics that lift your spirits.

The Covid outbreak has dramatically changed people's lives, including their relationships. For instance, because of the imposed restrictions, many people are thrown into much closer contact than usual with those who share their homes, whether partner, spouse, or family. For some people, this is 'heaven on earth', and for them their relationship will become more intense. For others, however, it can feel stressful, even unbearable and the relationship will be (further) strained.

Since the challenges of the pandemic are expected to last for some time, we believe that pandemic-specific ideas must be highlighted. In this book, we will discuss many options that can be used to maintain healthy relationships during these trying times.

For instance, it's worth trying to be extra patient and understanding, not only with each other but also with yourself. This is particularly true in a situation where time is no longer the problem but its surplus maybe.

In a situation of unexpected closeness, it is not the very big problems that should take priority. On the contrary, it is more important that both individuals agree on all those small, sometimes very trivial points, which, though of minor importance, can give rise to big disputes.

To avoid this from happening in a lockdown situation, a smart couple should pragmatically agree on some basic rules of conduct. This will help in making the unfamiliar close living as conflict-free as possible. For instance, the couple can agree on planning the day, sharing or alternating use of space, and deciding on who will look after the children, as well as sharing ordinary household tasks like washing the dishes, cleaning the house, garbage disposal, and shopping.

In case the couple is separated by the crisis, the same principles of working out a long-distance relationship will apply. Both partners can stay in touch by means such as phones and social media. This is especially important if either is surprised by the separation, not used to living alone, feeling lonely, or afraid about what is happening in the relationship. Hearing a friendly, familiar voice, or reading a message from the partner you care about is important for mental balance.

In addition to these general principles, there are also actions you can take to boost your happiness during a crisis:

- *Try to be closer to your partner:* When you are locked up with your partner, love becomes a very important aspect. You can cultivate and nurture your feelings for each other by taking out the time for intimate togetherness.
- *Connect with other people:* Though difficult to achieve during the pandemic, it would be good if you can do this as social distancing often means that you cannot be physically with the people you care about. However, technology can be very helpful and by using platforms like Zoom or FaceTime you can talk to friends in real time.
- *Do nice things for others:* When you think about the happiness of others rather than your own, you may get a new perspective on your problems and find that they seem less overwhelming than before. For instance, if you help an old neighbour with shopping, it can have a positive effect on your happiness. This is particularly true at a time when everyone is struggling.

Example: Maria, a soprano singer, lives in Rome. Even though she is under house lockdown, Maria feels joy every evening when she stands on the balcony of her apartment at 7 p.m. and sings for her neighbours, who are also under house lockdown. Her voice touches their hearts, and she finds happiness in their chorus of 'Bravo!'.

Tip: One of the best and the easiest ways to make yourself happy is to make others happy. So ask yourself: *How can I make others happier?*

- *Seek intellectual stimulation:* Often job-related and private-life-related activities consume most of our time, and as a result, there is little or no time left for intellectual stimulation. But the Covid restrictions provide opportunities to fulfil this part of life. For example, you can use this time to finally pick up the unread books on your bookshelf.

- *Sensual pleasures:* These are extremely important for a good life and happiness. Sensual pleasures don't just mean sexual activity but everything that is connected with the body such as wellness, good food and drinks, and creative pursuits.
- *Setting new goals:* You can also consider creating new goals for yourself—for instance, becoming a more caring spouse, spending more time with your aged mother at the senior care home, and checking in with those close friends for whom you didn't have enough time prior to the crisis.

Example: Patrick, a car dealer, was dismissed by his employer due to a decline in sales during the Covid pandemic. He was shocked at being suddenly unemployed, but at the same time felt relief because he didn't like the job and found it meaningless. He knew he only worked at his job for the money. After accepting the fact that he was unemployed and spending some time thinking about his life and what he wanted, he realized that he wanted to be his own boss and pursue his passion for cooking. He converted this small apartment into a plant-based kitchen and used social media to advertise his healthy meals. He received a lot of orders and delivered them through the many available online delivery services. His project was a success. He generates a substantial income and receives great feedback from his satisfied customers.

- *Learning:* Training for an advanced degree, for instance, may not always be enjoyable, but once you have achieved your goals, you will be proud and happy.
- *Being open to change:* When you are open to change—instead of harking back to the pre-Covid situation—you begin to look at the possible characteristics of the anticipated 'new normal'. When you see that conditions affecting your environment change and things develop in a different way than expected or hoped for, you should give yourself permission to change your mind and not rally against those changes. An important step in adapting to change is building new routines.

Even though for some everything may seem out of control, you are already constructing your new normal.

Example: Adam lived in an extremely rainy country. When leaving home, it was a routine for him to pull out an umbrella from the umbrella stand next to front door. After the Covid outbreak, he hung several face masks on a hook next to his front door and made it his new routine to pull them over his face when he left the house. Unlike some of his colleagues who refused to wear masks, he had adapted to the new normal.

In this example we see that Adam was happy doing this because he understood that it wasn't just joy and pleasure that brought happiness but also a sense of purpose. He didn't want to focus on the negative aspects of the current situation because he knew it wouldn't make him happier. Instead, he accepted the new realities and wanted to make a positive contribution to the well-being of his community by reducing the risk of infection, not only for himself, but also for others.

2

HAPPINESS IN RELATIONSHIPS

LOVE AND HAPPINESS

> All you need is love.
>
> —The Beatles

Love can be a significant part or maybe even the only reason for your happiness. But you can also be happy without love. So, what role does love play in your happiness? You may say that love plays an essential role for your happiness, but alternatively you may also say your happiness—before you even fall in love—may positively influence your chances to fall in love and be loved. This is because your own (pre-existing) happiness may positively affect your chances for success with your (future) partner.

To better understand the relationship between happiness and love, it's necessary to take a closer look at the complex idea of love.

When we talk about love in connection to happiness, we

are referring to the emotional and not the compassionate love taught in Buddhism.

Emotional love is the type of love, which, hopefully, all of you have experienced or will experience during the course of your lives. This type of love involves intense romantic feelings, sexual attraction, and a commitment to long-lasting partnership. In contrast, compassionate love is less intense emotionally; it is transitory, and more based on feelings of mutual respect and affection.

> Real love is always chaotic. You lose control; you lose perspective. You lose the ability to protect yourself. The greater the love, the greater the chaos. It's a given and that's the secret.
>
> —Jonathan Carroll, American fiction writer

For some, love is a disorderly and chaotic feeling, which does not immediately equate to happiness.

Indeed, the 'chaotic' phenomenon of love is an inexplicable mixture of feelings and emotions, romantic fantasies, and dreams and longing. On the one hand, love can give you a 'high' so much so that you want to sing out loud, but, on the other hand, it can also—if your love is disappointed—lead you into a deep black hole. When your love is reciprocated, you feel happy, even if there are other elements in your life that, under normal circumstances, would negatively influence your feeling of happiness. But if it is rejected or disappointed, you feel unhappy, even if other elements that influence your life would make you happy under normal circumstances.

TRUE VERSUS FALSE LOVE

Just like happiness, there is no absolute definition of love. However, you should be able to distinguish between two common categories of love: true (genuine) love and false love. This is important for our discussion because these two types of love have different effects on the happiness quotient of loving partners.

Similar to the feeling of happiness, you can instinctively feel whether you have fallen into true love. It is quite distinct from engaging in an unhappy false love relationship. It is also different from being merely attached to a person. In a false love relationship, there is often no real affection between the partners, coupled with a lack of interest in each other. Such a love manifests itself in an excessive and selfish desire to control the other, and it is characterized by jealousy and the intention to keep the partner from living their life. Frequently, relationships based on false love resemble more a 'community of purpose' than a true relationship. In none of these cases, a true feeling of happiness can be generated.

> There is no disguise that can hide true love for a long time, or fake it where there is none.
>
> —François de la Rochefoucauld

Example: Jack is a member of a wealthy family. He boasts that he has never had to work for a living and will not have to do so in the future. He is extremely cheerful and charming and known to be a typical partygoer. He never misses an opportunity to have fun, sometimes excessively. Jack is proud and happy when he sees himself surrounded by many scantily dressed, beautiful young women in photos. It has often happened that one of the young women has fallen in love with him and his charm. But none of these relationships lasted long, even when he felt that he was in love too. The reason for this was his attitude to see and treat his partner as an investment. The lack of warmth and the feeling of being overly controlled by Jack, led again and again to the young women leaving him disappointed. As he grows older, Jack is alone despite his many social activities, and he still doesn't see an alternative way of life that might bring him happiness.

When you always want something new to satisfy yourself, you're just being egoistic. If you're really honest with yourself, you will realize that you don't actually know how to be satisfied and happy.

The endless desire for amusement and changing relationships following from this attitude can create a vicious cycle from which it is difficult to escape.

Another variation of false love is, when you think that you are in love with someone, but only when they do what *you* want them to. The desire to govern by one partner can make the other partner feel unhappy.

Example: Henry loved it when his friend Zoe dressed in sexy and revealing clothes. In some cases, it was also fun for her, and there was no problem between the two. But sometimes Zoe didn't feel like dressing conspicuously and preferred sneakers and jeans. But Henry would not tolerate this and tried to force his will on her. At times, Zoe resisted his pressure successfully, but often gave in reluctantly under his pressure. When he kept insisting that she fulfil his wishes, fights ensued. When this situation was repeated over and over again, Zoe started to feel unhappy. One day, Zoe lost her temper. She shouted at Henry and asked him whether he was loving and respecting her, or just wanted to use her as his figurehead and mascot.

If you have doubts about whether you are in true love or your feelings are misguiding you into false love, you just have to listen to your gut feeling. Ask yourself whether your feelings correspond to what you experience and expect, for instance:

- Certainty as to whether the relationship is only superficial and only held together by common (materialistic) interests, or whether there is a true emotional and mental closeness.
- The ability to find happiness in the other person's happiness, and your unconditional willingness to share your personal happiness with your partner.
- The opportunity to grow together alongside your partner.

- Mutual acceptance of each other just as you are, including strengths and flaws.

Some believe true (genuine) love is only when you give your love to someone and get loved in return. This is erroneous. It can even lead to unhappiness when you get disappointed. Ideally, true love is unconditional, and you should not expect something in return.

> True love begins at one end like the flame of a match.
>
> —Buddha

The desire for unconditional love, like for recognition, respect, and self-realization, is among our basic needs. This means that to appreciate and love your partner just as they are—including all their strengths and weaknesses—without imposing conditions.

But there is a difference between true love and just being attached. To love each other means that both partners let down the walls they have built around themselves for reasons of self-protection. When you are in true love, you let your vulnerabilities show. This is because you trust that your partner will not hurt you and will unconditionally commit to the relationship. This goes beyond all other forms of attachment. Whereas, just being attached means that you fear being alone, so you have entered into a relationship to avoid your loneliness from affecting you negatively.

LOVE AND ATTACHMENT

> Attachment is an element that is helpful for survival. As humans, our body has a positive element on the emotional level that brings us to have attachment to someone or attachment to our own happiness.
>
> —The 14th Dalai Lama

Under favourable circumstances, for example when pursuing common hobbies, sports activities or shared interests such as jazz, classical music or

painting, people are, in principle, relatively easily attached to each other. In other words, they like each other.

Some people may even believe that they are in love with someone when, in fact, they are simply attached to them.

Buddhism teaches to distinguish between love and attachment, though there is only a fine line between the two. If you feel loved, you necessarily feel attached because you can hardly be in love without being attached.

As opposed to a partner who is merely attached, a true lover will do everything to make the partner happy. The special relationship that true love creates between two people allows one partner to be completely absorbed by the other and be completely open. People who just feel attached to each other are merely focusing on a selection of perceived positive sides of their relationship. They are 'blind' to see their partner's true personality.

Example: Rick is a young, gay freelancer working in the marketing sector. He is closely attached to Donna, a young female executive who enjoys her many relationships with handsome, young men. Rick and Donna have discovered that they have a remarkable spiritual kinship with each other. Therefore, they often go on holidays together. They exchange views and information almost daily, confiding their worries and sharing many joys. Though they are strongly attracted to each other, they are not in love. Their relationship is more of a soul relationship like twins or close siblings can have.

Attachment is more based on necessity, co-dependency, the need to avoid loneliness, and to fill up emptiness. People with an anxious or dismissive attachment to another person tend to feel emotional hunger, and they frequently cling to their partner just to rescue or complete themselves or to feel being taken care of. But if the attachment is no longer in their interest, they can push their partner away anytime. Others are attached but afraid to get too close to their partners and find reasons to withdraw when it seems convenient to them.

As opposed to mere attachment, love is stable as it requires security to allow full openness and a free exchange of give and take. It is this stability that can lead to enduring happiness. In contrast, attachment is volatile and does not provide a secure basis that would allow both partners to be who they are and be happy in the long term.

Example: Max and Xenia have been a couple for two years. They met playing golf and have come to feel an attachment to each other. What they had in common was their sport and the many relaxing hours with other golfers at the golf club bar. Though they saw themselves as a couple, they had not moved in together in order to maintain their respective independence. Xenia had noticed that Max did not care much about his apartment. So, she came regularly to clean, wash, iron, and cook for him so that he didn't only eat home-delivered fast food. Max was enjoying her service because he liked to be spoiled. Xenia, on the other hand, did this because she felt needed. She knew that they shared nothing important except for their love for golf. In fact, she was not even sure whether she liked Max but continued because she feared being alone. For a while, Xenia believed that she could tolerate Max's indifference and disinterest, but without love, it was difficult for her to swallow her growing resentment. Her anger and remorse started to build, and eventually she realized that her relationship with Max made her unhappy.

Buddha taught that one can be free from any attachment. This statement does not only refer to material possessions but also to people—and even those you love. According to Buddha, it is possible to love, live in peace, and be happy, even if you stay detached from attachments. This is feasible because you do not seek love to fulfil your own self-centred wishes. Instead, you are ready to give your true love to your partner (or loved ones) without expecting anything in return and wishing the other person to be happy. It is the mere act of giving which makes you happy and fulfilled.

Example: Nora and David were in a close live-in relationship for more than five years. One day, they went to a reception together. Right at the beginning, David met an attractive lady who was an old friend from high school and immersed himself in a conversation with her. Nora got bored by their conversation and, unnoticed by David, she moved away. When the conversation with his school friend was over, David missed Nora. He looked out for her but it took him quite a while to find her. She was engrossed in a conversation with another person he didn't know. As he didn't not want to disturb her, he walked to the buffet waiting for her. Only after what seems like forever, he saw Nora again in the crowd of guests, obviously looking for him. David walked over to her and reproached her for having distanced herself from him and leaving him alone. Nora reacted outraged because she felt wrongly accused. She insisted that even as his close partner, she had a personality of her own. She did not feel the need to stick to him like an appendage and had the right to look for her own interlocutors. They got into an argument and left the reception to go home. After a drink at home, Nora apologized for her aggressive response. She explained to David that she got upset at the beginning when he was talking to his old schoolmate about events she wasn't interested in. She left him and his friend because she felt left out. David accepted her apology and they were good again.

This example illustrates a situation where a partner in a close relationship reacts aggressively when the other partner is branching out and away from them or seems to care more for someone else. The instinctive reaction of the seemingly abandoned partner is to bring the other back under their control in an attempt to possess them.

The difference between attachment and healthy love is whether you can step back and allow your partner the freedom to be their own individual person. If one partner tries to exercise control over the other or imposes restrictions on their freedom, sooner or later, the controlled partner will want to escape from what they would perceive as a prison. If, on the other hand, both partners decide generously and trustingly to allow and give each other space and freedom, they will be happy together.

Example: The same principle applies to parents who impose their wishes and aspirations on their children. They are full of expectations with regard to their offspring's life and often project their own desires on to them. But birds kept in cages merely exist and do not truly live. In the same way that birds want to fly freely and not to cling to bars, children also want freedom. If children aren't allowed to grow up in freedom, then they'll become unhappy, suffer, rebel, and will forcefully break out of the cage they're imprisoned in.

In some cases, when this 'escape' takes place, the parents do not feel pity for their children's unhappiness. Instead, they complain about their misguided children and become unhappy about it.

JEALOUSY

It may seem normal for a man or a woman to become jealous when the partner seems to care more about other people, or becomes excessively occupied by a hobby or any other activity which excludes them.

Example: For many years now, Tony has been watching the *Antiques Road Show* on TV every day. He began to develop an interest in collecting toy cars, and soon he was hooked to this hobby. So far, his wife Sandra had tolerated that all the free space at their home was occupied by his collection. To his family's distress, Tony spent most of his free time collecting and only looked for vacation spots where he could possibly find new collectors' items. But one day Tony seemed to have overshot the mark and crossed the border of Sandra's tolerance. When he told her, that he would spend the next Easter weekend alone at a collectors' fair outside their home city, she lost her temper and shouted at him. At this moment, he learned for the first time that she felt abandoned by him because of his hobby, and she wanted to vacation at locations that were not necessarily selected because of their antiques fairs or flea markets. He finally understood that his frequent absences made her feel lonely and unhappy.

In principle, jealousy is born out of insecurity or possessiveness, and it is likely to develop a destructive effect on the relationship. However, not being jealous at all and being disinterested could also signal a problem.

Example: Sarah said to her husband Gabriel: 'Do what you want, I don't care.' Her indifference upset Gabriel. He felt that love was missing in her response, and he asked himself why this was so.

In a well-functioning relationship, a certain level of jealousy can be seen as an expression of love. In such a case, jealousy can be tolerated as long as it is done right and arises from the desire to keep the relationship intact.

Example: Martin was an associate lawyer in a renowned local law firm. His goal was to become a junior partner in that law firm within twenty-four months. In return, he was willing to work long hours, on weekends, and even on holidays. His young wife, Tatjana, initially shared his enthusiasm. She also worked as a lawyer but was less ambitious because of her poorer exam results. But when she noticed that Martin came home exhausted late every night and fell asleep immediately after dinner, without enjoying any free time, she began to worry about his well-being. When she talked to Martin about this, he reacted angrily accusing her of being jealous of his looming career. Tatjana knew that he was referring to a remark she had made after his exams, referring to herself as 'the better lawyer' despite her poorer results. However, she rejected this accusation by calmly retorting that she had only brought up the issue out of love for him. Her only motivation had been her genuine concern for his health and well-being.

Tip: Openness, communication, and understanding for your partner are the key to keeping the relationship a happy one. Therefore, let your partner know that you care about them. Take part in their professional and leisure activities or just show interest, the same way you expect them to do for you. In cases of doubt, try to understand your partner by talking to each other. This will clarify the situation.

THE FEAR OF LOSS AND THE WISH TO CONTROL

> Fear is misfortune, therefore courage is not happiness, but fearlessness.
> —Franz Kafka, German-speaking Czech writer

If you feel a constant desire to control your partner, you should recognize that it is your lack of trust and your fear that is making you do so. You fear that your partner may no longer be interested in you alone, and therefore want to counteract this with control measures. The fear of loss becomes even stronger if you fear losing your partner completely.

Example: You want to know every last detail of what your partner experienced with friends yesterday when you were not present, for fear that he might have had 'something' with another person; or, you ask your partner, 'Tell me that you love me, so I can think that you won't leave me and I can feel safe.'

This can lead to uncertainty and confusion or even fear of loss, especially if your partner fails to involve you or communicate with you. Your insecurity about what your partner is planning or doing when you are not together can cause discomfort, and this can trigger defensive measures.

Example: In his mid-50s, Donald decided to get into local politics. He quickly made a career there, was appointed chairman of committees and his party fraction, and had chances to be nominated as the next candidate for mayor. His wife Olga was not interested in politics. Donald, therefore, did not feel it necessary to tell her about his political activities and ambitions. Despite her disinterest in politics, Olga began to suffer from the fact that her husband did not share what he was doing in the political arena. When she accidentally discovered his photo in a newspaper, showing him at the side of an attractive woman who wanted his autograph, she felt, for the first time, a fear of losing him.

In cases like this, usually, the ignored partner's self-defence mechanism will begin to work by fighting and protecting against the envisaged possibility of loss. But you should be aware that your attempts to regain control over your partner through hard words or 'check-ups' will most likely lead to dispute, *inner termination*, or worse, your partner will want to run away.

For continued happiness in a relationship, 'inner termination' is the most dangerous measure in a partner's self-defence toolbox against the fear of loss. While the partner's behaviour remains unchanged on the outside, internally, and as a result of a creeping process, the partner has long decoupled themselves from a commitment to the relationship and has increasingly given way to resignation.

This can manifest itself in loss of interest in the relationship, further reduction of common activities, social withdrawal, cynical or critical distance from the other or their activities.

Tip: Read the signs on the wall. Inner termination is so dangerous because the process leading to it remains invisible to the partner concerned for a long time, especially if they are not sensitive enough to correctly interpret the signals from the other side. It is, therefore, possible that the problem has existed already for a long time and only becomes an issue between the partners when it is too late for an amicable solution because the relationship is irreparably broken or a third person has entered the partner's life.

It should be noted that in the case of fear of loss, the struggle of a partner against the possibility of loss takes up a large part of their attention and energy. This attention and energy would be put to better use if it were used to creatively shape the common time with the other or partake in joint activities which have the potential to bind the partners together.

The same principles discussed for managing fear of loss or fear of losing control can be applied to other types of relationships such as parent and child. Well-advised parents raise children with full care and affection. But at the same time, they also understand and respect that they are small people full of their own individual characteristics. They will grow into their own lives, which will be shaped by them. Parents facilitate the process of breaking away from parental care by equipping children with the tools to manage their lives on their own and become independent. The same goes for partners in a relationship.

SPACE TO BREATHE

When you fell in love, you probably accepted your partner as an independent individual with a distinct history and personality. This personality was possibly shaped and guided by an education system, a culture, a package of totally different (childhood) experiences, and other influences that may differ more or less from yours. In fact, that is what you fell in love with.

As a consequence, you should welcome and support the changes your partner may want to introduce to your life. This will only work to enrich your life. In return, you will expect your partner to be open to any addition and new elements that you may want to introduce in their life. This may be the way your partnership would grow into a mutually enriched relationship with its own distinct personality.

Example: The German engineer Karl had married Nui, a former air hostess from Thailand. Both Karl's German and Nui's Thai families were sceptical about how long a relationship between a German and a Thai would last. Both stood for completely different cultures and life stories: Karl came from a wealthy home and had received the best education. His parental home was liberal and anti-religiously oriented, which influenced his attitudes to this day. He had quickly made a career in his profession and, through his many activities abroad, he had become truly cosmopolitan. Nui, on the other hand, came from bitterly poor circumstances in northern Thailand, had grown up as a Buddhist, and for a long time in her life, worked to pay back a loan she had taken to finance her education, including intensive English-language classes. Contrary to what the sceptics expected, Karl and Nui had a happy, long-lasting relationship. Karl had become accustomed to Nui's varied spicy Thai cuisine, had successfully resisted Nui's quiet desire to make him a Buddhist, and had come to terms with the important role Nui's Thai family played in her life. Nui, on the other hand, was impressed by the reliability and precision that Karl brought to the marriage and enjoyed discovering with him a culture she would never have known otherwise. Both gave each other the freedom to pursue their respective interests without reacting with rejection, jealousy, or a know-it-all attitude. Karl and Nui felt free and independent within their relationship and were both proud to talk about or share their respective activities with the other.

In order to encourage a partner to contribute to an enriched relationship, it is important to first give them the freedom and space to be themselves. In principle, this is an easy task because you just have to wish your partner to be happy.

Tip: Give your partner space and they'll come back. Force your partner into a cage and they'll try to escape.

Give your partner words of encouragement and express your love in a way they appreciates. To truly love a person is to recognize them as a distinct individual. So, give your partner space to breathe the same way you will expect it for yourself. This also means that you must be generous by not setting unrealistic expectations that would put them under pressure. Further, it also means to be forgiving and allowing the partner to be imperfect and make mistakes, and, above all, to not to be vindictive.

> You must love in such a way that the person you love feels free.
>
> —Thich Nhat Hanh, Vietnamese Buddhist monk

In this context it is interesting to see how the philosophy of Buddhism can help in understanding attachment, love, and control.

In Buddhism, to be free from suffering, one must first get rid of all attachments, because they are the cause of suffering and unhappiness. The term *updana* refers to clinging or attachment, and by clinging to your desire, you make yourself an object of suffering. If you do not get the object of your desire, you suffer; or, alternatively, even if you get your object of desire, it may eventually change or fade and you suffer as well.

However, it is difficult to distinguish between love and attachment. When you feel love, you will feel attached to the other person, and then you would want to control them. You may think that you want to control and own your partner out of love, and wouldn't feel this way if you didn't love them. But, on the contrary, true love is just the opposite. True love is not binding but free giving. It is not controlling, but it wants the other person to be happy and free.

On the other hand, there are people who develop anxieties and cultivate unjustified fears because they fear losing their partner, thereby denying themselves the full potential of the happiness that love produces.

> Love is free giving, but if you expect something back from love, love dies.
>
> —Unknown

With love, one has full trust in one another. You know that the other person accepts you completely, and you feel freer in such a relationship than you have ever felt alone.

Yet, instinctively, you may want to defend yourself against possible threats of loss by clinging to your partner. You might want to know what your partner is doing; you constantly check up on them, just to make sure that you are the focus of their attention. But the harder you cling on, the closer you get to failure because you cannot control others. The more you control, the more uncomfortable they feel and want to run away.

> It's dark because you are trying too hard. Lightly child, lightly. Learn to do everything lightly. Yes, feel lightly even though you're feeling deeply. Just lightly let things happen and lightly cope with them.
>
> —Aldous Huxley,
> English writer and philosopher

Example: Dan was a tax attorney working for a multinational company. He was constantly overwhelmed both by the amount of work he had to do and by the complexity of the tasks for which his management expected him to find solutions as quickly as possible. While he was working hard in office, his childless wife Mary-Ann was bored at home and had nothing better to do than call him several times a day just to tell him on the phone that she loved him. She didn't know that her frequent calls would disturb him at work and thought he would appreciate it. At first, he tolerated these disturbing calls because he knew that Mary-Ann meant well. Even as the number of daily phone calls increased, he did not dare tell her to stop because he was afraid of hurting her. But at some point, when she called at a particularly inopportune moment, it became too much for him. He couldn't control himself in this situation. He lost his composure and harshly told her to stop making these calls in the future. As a result of his outburst and despite his subsequent apology and explanation, the harmony between Dan and Mary-Ann was disturbed for a long time.

In this example it is demonstrated what could happen if a partner makes the mistake, albeit emotionally, of holding on too tightly.

Maybe that in this example, Mary-Ann wasn't sensitive enough to acknowledge her husband's stress, maybe she was just bored, or maybe she had fears over 'losing' her husband to his job. Maybe, instinctively, she wanted to defend herself against possible threats to her desire to possess her husband 100 per cent by clinging to him even when he wasn't physically present.

But, as demonstrated by this example, the tighter you cling, the closer you may get to failure because you can't control others without the risk of doing the opposite of what you desire.

Dan's annoyance could have been a first indication that his wife was getting on his nerves instead of supporting him with unselfish love. Mary-Ann acted wrong because when she decided to make her calls, she didn't have her husband's happiness in mind. Had it been otherwise, she would have allowed him to work undisturbed, instead of showering him with unnecessary calls.

Other disharmonies between partners can arise when there are conflicts over issues such as raising children, money, parents-in-law, home design, or the organization of leisure time. In case you happen to detect a certain level of disharmony in your relationship, you should not immediately start worrying as this development may perhaps not be bad at all. This is because allowing a certain level of disharmony is acceptable, and this should be part of your tolerance threshold to give your partner 'space to breathe'. Your happiness with your partner should not be affected.

Relationships in which the partners always say 'yes' and live in seemingly total harmony are not realistic. It's even likely that there is only a semblance of happiness and that in reality, the alleged permanent harmony may be hiding unresolved conflicts or unacceptable concessions that one partner makes for the other just to please them or avoid conflict.

Therefore, you should not immediately start worrying as disharmonies or disagreements in a relationship are not always bad. At first sight, perfectly and permanently coordinated or even matching expectations between partners may look very reliable, but they are not really 'tingling'.

You feel happy in a relationship if you can trust your partner deeply. This trust requires honesty on both sides. Mutual honesty in a relationship also includes the ability to say a clear 'no' to the other person when it is appropriate. If both partners have a positive attitude towards each other, then a clear 'no' can even be interpreted as an expression of love because it is honest and behind an honest 'no' there is usually nothing hidden that is deceptive. This could, theoretically, also be the case behind a 'yes, but...' or a 'false yes'.

Tip: In order to avoid misinterpretation of your 'no', it is recommended that you give an explanation as to why your answer is negative. This will provide clarity about your motivation and intention. This transparency will let your partner feel that you treat them as a true equal partner.

ROMANTIC COMPLICITY

Mutual trust expressed in this way can also be used to create an especially intimate feeling of mutual complicity.

The loyalty and solidarity inherent in complicity makes it a preferred model for a happy relationship.

Example: When one talks about accomplices or complicity, one thinks either of criminal outlaws or Hollywood films such as *Bonnie and Clyde*—the romantically veiled lovers who committed many crimes and were shot together in the end. In the latter, you might think less about the crimes committed. Instead, you probably sympathize more with the protagonists. This is so because the accomplices are positively charged because of their closeness, solidarity, and loyalty between them—something that would result in mutual happiness in a (marital) relationship.

As in crime, complicity in a relationship is an act of conscious will by the cooperating partners, motivated by reason and directed towards a common purpose. An important aspect of complicity is that both partners always have the opportunity to make decisions and participate in the course of the deed as equal partners. They are aware that the deed in question cannot be carried out without the consent (or rejection) of an individual accomplice.

Example: Markus and Stella have a happy relationship. They trust and respect each other, spend much of their free time pursuing their respective hobbies, individually or together. They are in love. In certain situations, they were able to demonstrate a loyalty to each other that went beyond the typical characteristics of a good relationship and made them accomplices. One of these occasions was when Markus got selected by his boss as one of two suitable candidates for a promotion. Markus did not know his competitor and was in the dark about his profile. It so happened that Markus' boss was convinced that a strong manager must have a strong woman. So, he invited Markus and Stella to dinner in a restaurant—as he did with his rival candidate, but separately. Markus recognized his chance. He knew that his boss preferred woman with an androgynous and self-confident persona. Together with Stella, he forged a plan in which way she could best impress his boss. Though, Stella wasn't really into acting, she agreed to do it for Markus. In fact, at the dinner, Markus' boss was enchanted by Stella. When Markus learned weeks later that he would get the position, he knew that Stella's performance had contributed a lot. In the meantime, he had also learnt that his rival candidate had a wife who was rather unimpressive. When Markus met Stella for dinner after he had received the good news, he took her in his arms, winked conspiratorially at her and whispered: 'You were my best accomplice, my darling.'

The core elements of mutual respect, trust and, in particular, loyalty inherent in complicity can lead to a conspiratorial intimacy between two partners. A love-based relationship with complicity can make an unusual cocktail of a relationship. As a result of the shared awareness of having a well-kept joint secret, the potential for partners to be happy together could even be higher.

DOES LOVE LEAD TO HAPPINESS?

Regardless of whether one is in a normal romantic relationship or in one with complicity, it can be assumed that happiness in a relationship is felt by everyone in their own way. This is because happiness depends on the individual person and their personal circumstances. But what seems to be certain is that genuine love that is the feeling of deep appreciation, gratitude, acceptance, and enjoyment, will, in most cases, make everyone happy.

When you are in love, you may realize that the genuine love you feel is somewhat detached from yourself and flows freely between you and your lover without conditions, limitations, or needs. This happens naturally and without your intervention. The result is happiness, which is not only caused by the fact that you have fallen in love, but also that you are loved by someone. This combined feeling of active and passive love creates the high that makes you happy.

At the same time, you should be realistic and remember that love does not always make you happy. As long as you are genuinely loving and being loved in return, there is no problem. But states of mind between partners can change and they do evolve continuously. If, for instance, change brings misery-making problems such as broken promises, cheating, lack of honesty, and the resulting frustrations, then the feeling of happiness can quickly give way to unhappiness.

Always remember that happiness is not just about good feelings but also the absence of bad feelings. You may be head over heels in love with your partner, but his behaviour may still cause you to develop bad feelings. Bad feelings initially generate resentment and are usually followed by concessions or compromise. But concessions or compromise have no place in a happy relationship, simply because a relationship is neither business nor a legal arrangement.

Generally, there are many uncertainties associated with loving another person, which can affect the feeling of happiness. These insecurities can manifest themselves in questions such as: 'Does he/she love me? Will she be able to adapt to my lifestyle? Will he/she ask me to marry him/her? Am I handsome/pretty enough? Does his/her family accept me?' Questions like these signal that the love between the persons concerned is burdened by expectations, doubts, projections, and other uncertainties and does not flow naturally and unconditionally. This can impact your happiness depending upon your particular circumstances and how much attention you'll pay to them (if you are at the receiving end) or how much importance you'll accord to them (when you impose a burden on your partner).

Tip: To ensure that love in a relationship leads to lasting happiness for both partners, your love should not be conditional or associated with high expectations. Instead, you should accept your partner as they are. However, if you enter the relationship with an expectation or if you make your love dependent on the fulfilment of certain conditions, your partner will soon recognize these by your reactions, even if they remain unspoken. Then there is the danger that your partner will think that you want to put a burden on them that they are not ready to bear. The reaction to this will naturally be resistance. This can first destroy the happiness in a relationship, and also love between the partners.

Example: Eva had fallen in love with Henry, though she knew that alcohol consumption and the use of cocaine were an important part of his partygoer lifestyle. Eva herself drank only very moderately, and she was strictly against the use of drugs. Despite Henry's weaknesses, she decided to enter into a relationship with him in the hope that her love would be stronger than his addiction and that in time she would be able to get Henry to change his behaviour. But contrary to what Eva expected, Henry revolted against her repeated attempts to dissuade him from taking alcohol and party drugs. More and more often it led to a quarrel between the two. Eva was unhappy because she didn't get what she wanted from Henry, and Henry increasingly felt Eva as a burden and spoilsport because she didn't let him do what he enjoyed. When they decided to separate amicably, Henry confessed to her that though it was true that she had done everything 'out of love' for him, her method had been wrong.

SELF-LOVE

> Dare to love yourself as if you were a rainbow with gold at both ends.
>
> —Aberjhani, American-born author-poet,
> in *Journey through the Power of the Rainbow*

There is no doubt that all of us want to love ourselves. If you don't do it instinctively already, the question arises as to how it should be done. It is

important to find an answer to this question, because self-love can be the recipe for a successful relationship with a partner. After all, if you don't know how to love yourself, how can you truly love others?

This question and the often-used statement '*you cannot love if you do not love yourself*' should not be misunderstood. It does not mean that if you have any problems with yourself or if you are plagued with self-doubt at some time, you will be unable to love another person.

Self-love should also not be understood as narcissism, self-centredness or arrogance; rather, self-love is an all-encompassing acceptance of oneself, along with elements of self-esteem, self-treatment, self-confidence, and self-value.

Example: For several years, Tina and Herbert have been in a relationship that she and her friends consider to be 'good'. However, there were indications that their relationship was not as good as it seemed. Tina had a bad relationship in the past in which she was disappointed, and which ended with emotional injuries and rejection by her partner. As a result, even in her present relationship, she suffered from the constant fear of doing something that could disturb Herbert and cause him to reject her. Out of her insecurity and her lack of self-esteem she saw problems where there were none. The weight of her past experience, her fear and projections dominated every situation and made her look everywhere for signs that things could go badly in her new relationship.

Without self-love, it is difficult to love other people. This is because self-love forms an essential part of the more comprehensive notion of self-esteem which not only determines our self-image to a high degree, but also forms the basis of appreciative interactions with other people.

Example: Hannah is regularly beaten up by her violent husband Dick. If it gets too bad, she normally flees to a relatives' home in the neighbourhood. But after each incident she returns to Dick on the grounds that she 'loves him so much'. Hannah's relatives and friends don't understand Hannah's decision.

Hannah's example demonstrates that the key to self-love rests within yourself. If your mind is occupied with other thoughts, you will not be able to develop the self-esteem required to love yourself. Therefore, the question about what ties Hannah to Dick is probably not true love but something else. It may be that Hanna draws all of her self-worth from the fact that there is 'at least someone' who loves her, even if he is violent. But

it can also be Hannah's longing for security, her fear of change, or her secret belief of her worthlessness is so strong that she thinks it acceptable for her husband Dick to treat her so badly. To love truly is different from needing another person to compensate for elementary perceived personality deficits. To really love means that you feel good in your skin, love yourself as you are, and have sufficient self-esteem even without your partner. It is this that allows you to approach them emotionally as they are, instead of just using them to fulfil your needs.

> When a woman becomes her own best friend, life is easier.
>
> —Diane von Fürstenberg, fashion designer.

It may then be asked—what is the right path to developing healthy self-love?

If you claim that it is difficult to love yourself, it will be understood as if you find it hard to accept yourself. In fact, if you have no self-esteem, or are plagued with persistent doubts about yourself, and believe that you are not worthy of being loved or loving yourself, then the road to happiness is blocked and you have a problem.

The way to solve this is through a frank insight into yourself. You need to accept both your good and bad sides, your flaws and errors. Take a good look at the mirror inside out, and try to better understand who you really are. This self-analysis will help you learn where your doubts, uncertainties, and self-projections stem from, thus allowing you to confront these issues head-on and ultimately receive and give love to others, including those you are not yet acquainted with.

If you decide to ignore this and are afraid of learning who you really are, then the question arises as to how another person who knows lesser about you than you do yourself should react to you.

> More smiling, less worrying. More compassion, less judgement. More blessed, less stress. More love, less hate.
>
> —Roy T. Bennett, American author,
> in *The Light in the Heart*

As demonstrated through Hannah's and Tina's examples, loving yourself is closely connected to healthy self-esteem. However, in the same way that you have to differentiate between genuine love and mere attachment, it is important to be cautious about this connection. Just feeling good about yourself or a high self-esteem does not necessarily qualify as the kind of self-love that may trigger another person's positive reaction towards you. If it is excessive, it can also be perceived (and rejected) as narcissism or self-entitlement.

An excessively strong self-confidence that is demonstrated outwardly is not only unpleasant, but can also be perceived as a challenge or threat by people who feel inferior to you. This will only provoke defensive reactions. Also, unfounded overconfidence usually leads to criticism and rejection, and it can negatively affect your self-perception.

> Love and compassion are necessities, not luxuries. Without them, humanity cannot survive.
>
> —The 14th Dalai Lama in *The Art of Happiness*

Tip: To embrace a self-love that is appreciated by you and others, avoid overdoing it. It can be helpful, for instance, to combine the development of self-confidence and the building of inner strength with emotions coming from your inner self, such as compassion and human affection.

Compassion and affection are both states of feeling that can be associated with love, and which go beyond attachment, goodwill, and friendship. In principle, affection and compassion include an element of devotion to others (and yourself), which are all helpful in reducing the risk of getting close to narcissism and excessively strong self-confidence.

Involving others in your reflections on self-love will prevent you from judging yourself too ambitiously.

On the other hand, negative thoughts and devaluing projections about yourself may also dominate your mind. In Buddhism, it is said that when you develop negative emotions about yourself, you cannot see reality.

In fact, if you are unable to succeed in remedying your prevailing negative thoughts, you may be confronted with difficulties in your attempt to develop true self-love.

What is commonly understood as 'inner critical voice' is probably the worst adversary when it comes to achieving balanced self-love.

The inner critic was created in your childhood. When you were a child, your parents had to protect you from harm. Therefore, they had to warn you, give advice, admonish, instruct, and correct you as needed. Naturally, you preferred to be praised and were also afraid of losing your parents' love or being punished, so you began to admonish and criticize yourself. This is how the inner critical voice is developed in an individual.

However, if you are unable to manage your inner critical voice as an adult, it can lead to problems as it will gradually damage your self-confidence.

Therefore, when your inner critical voice wants to take over your mind, try to switch to a 'positive programme' and focus on positive and helpful thoughts that can distract you from bad or (self-) critical thoughts.

Another possible option is to make your inner critical voice your ally. Look at the points of critique with the eyes of your best friend and treat yourself like your best friend. Tell yourself that you shouldn't be so hard on yourself. Be more patient with yourself, take the time you need, and be proud of what you are doing.

Never stop building yourself up in a positive way. Many people experience negative or defeatist thoughts, such as 'I'm totally useless.' 'Man, am I stupid?' 'Wow! How fat I've become!' Such ideas will do you no good and will never be helpful for strengthening your self-love. Instead, you could think about why you're great the way you are. Tell yourself that you love yourself and/or what you are doing because … [fill in the blanks] of so and so reason.

There are some practical ways through which you can change the way you think about yourself, remove possible negative thoughts, and make progress on your goal of self-love.

To truly love yourself, it is first necessary to accept how you live in the present. Of course, there are always things that you won't love about yourself and which you will want to change in the future, but as part of your self-analysis, you should also be able to find a number of things you are content with.

Example: George is a junior manager in a food processing company. His job performance is highly regarded by his superiors. George's weakness is his forgetfulness. It only affects so-called small things like forgetting his keys, passwords, his smartphone, his identity card, or the names of business partners. But his colleagues often tease him and at internal meetings, he has already become the target of their ridicule. George is neither pleased with his weakness nor with his colleagues' mockery. However, instead of getting angry at his colleagues and at himself, he decided to focus on the more important things, for instance, the fact that everyone appreciates him for his work and his balanced nature.

In the example, he tried to focus on positive things that better reflected his reality and those things that affected him directly.

Here are some handy tips that maybe useful when tackling with issues of self-love:

Tip: No matter what others say or what others expect of you, make yourself the No. 1 priority of your life. Do not let others tell you that this is selfish. It's not selfish because only when you feel good about yourself can you be there for others.

Tip: Write down things about yourself that you are grateful for and proud of, and which make you distinct from others. For instance, that you are a hard worker, that you are kind and generous to your friends, that you always have new ideas and are your own fun magnet, that you have ambitious goals and work towards achieving them or that you are healthy, and so on.

Tip: Make time for yourself and do what you enjoy. For instance, wake up a little bit earlier in the morning to write a blog or do yoga, sign up for evening courses in your free time, start creating art during the weekends, and so on.

Tip: Use your time more efficiently. For instance, ask yourself critically whether it is really necessary to attend to all requests and queries from your colleagues immediately, or if it is okay to decline and focus on yourself.

Tip: Don't help others because others ask you to. You can only help when you are doing well yourself and when you *want* to help, and not because

it is expected of you. If you only draw your sense of self-worth from helping others, you might become a person with an unusual strong drive to make other people feel better. This is something you need to avoid as it can cause burnout, the feeling to be exploited and depression.

British comedian Charlie Chaplin connected his experiences on the path to self-love with outstanding positive human qualities and came up with an excellent description of self-love.

- As I began to love myself, I found that anguish and emotional suffering are only warning signs that I was living against my own truth. Today, I know, this is AUTHENTICITY.
- As I began to love myself, I understood how much it can offend somebody if I try to force my desires on this person, even though I knew the time was not right and the person was not ready for it, and even though this person was me. Today I call it RESPECT.
- As I began to love myself, I stopped craving for a different life, and I could see that everything that surrounded me was inviting me to grow. Today I call it MATURITY.
- As I began to love myself, I understood that at any circumstance, I am in the right place at the right time, and everything happens at the exactly right moment. So, I could be calm. Today I call it SELF-CONFIDENCE.
- As I began to love myself, I quit stealing my own time, and I stopped designing huge projects for the future. Today, I only do what brings me joy and happiness, things I love to do and that make my heart cheer, and I do them in my own way and in my own rhythm. Today I call it SIMPLICITY.

- As I began to love myself, I freed myself of anything that is no good for my health—food, people, things, situations, and everything that drew me down and away from myself. At first, I called this attitude a healthy egoism. Today I know it is LOVE OF ONESELF.
- As I began to love myself, I quit trying to always be right, and ever since I was wrong less of the time. Today I discovered that is MODESTY.
- As I began to love myself, I refused to go on living in the past and worrying about the future. Now, I only live for the moment, where everything is happening. Today I live each day, day by day, and I call it FULFILLMENT.
- As I began to love myself, I recognized that my mind can disturb me and it can make me sick. But as I connected it to my heart, my mind became a valuable ally. Today I call this connection WISDOM OF THE HEART.
- We no longer need to fear arguments, confrontations or any kind of problems with ourselves or others. Even stars collide, and out of their crashing, new worlds are born. Today I know THAT IS LIFE!

> Not only do self-love and love of others go hand in hand but ultimately they are indistinguishable.
>
> —M. Scott Peck, American psychiatrist

RELATIONSHIPS

> To be happy with a man, you must understand him a lot and love him a little. To be happy with a woman, you must love her a lot and not try to understand her at all.
>
> —Unknown

RELATIONSHIPS ARE SMALL MIRACLES

The closest form of human coexistence is the relationship between two people, especially if it involves a marriage. Another form of human interaction takes place in the workplace, where the relationship between people is completely different in concept but also important for overall happiness of an individual. The general principle of happiness discussed previously—that it is more than just 'feeling-good', 'well-being', and 'pleasure'—also applies to all human relationships. To call a human relationship truly happy, other, more long-term-oriented emotional elements such as love or meaningfulness are required.

Doesn't it sound like an incredible fairy tale when you hear a story of two complete strangers running into each other by chance, falling in love, and entering into long-term relationships. In fact, it is fairy-tale-like if you consider that two people in question were most likely brought up under different educational principles, possibly come from completely different social and cultural backgrounds, own a different wealth of experience, and have different perspectives of the world. And, yet, we often find that such fairy tales do indeed happen all the time—of two strangers living together in harmony and happiness.

For those who understand the complexities of people and the distinct styles and conditions under which people usually live, this is a small miracle. It can be explained by the fact that love and attraction between two people—who were originally strangers to each other—and their feelings of happiness are not only the result of objective factors such as age, appearance, height, education, and education. There is more to it.

The happiness that people feel in such a relationship is rather the result of the interaction between objective elements *and* subjective elements such as how we think (cognition) and how we feel (emotion). They are, in fact, the subjective elements that are responsible for what we have described as fairy-tale-like. Our self-perceived (subjective) feeling of happiness or satisfaction are responsible for the 'little miracle' that makes something that seems objectively impossible possible in reality.

Example: Pim, a thirty-year-old woman from Hong Kong and Ken, a seventy-plus man from England fall in love with each other. Their families and friends initially believe that a genuine relationship will not be possible given the significant age difference. However, they have looked only at the objective circumstances—age difference and the possible difficulties that may arise from it, such as different lifestyles and life expectancy. Instead, for a balanced judgement, they should also have looked at the important subjective elements that, despite the great age difference, can lead to a great subjective well-being for both partners. These subjective factors include, among many others, the very personal disposition (e.g. Pim's preference for an older, more experienced partner) and, on the other hand, Ken's prevailing optimistic attitude in life, which, he felt, could only be shared by a much younger partner like Pim.

Love between two people is a commitment device working like glue. Part of the initial phase of love is that you typically view your partner as better than they may be in reality. This is underlined by the experience that people who are in love consistently rank their partner's qualities higher than other people would do, or they would do themselves if they weren't in love.

During this phase, the partner you're in love with is perceived through rose-tinted glasses. Small problems are overlooked, and all kinds of explanations for weaknesses are readily found. This is part of the happiness of new love.

But even in the state of greatest love and happiness, you should not get too far away from reality. One day, when your initial euphoria begins to weaken, you may realize that you were misleading yourself with regard to your partner's flaws.

Tip: Ask your partner directly about their frank perception of themselves and their idea of the kind of person they think they are.

Example: Frank likes to watch movies at night. His fiancée Judy shared this fondness for watching films initially. She thought that the hours spent together in front of the screen were proof of their intimacy. But this changed in the course of time when she realized that Frank's behaviour seemed to be a mania. He regularly rejected all her suggestions for alternative activities such as walking, bicycle riding, attending concerts, or meeting friends. When Frank told Judy one day that he wanted to buy an expensive new, larger screen with the latest technology, she refused. This led to an argument, and Frank told Judy quite openly that he was not interested in anything other than watching movies every night.

As shown in this example, a frank exchange can be helpful for both partners to see each other more authentically and in a way that matches reality. After talking to Frank, Judy realized that it wasn't the shared experience and the closeness with her that was at the forefront of Frank's passion for movie-watching, but the mere desire for non-stop entertainment and seamless distraction.

It often happens that at the beginning of a relationship, partners promise each other to change those habits and behaviours that the other does not appreciate. However, this does not always work out because very often one partner expects the other to change, even though the latter is reluctant to make this change.

The willingness to change established habits and behaviour is generally not very high. Especially in a longer relationship, it can happen that one partner expects behavioural change from the other but isn't willing to change themselves.

Example: At the beginning of her relationship with Arthur, Belinda liked to take on small and big sewing jobs. She had learned sewing from her grandmother and liked doing it. Later, when they had two children together, there was a lot of sewing to do but Belinda refused to do it.

Instead, she gave the work to a sewing studio. Arthur, who initially had been very generous with money, had become stingy after the birth of his children. He criticized her for her attitude and reminded Belinda that in the past she had always liked sewing. Belinda defended herself and pointed out that over time, her interests had changed and that she wanted to use her free time to train as a DJ. Arthur reacted insensitively and a dispute arose because he considered one activity to be meaningful and the other, pointless. Belinda was outraged.

Arthur and Belinda's example shows that discrepancies between partners that develop slowly over the years can split them so much in the long run that they both feel unhappy in their relationship.

RELATIONSHIPS CHANGE

It's quite natural for feelings in a marriage or a long-term relationship to mellow down. This is not unusual because you and your partner have become more knowledgeable about each other since the first time you met. You hardly have any secrets from one another now.

This is especially true when daily life together becomes a routine. It is natural that things that might have fascinated you and/or your partner (about each other) in the beginning will no longer have the same level of attraction.

Example: Bob always wanted to show his wife Tamara that she came first for him. When he was working on his computer or looking at his smartphone, he would turn the devices off immediately whenever Tamara came to be with him. But after a long time together, Bob had changed his behaviour and reacted less sensitively. When Tamara came to him, he no longer interrupted his activities to be with her. He didn't pay attention to her or even look up, but kept his eyes glued to the screen. In these moments, Tamara had the unpleasant feeling that she disturbed him with her presence, whereas before he was always happy about her company. Tamara was confused and worried about the change in Bob's behaviour, but for the sake of peace she said nothing about her observation.

Although you love your partner, happiness in your relationship can fade away. This process, however, can be slowed down or even prevented by constantly revitalizing and refreshing the relationship through new shared experiences, adventures and discoveries or, as mentioned previously, by becoming conspiratorial accomplices.

Example: You could compare a relationship to a book that tells a long story. In the same way that the chapters in a book are filled with exciting adventures, plot twists, and surprises, a relationship should also be about excitement and discovery. In a novel, the author usually divides a longer story into several chapters, with each having its own set of attractive details so that the reader does not stop reading.

The challenges for loving partners in a long-term relationship who are happy and interested in continuing to be so, are similar to those of a novelist. In order to keep the mutual love relationship as the source of their happiness alive, it would be helpful if the partners were to keep creating new chapters with new adventures and discoveries instead of getting bored in a daily routine or nostalgically referring to old chapters.

To achieve this, initiatives should be taken by both partners aiming at keeping the initial spirit of their relationship alive, fresh, and stimulating.

Example: The computer scientist Andy and the foreign language correspondent Rita still love each other as they did at the beginning of their relationship. They are happy together. But it does not remain hidden to them that it is their professional everyday life that forces them into routine activities such as time management, joint breakfast and dinner, catching up, cleaning, and evening television. One day, they did not switch on the TV set and openly discussed their fears that their relationship could be stifled in the daily routine forced upon them by the circumstances. In the end, they came up with the idea that instead of spending their free time separately pursuing their respective hobbies or together in front of the TV, they could use it for developing a joint project. It was Andy's idea to work on an innovative smartphone app that would make it easier for secretaries to handle foreign-language texts. Both Andy's and Rita's professional backgrounds allowed them to work on such a project in a promising way. The new project not only brought the couple closer together, but also gave them ample opportunity to meet, learn, and exchange ideas in their collaboration with third parties, in project-related meetings and in the search for investors for their start-up. The project idea had successfully pulled Andy and Rita out of their boring routine and brought a breath of fresh air into their relationship.

If Andy and Rita had not been interested in each other, if they had not been keen to revive their relationship with new adventures, and if they had not spoken openly about their situation, they would not have taken the initiative for their new venture. Without this change, their relationship would probably have become boring. They would either have gone their own ways and become estranged or become indifferent to each other, and consequently endangered their relationship and the happiness that they derived from it.

However, love and happiness in a relationship can not only be challenged by the seemingly inevitable routine but also by changes made by the partners in the early stages of their relationship such as in their social life and lifestyle, shared interests, and shared values.

Example: Hank and Mandy were Left-leaning green activists when they met and fell in love at university. Mandy made a career in a fashion company and was increasingly distancing herself from her former radical political positions. Hank, on the other hand, had become an elementary school teacher and was elected speaker of the radical green faction in the local parliament. When

Mandy told Hank that she was promoted to the position of deputy managing director in her company, Hank did not congratulate her but criticized her company for manufacturing clothes in Bangladesh using the lack of labour and environmental protection laws to their advantage. They got involved in a fierce political discussion. Mandy defended her company's position, saying, 'We bring jobs to a developing country.' Hank, however, maintained his initial radical Left-leaning position and accused Mandy of supporting her company which was shamelessly treating the Bangladeshi population like 'outlawed helots'. Their argument on this subject got very heated and ended with Hank recommending that she should seek the 'help of a doctor'. Mandy was shocked by his insulting remark and retreated to the bedroom to cry.

This example shows that changes in areas other than interpersonal emotional aspects can also have an effect on a relationship as well as on the common happiness derived from it. This is true even if the relationship is otherwise good and both partners seem to be happy. It can also happen independently of the fact that a partner can be accused of having made a 'mistake'. However, it could be a real mistake not to notice this trend towards change or not to detect it in time.

Another frequent source of conflict in a relationship is different needs for closeness. This is especially important when one partner misinterprets the other partner's need for distancing as rejection.

Example: Angie wants to spend more time together with her partner Xavier. But Xavier is always very busy, both professionally and privately with his hobbies. His idea of a partnership is different from Angie's. For him, partnership means two individuals with different interests living together, supporting each other, and meeting for common activities such as meals and sleeping, but otherwise pursuing their respective activities independently. He sees Angie's desire for more togetherness as a threat to his independence.

In this example, Angie is sad about her partner's behaviour because she interprets it as a rejection and a lack of interest in her. In her view, a couple that loves each other should seek closeness and spend as much time together as possible. Though Angie accepts Xavier's independence as a legitimate expression of his personality in theory, she is unhappy on a day-to-day basis about his constant unavailability.

In such cases, you run the risk of misunderstandings or upsetting your partner who may interpret your demand for change as them 'not being good enough anymore'. They may also feel that you are, in fact, looking for somebody else to replace them.

Tip: In situations where the conflict between two opposing interests is to be resolved, there is a compromise-oriented tactic that you should try. This tactic assumes that there is an overriding, greater interest you can refer to.

Example: In the example presented, the overriding principle for both Angie and Xavier are the preservation of their relationship and the continuation of the shared happiness that they derive from it. On this basis, they should accept that they must subordinate their individual interests to this principle. This is not about sacrificing one or the other individual interest for the sake of the overriding interest, but to show flexibility, which allows the possibility of a compromise on the basis of mutual give and take. A mutually acceptable compromise could be that Xavier agrees to reserve some time, such as weekends, for Angie and, on the other hand, she accepts that because of his interests, he cannot at all times be available for her. Such a compromise would take into account the individual wishes of both partners in a balanced way, fulfil Angie's insistence on more closeness, and bring both partners closer to the common goal of a lasting and happy relationship.

The overriding, greater interest in a partnership is its preservation, which aims at a balance of interests and mutually perceived happiness. It can be assumed that both partners agree on this goal, otherwise they would not want to be together.

When you propose changes in behaviour to your partner, it is important to let them know that you respect them as individuals. You must make clear that your demand for change is not only in your interest alone but also in theirs, and ultimately for the benefit of your relationship.

If you succeed in making clear to your partner that your demand is constructive, aimed at a balanced relationship, thus, in both partners' interest, your partner may be more willing to take into account what you propose and possibly also follow you.

If you find that your partner is making attempts to change something, let them know that you appreciate it and are enthusiastic about the good that it may bring. This will further motivate them and let them know that they are on the right track.

SHARING FOR HAPPINESS

SHARING

It seems obvious that in a relationship, the basic fundamental value the partners want to protect will be their shared love. But in addition to this, there are many other elements that partners should share to maintain a happy relationship.

Although people's hierarchy of priorities can differ individually, sexuality as well as physical and mental attractiveness and closeness are constructive factors that most couples want to share.

You would also expect a commitment by both partners in long-lasting responsible relationships to enjoy a certain level of intensity, unlimited trust, intellectual challenge, and the feeling of being safe. It's also lovely to be in a relationship with someone with whom you can share the same interests—for instance, a hobby. This, and the way partners react to each other's different interests and preferences, enhances their relationship.

Example: Joan and Peter have a happy relationship. There is only one issue: they don't have any common hobbies. Joan enjoys playing the piano. She practices every day. From time to time, she is invited by her community to make public performances. Quite distinct from her interest in music, her husband Peter enjoys the sports. He is a passionate soccer fan. He never misses an opportunity to watch matches between well-known teams at the stadium. At home too, he watches matches on TV. Joan finds football boring while Peter finds the 'jingling' on the piano, as he calls it, quite annoying because he is unmusical and has no feeling for music.

Despite the fact that they do not share their respective interests, Joan and Peter still have a good relationship. This demonstrates that there are additional elements that add to the bonds that keep a couple together.

In the example, Joan appreciates Peter's loyalty, his decision-making power, and she feels she can fully rely on him. He offers her a stable environment which makes her feel protected. Peter, on the other hand, feels strongly sexually attracted to Joan. He also appreciates her sensitivity and her ability to give him a relaxing, comfortable home. In addition, he appreciates her talent for cooking, which makes him happy at home.

Other elements that partners can share are experiences and memories.

Example: Alan and Thelma were spending a carefree holiday on the island of Mauritius. Their light-heartedness vacation ended abruptly when they were attacked by five men at their hotel gate one night. They were robbed, threatened with knives, and Thelma almost became the victim of gang rape. It was only because of Alan's courageous intervention that Thelma was saved from the worst. Despite all the disagreements and arguments that Alan and Thelma had afterwards in their relationship, they both could never forget the terrifying events in Mauritius. In particular, Thelma always felt grateful to Alan for freeing her from the five men's brutal attack.

But what constitutes the real foundation of a couple's relationship are shared basic values. They can include, for instance, the importance of mutual honesty, trust and communication, love and intimacy, marriage and family, similar religious and political beliefs, and common views on morality.

The importance of sharing basic values becomes apparent when big, life-changing decisions have to be made, such as decisions on moving together, marriage, having children or not, professional careers, becoming vegetarians, and so on. In these situations, the fact that you and your partner may share many common interests or having fun together, take the backseat.

The same can apply if a relationship mellows down and there are not enough common binding interests anymore. In this case, shared basic values can still provide a stable foundation for a happy relationship.

Example: Olga and Patrick met at ballet school and fell in love with each other. However, it soon became apparent that they had different views on morality that they couldn't reconcile. While Olga believed in a monogamous, romantic relationship between two individuals, Patrick believed that monogamy was 'unnatural'. He made clear that he wanted to continue using his 'natural freedom' and have affairs outside their relationship. Olga did not want to accept this, and she left Patrick because they could not agree on a basic moral value that she viewed as essential for a relationship.

This example shows that if the partners are unable to agree on shared core basic values, then there are no bonds left to keep them together.

Having said that, even if sharing of values is agreed upon, it's not a guarantee that no problems will arise in the future—for instance, in case the views of one or both partners change over time.

Example: For Macarena and Tom, the question of what food they ate every day was not an issue for a long time. Both consumed everything they liked to eat and did not make any big exceptions. That changed radically after Macarena was convinced by a close friend to become vegan. Abruptly, she changed her eating habits. In addition, she became a missionary in animal protection. She actively started convincing family members, friends, and acquaintances on the benefits of a vegan lifestyle. Her husband Tom was totally surprised by this development. He did not share Macarena's radical positions on animal welfare and food and began to suffer under her strict food regime at home. He made many attempts to change Macarena's new orientation, but without success. As a result, they quickly became estranged—partly also because Macarena preferred another group of friends as her previous friends had different views on animal protection and food.

The last two examples also show that it is not only shared key basic values that are important for the survival of a relationship. In addition to these, a mutual commitment by the partners to respect and tolerate one another, as well as the willingness to find a compromise in case of conflict are essential.

If you are not able to develop a common view with your partner on issues concerning changes in circumstances affecting the relationship, it is not advisable to promptly express signs of dissatisfaction, desperation, or even starting to fear the imminent end of your relationship.

Instead, in a positive and constructive move, you should try to develop a culture of common sharing between you and your partner, which will ultimately allow both of you to continue the relationship comfortably and be happy with each other.

When there are no common interests, shared experiences, shared memories, shared basic values, along with a failure to connect emotionally, then there is a risk that other superficial issues such as sex and money can gain importance and cause tension and friction in the relationship.

Some people believe that having children can play an important role in substituting the absence of such unifying factors by helping to 'bridge' the differences between the partners.

Example: Olivia and Kai married after one year into their relationship because Olivia was pregnant. Before they married, they failed to communicate with each other about their basic key values, including

principles relating to children's upbringing and the mother's and the father's respective role in the family. When the baby arrived, it had problems with drinking and sleeping. Olivia spent many long sleepless nights in bed. One day, when the situation was particularly tough, Olivia complained about Kai to her parents-in-law. She claimed that Kai categorically refused to take care of the babies though she needed his assistance, especially during the sleepless nights when the babies cried. She reported that Kai had justified his refusal by claiming that he needed his sleep more than her because of his stressful job and his hobbies. Olivia was disappointed by her father-in-law's response to her complaint. He protected his son Kai's position by referring to a tradition that views 'women as homemakers and men as breadwinners' and recommended her to adhere to this principle. Olivia was not pleased with his advice.

This example demonstrates that having children cannot prevent a conflict in a dysfunctional relationship. Such a relationship can usually *not* withstand the stress of a baby crying for many nights or conflicts arising at the time of the child's puberty. Raising children is a long-term engagement and the relationship out of which the child is born must comply with this principle by being solidly constructed. This requires a preventive agreement on the basic principles of living together and a continuous willingness to communicate with each other.

COMMUNICATING

In a partnership, one should communicate directly and intimately. The more open you become, the more authentic you are; and the more authentic you are, the better your partner gets to know you and the better your opportunities will become for you and your partner to grow together.

No matter, how well partners in a relationship know and love each other, and regardless of the fact that they often falsely claim to be able to read each other's thoughts, they usually cannot read each other's mind. Therefore, communication is needed in a relationship to establish trust, develop mutual understanding, and share intimacy. Note that intimacy is not only about the physical connection; rather, intimacy is something that only exists between two partners who are very close, trust each other, and do not necessarily need words to communicate.

Communication in a romantic relationship also serves to provide both partners a level of information that doesn't only allow one partner to better understand the other partner's views and position. Additionally, it also helps to avoid unnecessary misunderstandings that may cause hurt, resentment, anger, suspicion, or confusion.

In case of conflict, good communication can make it easier to find solutions and avoid the infamous 'war of words', which is so typical of relationships in crisis. To maintain an amicable atmosphere, the first priority is to make sure that your partner understands your positive bias and your good intentions to solve the problem.

It will be helpful in this situation, if you are not perceived as accusing, judging or condemning your partner. Also, it is a good idea to try de-escalate the conflict situation by refraining from jumping to conclusions or expressing something that could become toxic. Instead, you should restrict yourself to discussing mere facts aimed at better understanding rather than trying to 'defeat' the other. If you do not do this, it might result in a hardening of your partner's position which could turn out to be counterproductive.

In a debate, it is often tempting to distract or be distracted from the core issue. Bringing up other different but possibly related issues—even if they are close to your heart and important to you—only serve to distract from the main topic and lead to endless discussions without any results. The creation or acceptance of 'secondary battlefields' may, therefore, not be in your interest, especially when you are anxious to resolve the conflict. Creating a 'secondary battlefield' can be in your interest, however, when 'bridging' into another subject issue promises to be effective in avoiding a hardening of positions or finding a compromise.

In addition to staying focused in a discussion with your partner, do not attempt to sweep confrontational subject issues under the carpet. This is not beneficial to either of you. These issues continue to exist as unspoken and unresolved problems that have the potential to further spread their potential toxic effects over your relationship.

In situations when sensitivity is particularly high due to the increased amount of emotions on both sides, non-verbal communication can play an important role. Facial expression when speaking, making or avoiding eye contact, the aggressive 'bent-over' or defensively 'tilted forward' posture, and the aggressive or defensive gestures of the hands as well as the tone of voice—aggressive, loud, soft, conciliatory or guilty—can all express something that is not expressed through the spoken word.

Non-verbal means of communication can also reveal a lot about what your partner actually feels for you. It is, therefore, helpful to pay attention to such non-verbal communication signals, to interpret them correctly, and not to concentrate solely on what is being said. This could possibly lead you astray in your assessment of the situation because in most conflict situations you should assume that there may be a tactical element in your partner's communication.

In situations where it is not about 'victory' or 'defeat', but rather a compromise-oriented solution, passive communication can play an important role in addition to the active form of communication. By active communication, we mean both speaking and non-verbal forms of communication. Passive communication, however, is about listening, which is an especially important part of communication between partners. A good listener can encourage the other partner to speak more openly, intimately, and honestly and will frequently be awarded by growing trust leading to more openness.

Of course, this situation must be assessed differently if a partner's silence is meant 'politically', i.e. carries an unspoken message. In this case, the withdrawal into silence must be interpreted as a rejection in principle of what the other partner has to say and as a withdrawal from the partnership. If this happens, it doesn't make much sense to continue the discussion on the matter. Instead, and in case of continued interest by both parties, the blocking partner must be persuaded to learn to listen and react again. As a general rule, if the partner concerned cannot fulfil such a task, it requires professional help.

Tip: If you set aside time to talk to your partner, it is important your conversation is not interrupted by signals coming from smartphones, computers, or TV. In addition, it will be much easier to produce and share positive feelings if you put aside your own thoughts and interests for the time being and give your partner your full attention. It is very likely that your partner will appreciate your undivided interest and will become somewhat more obliging towards you. In contrast, your partner may feel more uncomfortable in a distracting environment, when your dialogue will suffer from frequent interruptions and a defensive or aggressive attitude. As discussed, non-verbal communication elements such as the avoidance of eye contact, a demonstrated lack of attention and interest, impatience, and arrogance will leave your partner unhappy during the discussion and thereafter.

THE SIGNIFICANCE OF MEANING

> You can't seek happiness; all you can do is seek meaning to your life and happiness will follow you.
>
> —Unknown

Another option to counteract fading feelings of happiness in a relationship is to give a new meaning to the relationship. New meaning refers to changing the dynamics of an existing relationship by giving it new purpose.

> Life has no meaning. Each of us has meaning and we bring it to life. It is a waste to be asking the question when you are the answer.
>
> —Joseph Campbell, American literature teacher

Example: For more than twenty years, Nanda and Harvey lived happily together as a married couple. They were close to each other, even though they had pursued different interests during their years together. During a quiet vacation, they shared an observation that they had become independent from each other. Quietly, almost unnoticed, the euphoric feeling of happiness in their relationship had given way to a certain sense of boredom. In the past, before they both passed the age of fifty, their relationship was characterized by many activities, shared experiences and trips, and frequent laughter. Also, they had always been charming with each other. But today, they were hiding behind their books or smartphones and sometimes didn't even speak a word for several hours. Nanda and Harvey agreed in their conversation that this development was not a growing lack of concern or interest in each other, but the result of their failure to establish a new meaning for their lives as an ageing couple. Since they still loved each other, they, therefore, started to think about giving new meaning to their relationship. After many long discussions, they finally came to the conclusion that at their age, partnership meant shared experience, continued personal development, growth, and change. As a consequence, they looked for an opportunity that would help them realize their new goal. When they learned that a new music hall was about to be constructed in their neighbourhood, they decided to found a private 'Circle of Friends of the Philharmonic Orchestra'. The mission of their group was to collect donations, arrange for sponsorships, and support activities of the concert hall. In addition, they met like-minded people

every month to listen to lectures and discuss topics related to classical music. This new task filled them both with new energy and joy of life, which made their feeling of emerging indifference to each other a thing of the past.

The new meaning that Nanda and Harvey gave their life opened many doors for them: They started cultivating a new purpose for their life and strengthened their relationship. This made them happier than before because their activities were soon widely accepted socially and positively valued as a contribution to the community's cultural life. In addition, privately too, they widened their social circle by spreading their idea, which provided them with an additional new source of happiness.

> Suffering is caused by a pointless life.
>
> —Victor Frankl, Austrian psychologist and holocaust survivor

To find out what the meaning to a relationship is, you can ask yourself the question whether the relationship as you live it is designed to a fulfilled life and if it creates equal satisfaction for you and your partner. The meaning is supposed to govern your relationship. It is essentially the establishment of benchmarks that serve as a guidance that you and your partner can use for your life as partners.

To define the meaning of your life and your relationship, you should not look at the goals of the relationship, but rather the direction in which you and your partner are going. You know the direction in which your relationship should develop once you know what and which values are important to you in your relationship. These values are like lighthouses that show you the direction you need to take.

The values assigned to your relationship are what you feel to be fundamentally important for the relationship, and what you and your partner absolutely need in order to be satisfied. These values are an expression of your and your partner's deepest inner conviction of what is important to the relationship and your shared life.

For instance, values can help you to make fundamental decisions that are not just based on a capricious mood but seriously considered over the long term. They are supposed to have taken into account what are ultimately the most important values in the relationship.

Example: If 'security' is an important value, then you probably won't give up your secure job to travel around Australia for half a year. And if 'family' comes first, and you are the breadwinner of the family, then you will always consider your family when choosing a job. You will probably not volunteer to manage the new branch of your company in a faraway country. Also, you won't cheat on your partner on a whim or a lure, because you know that the values 'loyalty' and 'partnership' are more important to you.

MARITAL HAPPINESS

Joke:

> Girl to fiancé: 'When we're married, I want to share all your troubles and worries.'
> Fiancé: 'But I don't have any troubles and worries.'
> Girl: 'I know, but we're not married yet.'

MARRIAGE: A TRADITIONAL INSTITUTION

To fall in love, to be engaged, and to get married. Though this was considered a central goal in life once upon a time, it is no longer so. In many countries, the number of marriages is decreasing from year to year, and the number of divorces is steadily increasing, not only among relatively young couples who have only recently been married, but also among those who have been married for a long time.

Joke: A man inserted an ad in the classifieds: 'Wife wanted.' Next day, he received a hundred letters. They all said the same thing: 'You can have mine!'

If you look at it superficially, the external conditions for a happy marriage seem rather unfavourable. But there are signs that couples who marry today and stay together, are happier than couples fifty years ago. This is despite the revolutionary student movement of the 1960s and 1970s that denounced marriage as 'the death of love'. This is because, in many parts of the world, marriages today, more than ever before, are equal and self-determined. The value of each spouse is better respected than it was in the past, and this usually leads to a more balanced relationship between the partners.

Though the views on marriage have changed, paradoxically, its underlying traditional values remain the same. Today, as in the past, its cornerstones are love, faithfulness, security, and connectedness.

Memo: The major difference of basic values between marriage and other forms of relationships is that those who marry, promise before the law to respect and uphold these values. There are no other differences except for those invented by professionally risk-averse lawyers.

The mention of the legal profession is a reminder that although most marriages are based on love, it must not be overlooked that a marital engagement is also a legal act binding both partners. A wedding is, thus, not only a romantic event, but from a legal point of view, it also triggers a wealth of rights and obligations. In the event of a separation, this can lead to serious legal consequences. This can include possible hefty financial obligations under prevailing post-divorce allocation of resources rules and judgements on child custody and maintenance. In many cases, the consequences of a separation can not only ruin financial status but also happiness of one or both partners.

Example: Mia, a spirited scientist, has met Lucas, a wealthy businessman. They fall in love with each other, though at first sight they don't make a good match. Mia is an intellectual who loves classical music, ballet, and other forms of art. In contrast, Lucas is neither interested in the arts nor in other cultural activities but prefers, in his free time, to go to bars and get drunk or watch soccer on TV. Despite their differences, Mia and Lucas decide to marry. Before the wedding, Lucas bullies Mia into a marriage contract under which she waives all her rights for financial compensation in case of a divorce. The time following their wedding is characterized by many turbulent ups and downs but despite the many fights, Mia and Lucas keep getting back together. After five years, Lucas tells Mia that he has met another woman and wants a divorce. Though Mia had waived all her rights for financial compensation by signing the marriage contract, her lawyer advises her to contest the marriage contract in the courts because of the threats and wilful deceit on the part of Lucas. The relationship that began with passion ended in an ugly, long-lasting legal fight over a lot of money.

Before the two World Wars, in some parts of the world, divorces were relatively rare occurrences. But that does not mean everything was better back then, especially if you take a closer look at the level of happiness in marriages from that era. At that time, marriages were generally much unhappier than they are today because people married, or were forced by their families to marry, not for love but because they or their families would gain something out of the union; in other words, they had alternative goals to happiness.

There are numerous reasons underlying 'planned', forced or 'arranged' marriages. They vary according to the social, cultural, economic, political and legal context. Forced marriages happen, for instance, because parents consider it their duty to 'place' their daughters because they are considered to be subject to parental authority, for mere economic or financial reasons, to save their family's honour, to prevent assimilation within a foreign host society, or because of perceived religious duties.

Also in the so-called West, the marriages of our generation's parents and grandparents were essentially marriages arranged for political or other factors, such as class, health, or finance. Often times, they were also a result of the parents' belief that a chosen partner would provide a safe haven for the upbringing of children.

In these cases, the absence of emotions often resulted in unhappiness, especially when the efforts of one partner to please the other partner ceased at the very moment they married.

> My wife and I were happy for twenty years. Then we met!
>
> —Rodney Dangerfield, American comedian

Cynical jokes about marriage, such as the ones quoted here, are a typical reflection of the situation for many people at that time.

Today, young people, in some cultures, can live together before marriage—something that was not common in the past. Many young people now have the privilege to gain experience, test living in a relationship, and get to know each other properly before they decide to marry. This then is no longer a romantically transfigured, emotional act but simply 'cool' as it is the result of the individual's autonomy allowing them to pursue their own contextually appropriate life course, irrespective of the norms, beliefs, and expectations of others which may still dominate their environment.

THE LIFELONG MARRIAGE CONCEPT

> A man can be happy with any woman, as long as he does not love her.
>
> —Oscar Wilde, Irish poet and playwright

Today, in many parts of the world, people enter into relationships much more quickly than was done 100 years ago. In some cultures, unmarried people live together in close relationships like a married couple, even for long periods of time.

However, they also separate much more

easily and more quickly, or divorce after only a few years of marriage. This is despite the fact that they would have promised each other a lifelong relationship when getting married. Increasing divorce rates don't seem to reflect these marital expectations. Instead, they seem to signal that there is something wrong with the model of a lifelong marriage as a standard.

The promise of lifelong love is either an instinctual consequence of the romantic 'search for happiness' or an empty promise made with the knowledge that momentarily experienced happiness will most likely not last 'until death', but just serves to maintain the momentary feeling of happiness associated with the wedding event.

Example: Until about 100 years ago, a marriage rarely lasted more than half a century. At that time, death was much more a part of life than it is today; people died earlier and for this reason alone, the phrase 'until death do us part' made sense. Today, it's different, not only because of a higher life expectancy but also for cultural reasons.

Notwithstanding these modern developments, there are still ideal couples who exemplify the principle that 'lifelong love' and 'lifelong happiness' in a marriage can work despite an increasingly dynamic and short-lived world.

This attitude is always evident when divorced persons remarry with the belief that *this* time, they will be spared the fate of divorce. Despite their negative experience, they are not discouraged and assume that their current new choice of partner would finally be the only 'real' partner and their love for them would be the first 'real' love they had been waiting for all their life. This process can be repeated as often as desired without the formerly divorced partner losing faith in the prospects of their final 'right choice'. Therefore, one can see people trying again and again, despite all unhappiness they may have endured in former marriages.

In consideration of this phenomenon, it seems that the model 'falling in love, getting engaged, and marrying' is deeply implanted, over many generations, in the subconscious mind of people, so much so that its repeated failure doesn't deter them.

Example: After nine years, Mickey's marriage with Grace was doomed. There was nothing left between the two of them to spark a passion.

They divorced. Soon after, Mickey met Anna with whom he started a relationship. They got married but separated after three years. For professional reasons, Mickey had accepted a long-term foreign assignment in an African country. Anna could not follow him because she was allergic to insect bites. His assignment took three years, much longer than planned. Anna did not appreciate having a long-distance marriage and divorced. After some time as a bachelor, Mickey met Yasmine. He told his friends that he had finally found the 'woman of his life'. After a very short time, Mickey and Yasmine married. Mickey was very happy because after being alone for so long, he was longing for a close relationship. He was aware that his third marriage might end the way his two previous ones did, but he wanted to trust and believe in the promises made between him and Yasmine.

This example shows that the perception of marriage is not as negative as many people may think. Most people still believe in the concept of marriage—even those who have had one or more bad experiences.

This also shows that it is not marriage that is the problem, but rather the notion of a lifelong relationship and the pressure to adhere strictly to it that causes trouble.

It seems to be more widely acknowledged that a lifelong relationship does not mean you stay in one relationship for the rest of your life. Rather, you may go through a series of relationships—or, expressed differently, a serial monogamy—before finding the one that is truly going to give you happiness for the rest of your life.

There still remains the question whether, despite all the negative reporting, people's willingness to remain loyal to the concept of marriage in principle has anything to do with their preference and longing for 'true romantic love'.

Among the different types of love, 'romantic' love seems to have the highest acceptance among people who are in love. This is the case, though we know that the concept of a lifelong marriage offers in principle little opportunity for romance and passion because it is designed for eternity and based on a long-term concept. In contrast, romance is a more short-term concept, as it diminishes in strength after a brief period and possibly dies off completely in the long run.

> The great enemy of love is romanticism [...] It teaches us that true love is without words and that a perfect relationship consists of a mystical union of two souls. This is not very helpful.
>
> —Alain de Botton, French philosopher

This quotation by Alain de Botton warns against associating romantic feelings with love, because such an association has a staggeringly high potential for failure.

The reason why people are so concerned with romance also has something to do with the ideas of love and sacrifice that are at the centre of romantic stories.

Example: In the tragic-romantic story of *Romeo and Juliet*, the young lovers die, as a result of the obstacles in their way to unconditional love. Instinctively, we ask ourselves whether, in a similar situation, we too would have killed ourselves.

These kinds of thoughts may give rise to great ideas of what love is, but mostly, they have nothing to do with reality. Although, we don't know exactly what really happens when two people fall in love, it seems certain that people in love imagine their future to be rosy. They do not think that their love could ever break, even when the loved partner snores while sleeping or has other deeply disturbing habits.

People in love usually have illusions about love as their feelings are typically deeply romantic. This is fine, but only if they do not lose sight of reality.

You may think of this to be a plea for disillusionment, but you should simply accept that in reality, love and happiness can neither be perfect nor eternal. It is understandable if you like to be fooled by your momentary romantic feelings. At least for a certain time. But if you are realistic, your great expectations—possibly inflated by romantic feelings—have the potential to stand in the way of your happiness. Expectations bear the risk of not being fulfilled. This is especially the case once the inevitable daily routine and habituation coupled with the ever-growing desire for something diverse or even exotic and a break from normality will take possession of the relationship.

When you understand this as a principle, you may be able to become happier in the long run.

This insight also refers to the feeling of satisfaction resulting from marriage and the subsequent companionship. In this case, you should also be careful not to confuse a feeling of momentary satisfaction with the true feeling of happiness.

You may have experienced it yourself, but true happiness does not totally elude rationality because it is built upon it; for instance, the principle of being at peace with yourself. Therefore, the importance of 'reality' as a factor must be considered. In this context, it would be helpful if you avoid deluding yourself with something that does not exist in reality.

But many searching happiness describe it unsatisfactorily with metaphors, such as 'having butterflies in one's stomach', which signal irrationality. Interestingly, in this metaphor, the word 'stomach' and not 'brain' is used. This can be interpreted as a small indication of the emotional irrational prevailing in this field.

Keeping the importance of 'reality' in mind, the traditional imperative of 'lifelong marriage' has the potential to contribute to the destruction of what it claims to accomplish. Instead of promoting happiness, it has the potential to destroy it.

Example: Over time, Roger and Caren's initially 'passionate love' had lost its vitality. After close to fifteen years as a couple, Roger spent most of his evenings at home sprawled in front of the TV with beer and crisps. Caren, on the other hand, was glued to her smartphone, posting on Instagram and Facebook. Their lives were drifting apart because of a lack of mutual interest in each other. There was little to no communication between the two except for the essentials such as food and their thirteen-year-old son.

Both seemed to be bored with each other and were increasingly looking for distraction from the outside. Roger had already had a number of short-term affairs. Until now, Caren had felt a bit trapped to do something similar because she had to take care of their son, but this situation was slowly changing as the boy grew older.

So, it's quite frequently that people find themselves in a relationship with the following qualities:

- They *feel trapped*, either out of habit, comfort, duty, sociocultural, and other obligations or responsibilities.
- Some resign themselves to a *lifetime of misery* because they can't, don't dare or won't make the decision to separate from their partners.
- Other couples experience and complain about increasing *boredom*, indifference, disinterest, inattention, cynicism, bad manners, and let themselves get sloppy.
- Some others seem to be unable *to adapt to the changes* in their life circumstances.

The basic flaw in the assumption that a lifelong bond can be promised at a relatively young age is the failure to recognize that the initial circumstances will not remain the same throughout the years, that is in good times and bad. In reality, like in any other relationship, marriage is not static. As discussed before, in addition to underlying circumstances, the personalities of the two partners are also likely to change and develop with time; for instance, in case of job changes or after the birth of children.

When a marriage becomes routine, dull or boring, and the partners believe they have exhausted all possibilities for reviving the relationship, their usual reaction is to search for new avenues for excitement. Here the partners have the choice to make a change for the better.

Either they remain loyal to each other in the relationship and undertake these attempts together, while behaving like the previously mentioned accomplices. This includes the possibility that they will continue to be happy with each other. Their efforts will only be aimed at maintaining their partnership and the happiness they derive from it in the long run.

Or, alternatively, openly or secretly, the partners decide to go their own ways. By opting for this method, they risk not only the continuation of the relationship, but also the happiness they derive from it.

> An era can be considered over when it's basic illusions have been exhausted.
>
> —Arthur Miller, American playwright

Another option for the partners is to stay together the same way as our grandparents and earlier generations under the traditional imperative of a lifelong marriage used to do. In this case, it would soon become apparent that this traditional model is not be helpful but detrimental to promoting the partners' happiness.

This is when the traditional lifelong expectation—categorically formulated as a dogmatic norm—can cause tremendous unhappiness, especially when the partners involved and their circumstances have changed completely in the course of time.

Example: Sacha and Louisa married and were a happy couple for more than nine years. They had two children. Their happiness changed dramatically after Sacha had met his old college buddy Rowan who, in Sacha's memory, had always been gay. Amongst other topics, Sacha's and Rowan's conversations also covered some college experiences which, over time, Sacha had forgotten about. This included a homosexual experience between the two friends. After meeting Rowan, the memory of this experience never left Sacha. One night when Louisa and the kids were traveling, he went to a gay bar and had a sexual adventure. It was very intense and Sacha couldn't forget it. He followed up and had more homosexual adventures. After a while, Sacha realized that, in the end, he was sexually more attracted to men than to women. For a long time, Sacha hesitated, but finally he opened up to his wife. Louisa who was very much in love with her husband was shocked by his revelation. Sacha proposed a separation but Louisa categorically refused, referring to the two children and particularly citing her promise at the wedding to stay together 'till death do us part'. Coming from a conservative family, she took this promise very seriously but her main motivation was her hope that Sacha's homosexual inclination would turn out to be a temporary lapse and that eventually he would return to her. In the following years, Sacha and Louisa entered into a kind of fictitious marriage that did not let either of them be happy.

This example demonstrates that the real issue behind the problem of infidelity in a marital relationship is not so much the institution of marriage or the principle of monogamy, but the underlying idea about a lifelong relationship.

THE PRIORITY OF HAPPINESS

Joke: Recently, an old couple, married more than seventy-five years, was interviewed. When the husband was asked about the happiest time in his long life, he looked at his wife with a smile and said: 'The five years I spent as a prisoner of war.'

The strongest attraction for a partner who is cheating is usually boredom and the search for a new thrill. Some cheating men refer to something they call 'instinctive biological search for optimal genes' or their natural unbridled urge to multiply. Ignore these explanations. They are nonsense!

This is all the more so because society generally expects too much from its standard marriage model, which is supposed to provide two people with lifelong happiness, love and sex, mutual interest and passion—today and forever—along with friendship and companionship long into old age.

This critical view of the standard marriage model should neither be misunderstood as a rejection of marriage, nor should it be seen as a justification for an unbridled and unattached, and, in some cases, irresponsible way of life.

Some people argue categorically that marriage does not guarantee happiness. This cannot be advocated in such an all-encompassing manner. There are people who live in a marriage-like close relationship and are as faithful to their partner as if they had made a vow of fidelity during a wedding ceremony. Others are married, have formally sworn fidelity, but do not keep their promise.

It is understood that everyone has different reasons for why they want to be married or stay unmarried in a close relationship. When you think about entering into a relationship, you may, therefore, decide that it is not important for you which type of relationship you choose, but that you prefer to choose the kind of relationship that will help you to feel sustainably happy in it.

This decision makes happiness from the relationship your priority and, as a consequence, also the internal and external factors that affect your personal happiness within the relationship. You will find out that your autonomous, 'cool' decision to stand above restrictive social, religious, and sociocultural norms will make you feel free. You do this with the knowledge that these norms can change—as demonstrated in the history of mankind—but not your pursuit of happiness or your individual method of achieving it.

If happiness is your priority, no taboos and dogmas will hinder your independent, autonomous, and 'cool' analysis of all obstacles that stand in its way. Everything that prevents you from being happy has to be thoroughly examined and must be questioned, even the traditional principles of lifelong marriage. In this process, you must not accept any dogmatic principles or and religious, cultural, or social norms that can potentially put your personal happiness at risk. You deserve your happiness!

BONDING FACTORS

Communication within the marriage is of central importance to prevent you and your marital partner from growing cold and indifferent to each other. It needs to be understood that marriage is reciprocal, and the most important means to keep it alive is talking.

Tip: Talking in a marital relationship means foremost to share your expectations, feelings, fears, and insecurities that may affect the relationship. This will allow your partner to understand where you stand and what you aspire. When you share your anger, displeasure, and resentments, don't forget to also talk about the beautiful experiences you have had together with your spouse. This prevents the impression that all you do is complain.

Devastating situations, such as unemployment or the death of a loved one can plunge a marriage into crisis.

Tip: You can limit the negative effects by including your partner in your thoughts instead of isolating yourself and trying to work together to find workable solutions.

Tip: To prevent problems from blowing up so much that you need couple therapy, you can set aside time for yourself to spend together and talk. This can take place at home in a quiet environment, without distractions from TV, smartphones, computers, children, family or friends, or during a specially planned change of location to a quiet place without outside disturbances.

Whatever the cause be for communication, its success depends on the mood of the partners at time of communication.

In principle, both partners should start the conversation with a positive basic attitude. A basic attitude is positive if both partners intend to behave constructively and purposefully, i.e., to do everything possible to solve the existing problems and restore harmony in the relationship. A positive attitude towards the partner and the relationship can be signalled by conducting the conversation with an open mind. An open mind is when the partners are willing to listen to each other and seriously consider their respective points of view on the basis of mutual respect and respect for the relationship.

In order to create a positive climate for the discussion, you could also consider introducing elements in the conversation that act as small 'bonding factors'.

Example: A bonding factor can be the mention of shared experiences that trigger a positive memory in both partners. For instance: 'Do you remember how we argued back then about whether or not we should actively join the anti-nuclear movement and how we loved each other afterwards though we were fighting so hard. At that time, our different points of view didn't divide us! Why should the topic we are discussing today do it?'

You should also take great care to refrain from trying to change your partner's position. This will rarely work. Instead, it might lead to a hardening of your partner's position and thus have a negative impact on the outcome of the conversation. You shouldn't forget that the purpose of the conversation is not to change your partner's opinion but to create a basis for a rapprochement in the relationship based on mutual respect and tolerance for each other. Partners in a relationship have the right to have their own opinion, even if it differs from the other. The only decisive factor is to make the relationship strong enough to withstand differences in opinion.

> Couples who have had fewer than five positive interactions in one negative interaction are likely to divorce.
>
> —John Gottman, American researcher and clinician

Relationships between partners who have different points of view can be exhausting. But relationships continue to be a goal for most people even when they believe that they may have become used to their relative freedom outside a relationship. In fact, even those who became increasingly self-centred and unable to accept compromises often look for relationships.

The reasons why men and women need close relationships can be different—for instance, creating stability in life, increasing emotional well-being, having someone to count on and trust in times of need, and feeling a sense of happiness on being loved. Closeness does matter in our lives and that is the reason why we tend to gravitate to others and like to share life experiences, activities, and hobbies as well as our love and happiness.

Relationships not only allow us to love but show us how it feels to be loved in return. Having a trusting relationship enables us to truly be our true selves. For instance, if each partner perceives the need for solitude in himself and, at the same time, accepts it in the other, both partners can develop a cool feeling of independence which will possibly result in a strengthened partnership.

Tip: Look at your relationship like building a house. It is hard work and requires a lot of effort and dedication.

POSITIVITY

In this section, we will discuss some of the 'bricks' you should consider when you have decided to undertake the hard work of building your relationship.

The question is how can couples remain communicative and maintain a receptive attitude to differences between themselves? As discussed before, the key factor is to be positive and constructive, to listen effectively, be prepared to give and take feedback, and not to make projections on your partner that may lead to misinterpretations and misunderstandings or put them on the defensive. You can keep the tone positive by making a shared commitment to communicate dissatisfaction in a constructive way, and by accepting and celebrating differences.

In case of a controversial discussion, you might want to try balancing negative remarks with positive asides. The idea behind this is that you don't suppress your criticism of your partner but you criticize in a way that doesn't sound aggressive but conciliatory.

Example: Scarlett had a problem with her husband Levy. Even after she told the children to go to bed, he started playing a new game because he enjoyed his time with them. Scarlett was upset because his behaviour did not only undermine her authority but took away the time she wanted to share with her husband. She complained about it, but Levy didn't care about her concern and continued. The next time Scarlett talked to Levy she did not complain saying, 'I told you several times already not to do this, and you haven't bothered to listen to me!' Instead, she chose her words carefully and said, 'I really appreciate the fact you play with the kids every night, but please realize that it means a lot to me to talk to you at night without being disturbed by the kids.' This time, Levy got Scarlett's message and started to make an effort to devote more time to his wife.

Always try to keep your mind focused on the positive aspect of the relationship and talk more about the future and what the things you want to do with your partner than the past. It will be fine, however, when you draw on memories that connect you and your partner with feelings of love and happiness. Alternatively, you can ask your partner relevant questions, like 'since we decided to be together, what was your happiest memory of us?'

EXTERNAL AND INTERNAL INFLUENCERS

There are a number of external and internal factors that can negatively influence your relationship.

Example: Theo, Abigail's husband, has a problem with his boss at work. For this reason, Theo comes home every day in a bad mood. He is grumpy, irritable, and refuses any conversation. Theo can't separate the professional from the private and Abigail suffers as if she too had a problem with Theo's boss. This has been going on now for more than six months, and it has started to have a lasting negative impact on Theo's and Abigail's previously happy relationship.

When talking to each other about negative influences on your relationship, it is helpful to clarify who or what contributes to the deterioration of the climate in your relationship.

Tip: Write together a list of all external and internal factors, such as job stress, boredom, lack of money, worries about children, arguments with relatives or friends, and so, that is causing trouble in your relationship.

Based on such a list, you may realize that some of the points are so important that they need a solution-oriented conversation. But it can also be that many of the points on the list are of no or little importance for your relationship. But over time, because they have never been discussed, they have gained a disproportionate importance. In this case, you may realize that you have just been nit-picking. Here are some mundane examples worth considering:

- Don't leave your handkerchief on the table.
- Switch off the lights when leaving the room.
- Don't let the water run when brushing your teeth.
- Switch off the TV when you're not watching.

What you can learn from this exercise is to develop some self-discipline that will help you distinguish important issues from unimportant ones. It will also prevent unimportant issues from poisoning your relationship and help you focus on those factors that have the potential to really harm you both. Sometimes, you might even find that the negative influence is not your partner's fault but that your relationship is being influenced by an external factor.

Take time to identify and categorize these factors appropriately and come to a resolution on how to deal with them. This approach can be helpful to maintain or restore happiness in your relationship.

SPACE TO BREATHE

If you truly want to spend a lifetime of happiness with your partner, then you need to give the love between the both of you 'space to breathe', accept differences, and be receptive to change. Practice tolerance by understanding your partner, respecting them, acknowledging their flaws, and learning to let go of your expectation of changing possible differences based on your perception of what is right.

Tip: Define what you perceive is the other's greatest weakness or flaw (this should not be difficult for either partner). *Example:* 'You nag about everything.' Behind each of the statements you write down your personal strategy for dealing with the other's weakness. *Example:* 'I will not always feel personally addressed, fight back or feel accused right away.' Afterwards, share what each of you wrote. You might find that your partner has a better idea than you on how best to respond to his moments of weakness or times of conflicts, and you too can learn from it.

You and your partner should find a mutually acceptable attitude towards your common human weaknesses and flaws. When you married, you accepted each other's flaws, and it would be unfair to suddenly make these weaknesses an issue determining the happiness in your relationship.

Tip: If you notice that you are starting to get upset about some of your partner's flaws, you should take a moment to reflect and ask yourself how you would react if your partner would suddenly start to nag you all the time about your weaknesses.

Probably, you wouldn't be too happy about your partner's criticism.

SECRETS AND TRUST

If you decide to keep something from your partner, it can raise suspicion and some people even say that it can act as a 'relationship killer' because secrets separate partners from each other like a transparent wall.

> Knowing everything about your partner disenchants him.
>
> —Unknown

In real life, everyone who lives in a long-term partnership walks a fine line that separates the *unsaid* from the *said*. The question is whether secrets are really 'relationship killers' or whether they give a relationship an additional exciting feeling, because with their help, it is possible to keep a sense of curiosity alive.

How many secrets (and of what quality) a couple have in their relationship—without breaking it apart—can vary greatly.

When assessing the influence of secrets on the happiness in a relationship, one has to make a distinction between secrets that are unintentionally created over the years and those that are from the past.

Example: Sometimes on Saturday mornings, Ara would pack her sports bag, put on her sneakers and headphones, and leave the house. Three hours later, she was back. Her husband and the children assumed she had been to the gym, but in reality, she had gone shopping wanting 'to be alone for a little bit and reward herself'. She hid this from her husband because he hated shopping and not only would he never go shopping with her, but he also hated to see her do it alone.

Other secrets are due to embarrassing incidents from before the marriage or things that might be disturbing to the other partner.

Example: Diana only had sexual relationships with women before she met her husband Richard. She kept this as a secret from him for many years. Her sexual attraction to women surfaced again, when Richard mentioned his dream of experiencing a threesome relationship with another woman. Diana was embarrassed because she didn't know how to react. Although she was interested, she feared that her secret would be disclosed if her husband went ahead with the idea from his dream.

These two examples show secrets that can strengthen a partnership because the secretive partner is familiar with the other partner's sensitive areas and understands that revealing the secret might only hurt the other. This is considerate, contributes to the partner's happiness, and strengthens the relationship.

However, how far an individual would want to go with hiding things varies from person to person. Also, people have different thresholds for guilt.

Secrets become a serious issue, however, when they involve betrayal, fraud, or the concealment of facts that the other person would have the right to know—for instance, a past crime with subsequent imprisonment. In these cases, a secret can quickly turn into a lie because it is a lie which is an instrument to keep the secret a secret, and a means for the liar not to exonerate themselves. If this is the case, neither in a relationship can be happy, because it cannot be excluded that, one day, the secret will come to light unintentionally.

FIREDOORING

An emergency exit, like a 'fire door', can only be opened from one side. With this artificial term, one describes a one-sided relationship in which one partner takes care of the other while little or nothing comes from the partner at the receiving end. In a romantic relationship, this disparity cannot really contribute to the happiness of the partners, because a happy marriage needs equal partners in a balanced relationship.

Example: Emmy always had good ideas to show her husband Harry how much she loved him and how much she liked to make him happy. But her many little attentions were taken for granted by Harry. Last time, when

Emmy had brought him his favourite chocolate from her shopping trip, once again he had not bothered to thank her or let her know that he appreciated her little gesture. There was neither a word of thanks from Harry, nor a kiss, nor a caress. Instead, he had immediately started to eat the chocolate without offering her a piece of it. When she, in her disappointment, dared to give him a hint that she had actually expected a small word of thanks and would have been happy about it, he took it as criticism and was offended.

The question is, how long a loving partner can go along with this behaviour. As in all relationships, the linchpin is self-esteem. If one partner is suffering from a weak self-esteem, they will be more prepared to be taken advantage of under the assumption that to get recognition, friendship, or also love, you have to make an effort with the hope that at some point you will get something back. The receiving partner, on the other hand, is selfishly looking out for their advantage. They think it's ok to be cared for, courted, and desired but lack the empathy to see that a happy relationship needs a balance of such efforts.

If the relationship account on your side is permanently 'in the minus', while your partner permanently enjoys the 'plus', it is time for a clarifying conversation between you too. This should take place without reproach. The giving partner should make it clear, however, that they feel taken advantage of. In addition to this, the conversation can also help the giving partner to find out whether they were attentive enough not to have overlooked the other partner's efforts. If the receiving partner has no insight, the giving partner should carefully consider whether they might not better use their commitment to people who appreciate their efforts and do not take them for granted.

> A good friend just told me that the key to a successful marriage was to argue naked.
>
> —Leann Rimes, American singer

DISPUTES

Arguments between partners in a relationship are inevitable and thus normal because living together with someone for a long time, inevitably means having to resolve many conflicts.

On the contrary, couples who pride themselves on successfully avoiding all disputes have often just conveniently swept their conflicts under the carpet.

In fact, the decisive factor for the quality and the continuity of a partnership is not the result of a dispute, but the way in which it is carried out. Continuing an ongoing dispute without any prospect of improvement is certainly dangerous for the relationship. But also, behaviour like justification, defence, attack and counter-attack, lack of objectivity, contempt, disrespect, and refusal to talk, can be harmful to the harmony in the relationship.

Long-term happy couples, on the other hand, succeed in largely avoiding these toxic behaviours in their conflicts and don't devalue each other but show respect and listen to each other. That way, at least, there will be a chance that, as a reaction, the other partner will avoid becoming mean, personal or behaving over defensively.

Another option to reduce and de-escalate tension is to signal closeness to the other partner. This can be done through physical touch such as a hug, or by saying that you understand the other partner's concerns, or lastly through humour which, in this situation of dispute, is best expressed as self-irony.

Remember, it's not too hard to develop a sense of humour. It can be developed with a bit of practice and can help to keep coolheadedness in a tense situation.

Tip: Take a step back, and view your situation as a third-party observer. This trick can help you see your situation with a new perspective. Next, try getting yourself to smile instead of making a grim face. Even if your face is fake it's okay as a fake smile has a tendency to lead to a genuine smile, which may pave the way for laughter.

> Raise your words, not your voice. It is rain that grows flowers, not thunder.
>
> —Rumi, 13th-century Persian poet

This downplaying of the conflict is particularly appropriate when the trigger for the dispute is a seemingly banal event such as sharing workload at home. This can, however, be the trigger for a more serious, fundamental conflict such as the accusation of belittling and humiliating macho-style behaviour, which can quickly arise due to incorrect communication.

A couple that is able to engage in healthy arguments and avoids bickering about issues over and over again, especially if they are of minor importance, can normally release tension quickly and return to normal.

If you are satisfied and happy in your relationship but still feel that a potential for conflict may exist, then you should not try to overcome all possible differences with your partner. Instead of spending your energy on potential or seemingly unsolvable problems, you should consider putting your own demands aside and avoid conflict.

LONG-DISTANCE RELATIONSHIPS

> The simple lack of her is more to me than others' presence.
>
> —Edward Thomas, British poet and novelist

For most people, having a long-distance relationship is an anomaly. But for many, it is becoming a reality. In most cases, partners did not choose to go long distance voluntarily.

Example: Already for seven months, Josephine has been living in a distant marriage with her husband Kevin. Kevin was transferred by his company to Shanghai on a temporary foreign assignment. Depending on the decision of his company, his assignment can last one year or more. Because of this uncertainty, Josephine refuses to send her three children to the International School in Shanghai and has stayed behind with them to provide them with a stable education.

In a long-distance relationship, important elements of a normal relationship do not work. For instance, partners who are separated by a large geographical distance don't have a chance in participating in the daily ups and downs of life of the other. They miss out on major events in their partner's life and are prevented from developing a shared joint memory. In addition, there is the constant underlying uncertainty which can dominate the partners' thinking.

Example: When he is alone in his hotel room in Shanghai, Kevin is thinking, 'Is this all worth it?' At home, Josephine wonders: 'Is he secretly meeting other girls?' Kevin wonders: 'Does she still feel the same way about me as she did before?' And, Josephine thinks, 'Am I kidding myself with all of this? Maybe Kevin is happy to be separated and I don't know it!'

The longer the partners are apart, the more these uncertainties can grow into an existential crisis of the relationship. To prevent this from happening, long-distance relationships need special attention of the partners and smart management to stay together.

This can only work if the partners, prior to their separation, discuss in all openness, all parameters to which this 'smart management' is subject to and how they envisage the continuation of their relationship under adverse conditions and what expectations they have of each other.

Tip: The spirit of these discussions should be positive. As loving partners, both sides should recognize the special challenges the other partner may be facing. Both partners should show readiness to support the other, instead of lamenting about how unhappy they are with the unwanted separation. This wouldn't be helpful in this difficult situation and only cause additional stress. Challenging or even attacking the other partner, whether justified or not, would unnecessarily incite further conflict. More effective than putting each other down through complaining, is holding back, shedding selfishness, and building up each other.

This mutual support requires a consensus between the two partners on what expectations they have of each other and how they plan to nurture the relationship under the more challenging conditions of a long-distance relationship.

EXPECTATIONS

It's important for both partners in a relationship to know that they are truly and equally committed to their relationship. If they wouldn't be committed, they will not tolerate that their relationship is subject to permanent change. Fuelled by the personalities of the partners, their respective inputs, joint experiences, and external influences, good relationships are continuously evolving. If this is not the case, then there is the risk that relationship will slowly die.

This is even more the case in a long-distance relationship. Therefore, it is recommended that in a long-distance relationship, partners engage in activities that help maintain the enthusiasm for and optimism in each other as they would have if they lived together.

One possible option to do this effectively would be to define a cause that unites you and your partner, despite the geographical distance. An example can your shared vision of a possible future together.

Example: Justin is offered a temporary position in his company's affiliate in South Africa. He has accepted because he will be paid generous allowances. In addition, his move will be an important stepping stone to a more elevated position in the company. For a number of reasons, his wife Audrey and the kids will not follow him to South Africa. Before Justin leaves, he and Audrey agree that during his absence, they will save as much money as possible to buy an apartment in their city, which at present they cannot afford.

Once you have agreed on a common cause, you can establish some milestones that advance your common cause and to which your partner can look forward to. Milestones could be, for instance, an agreement on the next time you both will be able to visit available apartments in the market, important financial decisions, decisions about your kids' school or education, holiday plans, and so on.

Another expectation is based on the assumption that a long-distance relationship cannot survive without the hope that the partners will soon be together again. However, the shared vision of being soon reunited again is not enough. The partners must also make sure that, during the separation, none of them will lose sight of their common goal.

Example: This would be the case if, in the continuation of the example above, Justin were to give in to the temptation to stay in South Africa for three more years because it would benefit his career. Audrey, on the other hand, out of defiance and anger, would accept an attractive offer from a friend to become director at her fashion salon in Paris.

COMMUNICATIONS

Long-distance relationships are easier to manage at present because advanced digital technology offers many options to contact and connect at any given time. Unlike in the past, where one had to write letters or make expensive long-distance phone calls, today, partners can stay connected using technology that lets them communicate in real time.

Tip: When you communicate electronically to share experiences with your partner, it is recommended that in these communications, you do not remain too general in what you say but to share details. For instance, don't just say, 'I went to a reception and met many people.' Instead, talk about the place where the reception took place, what kind of people you met, what you talked about, the food that was offered, and how the whole event and the people made you feel. Your partner will have a much better opportunity to imagine the event and to get closer to the feeling of having participated.

Technology also offers options to physically separated partners to have fun together. Distance-bridging alternative electronic forms of communication that previously seemed exotic to many, that were left to technology freaks and hardly used or not used at all by broader user groups, have become popular and a normal means of communication due to the pandemic-related lockdowns and other physical meeting restrictions. These include online games, discussion, and video-conferencing platforms. In addition, partners can use Skype to enjoy a movie night together and make 'good night video calls' even when they happen to be in different parts of the world. Similarly, digital streaming services can also be used to binge-watch multiple episodes of TV shows together.

Long-distance relationships that are going to stand the test of time need a plan for what happens next and assurances on when the distance relationship will end. This helps both parties because with this knowledge they can both work towards that common goal of being together once again.

When, due to the circumstances, 'physical closeness' is not possible, the question arises, whether a successful emotional and intellectual exchange is sufficient as a basis for a fulfilling and happy relationship. The answer to this question is contingent on two important factors: communication and trust.

> Nothing brings down walls as surely as acceptance.
>
> —Deepak Chopra, Indian–American author

To keep long-distance relationships going, you don't want to go long periods of time without seeing or talking to each other.

The positive reason for separated partners to communicate with each other is to provide the other with some insight into their lives, what is happening to them, what is exciting them, and what they feel bothered about.

In cases where misunderstandings can easily arise like in a situation where the partners are separated by a significant geographical distance, it is advisable to check whether the partners' communication serves the goal of maintaining a happy relationship effectively or whether it should be improved.

If you are in such a situation, you should have an agreement with your partner to maintain a high level of communication with a focus keeping a positive spirit between the two of you, which will, in turn, sustain the feeling of love. This communication should be frequent and open. The frequency of communication should be adapted to the prevailing needs and should not give rise to criticism that it is being misused by the other as a tool for control. Communication will be open when it is built upon the mutual trust that has already been developed between the partners *before* they were forced to live in a long-distance relationship.

The effectiveness of the communication does not depend so much on the form in which the partners communicate, but on the content communicated.

It would cause additional stress and frustration for the partners if their communications became a dumping ground for rants, tirades, and expressions caused by frustration, boredom and loneliness. Instead, partners should engage in an animated conversation, be entertaining, sharing, and supportive. But, above all, the content of the communication should be suited to keep alive and strengthen the feeling of love between the separated partners.

Having said that, insecurity can lead to one partner to check in on the other one too often. Excessive calls and messages can lead to tensions as the partner at the receiving end will be turned off by the constant monitoring and the checking partner, on the other hand, will probably never be fully reassured.

Tip: Communication is obviously important in any relationship, but *too much* communication is not always the best option in a long-distance relationship. The frequency of communication needs to be at a level agreeable to both parties. As a yardstick, one could say that it should correlate to the same criteria used when both are living under normal conditions.

Some people believe that rules could be helpful to manage the frequency of calls and messages. For example, rules to ensure that you speak to each other every night at a certain time or have a certain number of calls per week.

In reality, however, pre-scheduled communication often creates more problems than it solves; for instance, when one or both partners begin to resent feeling obligated to communicate. For this reason, the best way to avoid this risk is for long-distance couples to make all communication optional and spontaneous.

TRUST

Partners in a long-distance relationship can't be happy unless they fully trust each other. But trust is not readily available. It has to be built up in a step-by-step manner and is acquired through doing, experience, and learning. This is not easy in a normal relationship but in a long-distance relationship, it is even more difficult. In a long-distance relationship, the partners are additionally exposed to the challenges resulting from living apart such as loneliness, boredom, and jealousy. In this situation, both partners expect each other to fulfil their expectations of each other. In concrete terms, this means, for example, that the partners do not counteract possible loneliness with increased alcohol consumption, that boredom does not lead to a domestic person becoming a frequent visitor of bars, clubs, entertainment venues, and that jealousy does not lead to a control mania that restricts the other partner's freedom.

Trust in a long-distance relationship shows that the partners believe in their commitment to the relationship and, most importantly, their dedication to their partner. They view mutual trust with high regard as they know that it is essential for happiness in the relationship.

When you're confronted with incriminating symptoms of doubt and insecurity due to your long-distance relationship, you should keep making efforts to overcome the lack of intimacy by doing little things constructively and intensively.

Tip: To overcome the lack of closeness, you can suggest your partner to do regular or spontaneous video calls with you. You can also share videos, your whereabouts, update each other with photos and online 'stories' every day to day or even participate in group calls with friends and family during special events. In addition, invitations to participate in (group) discussions and chats, if available, can help to create closeness.

In a long-distance relationship, when, from time to time, the partners have the opportunity to visit each other, this becomes a special event in their life

characterized by separation. Such a visit will probably be perceived as a 'highlight' and, if possible, should be carefully planned and consciously organized. One of the aims of such a visit should be to revive, improve, and compensate for the temporarily lost (physical) intimacy.

During such visits, it may happen that the partners initially feel a certain awkwardness or that their expectations of the other partner's behaviour are so high that they can hardly be fulfilled.

Example: Donna, a mother of two children, is very much looking forward to visiting her husband Jeremy, who is on a job assignment in Nigeria for three years. Leaving the children with their grandparents, she felt relieved of all the responsibility and couldn't wait to feel comfortable with Jeremy, doing nothing and feeling the intimacy she has been longing for since he left for Nigeria. On the other hand, Jeremy, who was leading a new life in Nigeria, was not as sure if he would be able to take care of Donna when she arrived there. He felt a bit strange because he hadn't seen her for a while and had become used to being alone. Also, he now had a new circle of friends. In his ambitious attempt to keep Donna entertained, he packed the schedule of her visit with sightseeing tours of the many national parks and well-known attractions, including throwing her a party at his place and inviting his new friends as guests. As a result, Donna was very exhausted by the many activities that were imposed on her. She was unhappy about the lack of intimacy she felt throughout her visit and felt more distant than ever from Jeremy in his new surroundings. What hit her particularly hard was that she felt uncomfortable in Jeremy's presence as she did not know what to do or say as Jeremy now had seemingly entered into a new phase of his life that she knew nothing about.

AWKWARDNESS

When you are separated from your partner, it is normal that you start to make all kinds of assumptions, judgements, and projections that may be right but could also be wrong. In a long-distance relationship, this can manifest itself in various ways, including possessiveness, jealousy, frequent criticism, or even neurotic control mania. None of these behaviours is helpful, especially in a long-distance situation, as these reactions are mostly based on feelings and not on facts. In case you are exposed to such a situation, it would be better if you would be open with your partner and talk to them about your concerns. This will help avoid a negative projection of your feelings, which may endanger your relationship.

> Marriage is not merely sharing the fettuccini, but sharing the burden of finding the fettuccini restaurant in the first place.
>
> —Calvin Trillin, American journalist

A visit after a long separation make partners feel a certain awkwardness or distance in the first moment of their reunion. One or both partners may feel uncomfortable because they may believe that they no longer know the other as intimately as before. Or, it could be that they find the situation difficult because they are scared of expectations. If this happens, it should not be interpreted negatively but considered as a natural reaction based on fears of loss (of the partner). Behind such behaviour, one can normally find unexpressed desires or ideas that one partner has developed about the other during their separation and want to be dealt with.

To overcome such awkwardness, it is important that the partners decide to speak their mind. Never try to sweep under the carpet anything that disturbs you or otherwise concerns you. This is especially true when, for whatever reason, the destructive seed of mistrust happens to have already set in one of the partner's minds. In these situations, it's much better to talk openly instead of keeping the concerns to oneself.

In order to overcome awkwardness or shyness when meeting your partner again after a long separation, it can be helpful if you use this opportunity to remember your first meeting. At that time, you were still insecure and cautious because you both did not know each other well enough. Back then, a certain tension arose from this insecurity, which made the first meeting so exciting. The similarity of the situations can be used as an opportunity for the partners to win (back) each other again.

It is more difficult for the partners, if, at the occasion of the visit, one partner expects too much from the other partner. In such a case, disappointment can easily occur. Depending on how and how intensively the expectations are communicated, it can provoke the demanding person's partner to take a defensive attitude. In the worst case, this can lead to a process of alienation between the partners. A sense of '*you do not love me anymore*' can set in, which can make both partners feel that they are no longer understood by the other.

Mutual understanding is, indeed, the key word here because the best way for the partners to deal with possible awkwardness and exaggerated expectations is for each of them to put themselves in the partner's shoes to understand them better.

It can be assumed that in a long-distance relationship, both partners are aware of the challenges of living apart. However, what may be more difficult to understand is that each partner may react to these challenges differently. Mutual understanding for the others' reaction cannot arise solely from one partner's one-sided consideration of the other. Mutual understanding requires partnership, openness, and a positive attitude. These elements are necessary in order to recognize the concerns, wishes, and hopes of the other partner.

In any case, it is important that expectations and wishes are not expressed as criticism, but communicated positively and concretely.

Tip: Open criticism by one partner can easily be perceived as offensive by the other. Therefore, it is recommended to use a more moderate and positive way of expressing the wish for change. One option could be to formulate critique as an invitation for choosing an alternative way for doing something. Another option could be to reformulate a critical remark as a wish. This may come across even better when the wish gets 'wrapped up' in a way that it gets perceived as a hint as to how the partner could be made happy by the other.

Even if one partner regards the expectations and demands of the other partner as challenging or even as threatening, they could reinterpret the other's behaviour positively. For instance, one can interpret the other's expectations—even when exaggerated—as a positive indication that they are not indifferent. For instance, the partner's expectations may have arisen from a fear of losing their love. If there was no longer an emotional relationship, the partner would not have pinned their hopes in the other.

COMPLICITY IS A PLUS

Especially in a long-distance relationship, the principle of being connected in a 'complicity' becomes all the more important. As discussed in detail above, a 'romantic complicity' is a shared understanding between partners of mutual respect, trust, and loyalty, and is closer to 'conspiratorial intimacy' than a normal relationship. In a romantic conspiracy, small common secrets and conspiratorial bonds serve as a special connecting link between the partners. But unlike expressing your close relationship through physical actions, such as hidden winking, hand signals, head nodding, and facial expressions, in a long-distance relationship, new codes have to be created that work across physical barriers to highlight the shared understanding that characterizes romantic complicity.

But in a long-distance relationship, it is not the hiding, but primarily the discrete uncovering or the covert expression that creates the complicity. In this situation, complicity is based on an agreement between the partners on a common objective they want to achieve—for instance, maintaining a romantic relationship despite adverse circumstances.

Tips: In practice, the implementation of the partners' agreement can be rooted in a special intimacy between the partners. Such special intimacy can, *for example*, result from the creation and use of code words that only the partners can decipher, secrets shared exclusively between the partners, and the conspiratorial mutual sharing of information.

Example: Nathan and Lily are very happy and thankful that they have each other, even though they rarely meet as Nathan went abroad for several years for his studies, while Lily stays at home in New Zealand. Despite the distance, they make each other a priority, and the thought of the other is like a sting of faith that holds them together. They know that there is always someone there for them who loves and appreciates them, no matter what happens or how difficult the situation they find themselves in everyday life. Nathan shares with Lily the difficulties he has with fake friends who try to ruin him behind his back, and Lily shares with him the difficulties with her parents who are always fighting. The two share their secrets, hopes, and dreams, and they have developed full trust and complicity for each other, which has enriched their lives. Each of them helps the other to move forward on their own path, while at the same time they strive to be together again.

PROS AND CONS

With all these impediments couples have to overcome in a long-distance relationship, some evidence can be found that distance can actually make relationships stronger and lead to happiness.

Example: People in long-distance relationships miss their partners and thus are likely to express feelings of warmth and intimacy more willingly and easily. They work harder to stay in contact and are more ready to employ all available means to communicate with each other, including social media. Some people even claim that living apart can actually keep the spark alive in a relationship because there is no everyday routine from which so often a fatigue in marriage arises.

Nevertheless, there is a long list of considerations made by those who are critical about long-distance relationships. They believe that such conditions (of staying apart) are relationship-killers and are a detriment to the happiness of those who find themselves in these situations.

They argue that, sooner or later, issues will arise that will negatively influence their happiness. For instance, they may be plagued by doubts about how long their relationship can withstand the distance or be faced with acute loneliness for living apart. It is also said that when couples have to live apart, it makes them feel like they are still single, even though their decision to marry clearly demonstrates that they do not want a single status.

There are cases in which people who are separated from their partners feel even lonelier and unhappier in their long-distance relationship than a person who is truly single. Among other reasons, it maybe because unlike a single person, they cannot freely mingle with others or engage in flirtatious behaviour because of their existing loyalty to their partner.

Example: Hideo feels increasingly unhappy about his long-distance relationship with his girlfriend Ase, a top virologist from Taiwan, who has already been abroad for several months now. She is in Germany working to develop a vaccine against Covid and is unsure about when she can return. Suddenly, Hideo finds himself alone, and since he is the type of person who likes to socialize and have someone by his side, Ase's absence makes him unhappy. Though he is well aware that Ase left to pursue her career and is working day around the clock towards a good cause, subjectively, he feels the situation very unfair. He is now faced with two options: one, to be faithful to Ase, even though he is not sure when he will see her again, or two, start seeing someone new and take chances for his own happiness.

To cushion the possible negative effects of a long-distance relationship on your and your partner's happiness, you should examine and adopt as many generally valid principles that apply to a normal happy partnership. Your goal should be to make the long-distance partnership as close as possible to a normal partnership.

Example: Though you are physically separated, let your partner influence you, for instance, by asking them for advice. Turn towards your partner and attract their attention. Nurture your fondness and admiration for them, instead of turning away under the influence of your new life and environment. Talking about your personal challenges most of the time will not be helpful. Instead, listen more than before and continue to keep your partner intimately familiar with your hopes, worries, and fears. At the same time, try to understand your partner's views or problems as well, show interest in their lives by actively participating in problem-solving the same way you would do if you were present at home.

TIP: The trick here is to examine and adopt as many of these behaviours and practices as possible to see if they can be applied directly or in modification to the extraordinary situation of your temporary physical separation.

In your life, try working hard at your job, spending time with (new) friends, and pursuing hobbies to distract you from the loneliness of a long-distance relationship. Additionally, new contacts may also make you a more interesting conversation partner for your partner when you are finally reunited.

It's important for both parties in a long-distance relationship to continue living their lives in a wholesome manner and never consider hitting the 'pause button'. If you do this, you would admit to yourself and others that you don't have or don't want a personality of your own.

Such behaviour wouldn't be 'cool' either. When in a long-distance relationship, it is not advisable to isolate yourself from the rest of the world in a bid to avoid temptations. This follows from the fact that someone who lives apart cannot automatically be condemned to change their social life. Regardless of whether other friends or acquaintances like it or not, irrespective of prevailing social norms, and independent from self-imposed restrictions, the partner living alone should live freely as they deem fit.

As discussed previously, it is perceived as 'cool' when a person shows autonomy, independent judgement, and pursues their own course, irrespective of the expectations of others. This is in particular the case when prevailing social norms attempt to force a person in a long-distance relationship into 'compliant' behaviour.

A long-distance relationship becomes seriously unhealthy, when one or both partners are jealous and possessive of each other.

Example: In most cases, this can be seen when one partner checks on the other constantly, doesn't tolerate the other partner's activities and friends, doesn't take their views seriously, starts to nit-pick, blames them without reason, and makes attempts to manipulate or 'guilt trip' the other.

Your partner should not be jealous of your social activities, especially since they are also entitled to do the same. On the contrary, if you love each other and your love is based on trust, neither of you will be pleased to see that the other has socially excluded themselves only because of a temporary separation. Social self-isolation is not healthy for the psyche of the person concerned. So it then cannot be in the interest of the distant partners to see their beloved partners suffer.

In most relationships, partners may set healthy boundaries designed to ensure that you can get out of the relationship what you want without being excessive. Creating boundaries doesn't mean you don't love or trust your partner or that you suspect them of hidden agendas. On the contrary, boundaries exist to make both partners feel comfortable because the communication of the boundaries will make clear what each wants out of the relationship.

Example: Jim, a soccer fan, has a weakness. After attending soccer games, he regularly joins the supporter crowds and gets drunk with them. His spouse Mimi doesn't like it but so far, she has tolerated it and has taken care of him when he got home in an inebriated state. But now Mimi is worried. She has been assigned for a week to train her company's sales staff on new automated cashier systems. The training will take place in another city. During her absence, a major soccer game will take place and Mimi is concerned that Jim may take her absence as an opportunity for behaving even more excessively. Before Mimi leaves, she talks to Jim about her worries and even starts to cry because she feels he could harm himself or become a victim of an act of violence. Jim feels that her worries are genuine and understands them. He doesn't feel comfortable himself that Mimi won't be present to take care of him, when he would return home drunk. To calm her down, he discloses to her, that he always felt that he could get excessive, because he knew that, if shit hits the fan, she would be there to take care of him. As she wouldn't be around this time, he wouldn't know who would take care of him and where it would end. Therefore, he promised her that this time he would behave.

Such boundaries are even important in a long-distance relationship. Partners who are separated and are not in permanent communication need a clear framework on what is acceptable (or unacceptable) to each of them. This means the provision of clear parameters for boundaries based on openness and trust, which will make the relationship more comfortable for both despite the distance. In the absence of such a framework, the partners have to guess or presume their partner's feelings, and this can create misunderstandings.

However, in a normal as well as in a long-distance relationship, mutually agreed boundaries between partners must be reasonable and acceptable. Only then can they be called 'healthy'. They have to respect the partner's likes, desires, interests, and needs, and not restrict their ability to maintain their personal identity.

Example: Max was always jealous of his wife Mary's ballet classes. 'Too physical, too many beautiful bodies in daring positions', he used to say. Mary didn't take it too seriously and didn't care. She felt that he was just jealous of her male colleagues, but she knew that they were all gay. His remarks didn't diminish her happiness in the relationship. But when they had to live apart for half a year because of his foreign assignment, it suddenly became a contentious issue. He had forbidden her to attend classes during his absence because, as he put it, 'the temptation may be too great.' Though she had told him that her colleagues were not interested in women, he continued to be suspicious about their intentions. She couldn't tolerate his unfounded mistrust and they had an argument, which left her very unhappy.

Tip: Especially in a long-distance relationship, none of the partners should feel controlled or have their actions dictated by the other.

Both partners should accept the other's social environment, friends, families, and friends and not show jealousy but curiosity and genuine interest.

> The world's oldest man who recently died at age 112 in Japan, said the secret to living a long happy life was 'not to get angry and keep a smile on your face'.
>
> —CNN, 1 March 2020

It's normal to have arguments with your partner but in a situation of physical separation, it's even more critical to stay cool, i.e., not to get involved in the controversial exchange of emotional arguments. Instead, you should take the neutral position of an uninvolved third party and handle the controversy maturely as if it didn't concern you. A way to do this may be through a compromise between the controversial positions.

> That, 'you hang up *first* . . . no, *you* hang up first . . .' crap is really only funny the first 200 or 300 times.
>
> —Unknown

A dispute between partners is already difficult when partners argue face to face. However, it is much more difficult when it happens across the barriers of a large physical separation, perhaps over the phone or in form of text messages, which do not allow for eye contact.

But even in this situation, do not lose sight of the fact that the preservation of your relationship and your common happiness is more important (than your argument), and so it needs to be protected. Therefore, it is always better not to push the dispute to a peak, but to seek a compromise in time, i.e., before emotions begin to dominate. A compromise is neither a loss of face nor a defeat but a concession to the superior good, i.e., happiness in the relationship and the relationship itself.

It is not so much the resolution of the conflict that should concern you if the conflict is carried out without eye contact over the distance, as the way to resolve it. Conflicts should in all possible cases be solved in a fair, rational and, when possible, in a manner that helps limiting the damage.

You must also be aware that due to the physical distance, it is likely that your partner's reaction will be more sensitive than under normal circumstances. If your partner reacts irritably to you, it only gives you a hint that under normal circumstances, his reaction would probably be less insecure and irritable.

In a possible dispute between separated partners, both sides should grant each other a credit resulting from the special circumstances of living apart. This applies in particular to the partner who has remained in the familiar environment and must take into account that the partner living in a foreign country feels insecure and uncomfortable where they have been placed.

Tip: If you want to maintain a happy relationship with your partner, you do not want to hurt each other. Therefore, watch your language and do not further upset your partner by becoming aggressive, raising your voice or flinging insults.

Concentrate on the issue in question and do not get tempted to discuss other topics. This can either happen if you are not focused enough on the topic or if your partner wants to distract you because they feel their argument is weak or they are uncomfortable with the topic.

Example: Anita was curious to know why suddenly her partner Romeo, who was on a temporary foreign assignment, rarely responded to her calls and kept conversations very short. This behaviour was in contrast to Romeo's past behaviour when he seemed to enjoy calling her and sharing his experiences of the day. One day, she decided to call Romeo and ask him about it. During the call, Anita's two pet dogs were in the same room and started to make a lot of noise in the background. When Anita asked Romeo frankly what made him change his communication behaviour, he did not respond to her question but asked Anita why she allowed the dogs to be in the room even though he had asked to keep them outside. Anita frantically tried to move the dogs outside the room but they escaped and continued to bark loudly. Romeo got increasingly upset because unlike Anita, he wasn't very fond of dogs. He was especially uncomfortable with having them in the house. He started an argument with her about this issue and urged her not to do it again. Anita accused him of being cruel. One word led to another, and in the end, they hung up exhausted by their argument. Romeo smiled because his tactics had succeeded in making Anita forget her initial question which, for good reasons, made him feel uncomfortable. Anita was angry about Romeo's attitude towards her dogs, but she was angrier at herself for letting him avoid a discussion on the issue that was bothering her.

During a difficult conversation, it is recommended to use first person singular and plural (*I* and *we*) instead of second person (*you*). This can help ensure that what you say is not perceived as aggressive, finger pointing, attacking, or presuming.

Tip: If an argument takes place, you should exhaust all means to end the conversation in a conciliatory mood as you don't want the conversation to end in an argument. This would leave a bad feeling on both sides and has the potential to negatively influence the following conversation. If, in a long-distance relationship situation, a serious problem between the partners needs to be discussed and solved, it would be better if both partners would use some time to prepare themselves and chose the right time for their discussion. The clarification of controversial points should never be postponed to a later date and conflicts should never be left unresolved. If this happens, positions can harden and a solution can become more difficult. Generally, it is unfavourable to have a serious discussion when there is not enough time available or the basic mood of the partners is negative because of the preceding discussion of other, unrelated issues.

CONFRONTATIONAL RELATIONSHIPS

Whether you live in a normal or a long-distance relationship, it's important to realize that conflicts and confrontations are normal in relationship.

All of us have a certain level of tolerance after having dealt with countless frustrations in our lives. Tolerance and flexibility help us to manage divergent attitudes and behaviour. However, in a close relationship, the level of tolerance can be lower than with others outside. The reason for this may be that in a close relationship, you have the tendency to seek closeness and harmony but not conflict and confrontation, even if you accept disagreements to be a normal phenomenon of any relationship. This tendency generally make you react more sensitively to disagreements within your relationship resulting in less tolerance than shown outside.

But when dealing with serious disagreements in your relationship, and when you get the feeling that there is no way to reach agreement or compromise and you want to quit, then you have to pull the emergency brake. The first thing you have to bear in mind is that there was a moment in the past when you desperately wanted this relationship and adored your partner. At that time, you acknowledged that you were taking a risk to be with someone who is not the same as you. You also accepted the risk of exposing yourself to someone whose mind, personality, and character was influenced by a different environment and upbringing than yours. In other words, you had acknowledged that your perception and beliefs were uniquely yours and that you did not expect your partner to be the same as you.

The fact that each of us view things differently and are free to have our own opinions remains one of the main causes of problems in human relationships. This human capacity of showing individuality is illustrated by the following example.

Example: Two artists were commissioned to paint a landscape picture with mountains. The first artist's illustration was that of mountains against the backdrop of a barren, bleak landscape.

The other artist painted it as a lush green mountain landscape with vegetation and life.

The commissioner who ordered the paintings was surprised to see two completely different representations of the same theme. He said, 'No wonder why they are artists. They have their own way of seeing things.'

The ability to choose an individual way of looking at things is something that not only artists but all people possess. This human characteristic leads to the insight that even in a harmonious relationship there is potential for conflict. So, accept that there is nothing unusual if there are conflicts and confrontations in your relationship.

However, the answer to the question of how much confrontation a relationship can bear and at what intensity, depends entirely on the individual partners. Some people feel deeply uncomfortable with any amount of arguing, others have a high tolerance for confrontation and can return to 'peace' very easily.

When referring to a *confrontational relationship* one needs first to distinguish between two kinds of conflict: A constructive and gentle disagreement with your partner, on the one hand, and having a partner who is (permanently and) aggressively disagreeing on all major questions, on the other hand. In the second case, disagreements can concern both important issues such as the acquisition of a home or an expensive new car, or minor ones, like whether eating out tonight at an Italian Trattoria or a Chinese Dim Sum restaurant.

As signalled by the use of the word 'aggressively', it is not only important for the analysis of a 'confrontational relationship' to see *how often* couples argue, but *how they treat each other*, especially when the argument gets heated.

Example: In Damian and Kimberly's relationship, Damian is clearly the dominating partner. He has an opinion about everything, important or not, and finds it difficult to accept Kimberly's (or any other person's) opinion. During the first few months of their relationship, Kimberly ignored Damian's behaviour. She felt that she could tolerate it. But as time passed, she not only felt increasingly unhappy about Damian's permanent interventions but also about his tendency to move on to topics that had nothing to do with the original issue, draw arguments out longer than necessary, escalate disagreements to personal attacks, and his references to past disappointments or misbehaviours which she thought were long forgotten about. After such discussions, Kimberly felt exhausted, humiliated, and unhappy with Damian and her situation.

This example makes it clear that confrontations between partners that take place only occasionally or sporadically do not turn an ordinary relationship into a 'confrontational relationship'. To characterise a relationship as 'confrontational' requires a certain continuity and recurring, conspicuous patterns of behaviour. You can reasonably only talk about a 'confrontational relationship', if the partners are constantly at odds with each other on any subject, when virtually any situation leads to an argument, and the arguing becomes excessive, especially if it never ends on a positive note.

If occasional disagreements between you and your partner stay within mutually acceptable limits, don't produce lasting bad feelings, and do not interfere with other aspects of your relationship, your relationship is within the bounds of normality. Disagreements are also not toxic if arguments lead to something positive, for instance, a solution, a compromise, or even an 'agreement to disagree'.

In general, it is dangerous to romanticize or perceive aggressive or dominating behaviour, an uncompromising, bossy attitude, or excessive fighting in a relationship as a sign of passion, especially when it results in one or both partners' suffering and unhappiness. On the contrary, in an ideal relationship, a partner is supposed to be a source of happiness and not the other way round.

Though it sounds paradoxical, people who are closest to you can frustrate you the most because it is to these people that you have fully opened up to and lowered your defences. This is what makes confrontational relationships so toxic.

There are many warning signals that must be noticed and observed in order to stop the decline of what was formerly a happy relationship into a confrontational one.

Example: Typical warning signals include your partner's authoritarian, controlling, and aggressive dominance, the fact that you often feel sidelined—neither listened to nor taken seriously—and that your opinions are not valued. It is often the case that your demanding partner will not give up until you comply with them.

COMPETING PARTNERS

There are also cases where partners in a relationship are competing with each other. This can cause serious problems, lead to a confrontational relationship and negatively affect the partners' respective happiness.

Example: Rick, a young lawyer in training, fell in love with Martha, a young fellow student, who was also studying law. Rick and Martha married during their training. During their joint studies, Martha came to the conclusion that she was by far the better and more talented lawyer and expected to achieve a better examination result than her husband. But when Rick performed better in the examinations, Martha reacted angrily. She felt as if she was defeated. During the following years, she permanently let Rick feel her envy, which eventually caused her marriage to break up.

It would have been better for their relationship if Martha and Rick had discussed the problem frankly with each other to find a solution. This could have consisted of establishing a kind of working partnership in which they would have worked on their cases together, using their respective strengths and then sharing the success. Alternatively, they could have deliberately avoided each other's professional issues and concentrating on other topics of common interest.

There may be cases, when the partners won't even be fully aware that a competitive relationship is developing between them. They are subconsciously jealous of the success or superior social recognition of their spouse and desperately wishing they could achieve the same. In other cases, a spouse's jealousy and envy can drive them to make the partner feel worse than they are. In extreme cases, a jealous spouse can even engage in actions which could possibly harm the other.

If a wife feels superior to her husband and lets him feel her comparing, competitive attitude, her husband will probably feel unhappy because of his hurt pride, traditional male feeling of 'honour', or simply out of shame or sadness. In this case, he doesn't feel proud of his wife and doesn't want to provide support for her, but reacts negatively.

- One of the reasons for the man's negative reaction may be that he traditionally yearns for 'devotional love' and wants to be admired by his wife.
- However, behind his reaction, can also be a projection based on an outdated gender image that regards women as inferior in principle, and does not allow for any deviations from that cliché.

Example: Down-to-earth Leonardo and flamboyant Alexa run a restaurant together. He is the cook while she takes care of the organization, administration, and the guests. Over the years, Leonardo becomes unhappy with his situation in their partnership. Though he's working very hard every day, he feels that his glamorous wife is getting all the credit for the success of their restaurant. Whilst everybody seems to know her and praise her efficiency and charm, in Leonardo's view, nobody seems to take notice of him. He reacts to the alleged disregard in an offended manner and lets Alexa feel his frustration in bitter commentaries. She finds his attitude unfair and points out that in a partnership everyone has to play their part, and in their case his role happens to be in the kitchen and not with the guests. Still, Leonardo continues to be unhappy. He gets sloppy in the kitchen, begins to drink, and, in his free time, increasingly devotes himself to his old friends. Leonardo's worsening job performance costs the restaurant its reputation, and Alexa leaves Leonardo in an emotional alliance with one of the guests.

Tip: In situations of doubt about how you should deal with a troubled relationship and your trouble-making partner, you should always listen to yourself and your instincts first. Of course, your friends can also offer advice and guidance, but their suggested actions could be born out of other motivations such as envy, self-interest, or they could just be incompetent or prejudiced.

If you come to the conclusion that you no longer feel happy in the relationship, it is totally normal if, instinctively, you react defensively. Some people deny their unhappiness, and, others desperately look for arguments proving that the romantic relationship between the partners is still intact.

However, what you truly feel and what you personally observe doesn't just disappear because you do not want to admit it. The doubts remain and gnaw at you from the inside and eventually begin to burden you permanently. In such a case, it might be better for you to follow your gut instincts and face up to reality. This is that your relationship causes you unhappiness which can only be ended if serious consequences are drawn from the situation.

CHILDREN IN A CONFRONTATIONAL RELATIONSHIP

When children sense that their parents have a confrontational relationship, they can become unhappy. This is particularly the case when parents decide to stay together - just 'for the kids'.

Of course, the best environment in which children can grow up is a happy family with parents who are happy with each other. Therefore, it must be a priority goal for the partners to preserve the relationship. However, in the case of a confrontational relationship characterized by permanent quarrelling or violence, separation often seems to be the better way out—also with regard to the well-being of the children.

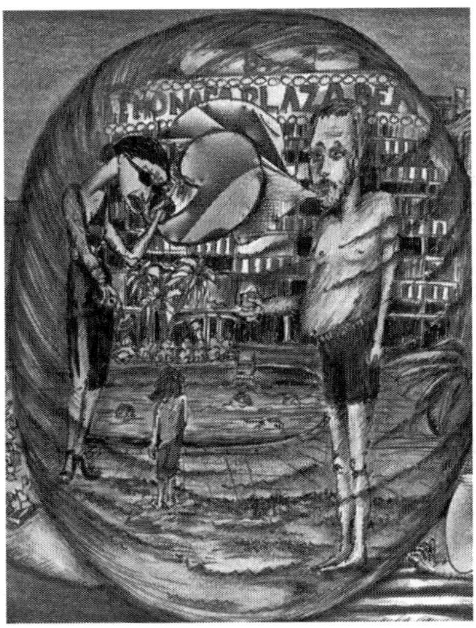

Younger children, in particular, need security, trust, harmony, and continuity for their healthy development and happiness. For this, they have to be able to rely on their parents because they are completely dependent on them.

Therefore, parents in a confrontational relationship often face a real dilemma. On the one hand, they know that their children need an intact family to be happy, and, on the other hand, they realize that a separation is inevitable because there is no way to work out the differences in the relationship.

To protect their children, parents frequently suppress or postpone their relationship problems and believe that by doing this they are acting for the good of the children. In the end, however, there will only be losers because everything that makes up the harmonious family is fake and not authentic. Children are very perceptive and will instinctively feel it.

In addition, the stronger the social, professional, and family ties are, the more difficult it becomes to change or break them. Many remain in deadlocked relationships because change or a new beginning is hardly conceivable or would actually involve considerable technical, organizational, legal, and other difficulties.

Example: Chuck is an engineer and his wife Joanna gave up her job when they were expecting their first child. As a result, she has become financially dependent on her husband. When things started to go downhill in their marriage, Joanna suppressed the thought of separation. As a single mother, she was afraid of not being able to find a job and as a consequence, becoming dependent on alimony and state benefits, and not being able to offer the children their usual standard of living.

But these concerns are not a good reason to continuing a partnership. For a child, it is sometimes better to see their parents separated but happy rather than constantly fighting with each other. In case of the former, the couple can then work out a *'modus vivendi'* by mutual agreement to get along well with each other. The more effort parents put into presenting a picture of a well-functioning, perfect family to the outside world, even though they live in a confrontational relationship, the more difficult and stressful it will be them to find their way back to themselves after the pressure has been lifted, for instance by separation or when the children have left home.

BAD BEHAVIOR

As said before, it is not only important for a relationship to see how often couples argue but how they treat each other. A confrontational relationship provides motivation to learn how to manage outburst in the sense of explosive rage, reckless discharge of anger, and intimidation. These outbursts can be caused by many different reasons such as frustration, fear, hurt, banal everyday annoyances, and other (marital) issues such as cheating, dishonesty, or lies.

The expression of, *for example*, anger can be different in each relationship based on the partner's individual personality. Some people have a talent to disguise their anger, while others magnify the issue they are angry about and engage in offending and aggressive behaviour—sometimes in a way they may later regret.

In a confrontational relationship, outbursts are not necessarily caused by individual events or reactions to the partner's behaviour. They may also be the result of a more fundamental problem, such as a congenital predisposition or a reflection of a psychological issue.

> Better to live in a desert than with a quarrelsome and nagging wife.
>
> —Bible, Proverb 21:19

Also, outbursts are not necessarily caused only by angry husbands. It could also be wives who, for instance, simply can't stop criticizing and nagging their husbands.

It is difficult to point out a sure-fire way on gaining control over outbursts but one method may be to embrace an 'appreciative mindset'. You develop an 'appreciative mindset' when you stop judging and feeling negative about others. Instead, you start being positive, recognizing the good, trust and appreciate them.

Obviously, it is difficult to express appreciation for a partner who has caused anger. However, we recommend that you stay 'cool': You neither get impressed by the outburst, nor you get engaged by the partner's anger. On the contrary, instead of engaging, you are disengaging.

Example: Gavin and his husband Ian are in complete disagreement on the issue of Covid face masks. Ian is following the news and is an enthusiastic newspaper reader. Gavin is not interested in informing himself and picks up his news over a beer at the pub he's regularly frequenting to see friends. While Gavin argues that wearing a mask violates his 'human and constitutional rights' and limits his freedom of choice, Ian believes that wearing a mask is a social duty. They got into increasingly heated arguments about this issue on several occasions. The last time, Gavin had not shied away from personal attacks and insults. He shouted at Ian and called him a 'Left-wing fascist' who needed 'medical help'. Although he was angry about Gavin's outburst, Ian did not get carried away. He didn't shout back but left the room and tried to understand Gavin's reaction. He told himself that Gavin's views on not wearing masks came from his ignorance resulting from little factual information. After some time, Ian returned and calmly asked Gavin why he would automatically fasten his seat belt when driving a car. At first, Gavin didn't understand the meaning of the question and looked at Ian in an unsettled way. But then he replied insecurely that it was for his safety. Ian grinned and slapped Gavin on the shoulder without saying anything. The next day, when the media reported that more than 290,000 people a day were now getting infected in their country, Gavin was shocked. He casually asked Ian whether, by any chance, he had a second mask.

The way you disengage is by acting 'cool', like an unrelated third party observer wo is not concerned personally and who takes a neutral look at the other person and the situation. This will prevent you from using your own, possibly, emotional reaction that, for sure, would only serve to add fuel to the fire. Instead, you should look at your partner with an emotionless analytical mind, try to understand the motivation and rationale for their outburst, and then focus on the 'good' in them. This 'cool' process will enable you to arrive at a more balanced and relaxed reaction and avoid further conflict.

Tip: If you don't manage to react coolly in such a situation and feel that you are getting overwhelmed by your emotions, then you should use a simple trick to outsmart yourself and get back under control. Look at yourself in the mirror when you rage and scream. Or, imagine your outburst being observed and videotaped. It is very likely that when you see yourself in the mirror or on the screen, with your face distorted with rage, you will begin to laugh at yourself, especially if there happens to be a gap between the significance of the cause of your rage and your own extreme behaviour. This trick should give you a more objective and controlled perspective on your behaviour, and may lead to an alternative and more reasonable way to vent your anger, like, for instance, boxing, weight training, deep breathing, yoga, painting, and so on.

Similar to outbursts, the use of blunt language in relationships rarely leads to success. Therefore, when dealing with sensitive topics, you should be as careful in your choice of words as you are in your choice of time and place to talk to your partner. The language you use when discussing your partner's flaws or mistakes must be appropriate, i.e. not hurtful, derogatory or insulting, but tactful. The wisest thing would be to intentionally overlook your partner's flaws or remain positive when talking about them.

Example: Instead of telling your husband, 'You have bad body odour', you could say: 'I like when you wear your favourite perfume.' Or, instead of saying, 'You are an excessive drinker and drink too often', you could say: 'I am worried about you. Drinking in large quantities would not be good for your health in the long term.'

Also, instead of telling your wife, 'You look terrible in that fluffy pink dress', you could say: 'You look amazing in little-black-dress type of outfits. Simple outfit suits you best.'

Such a compliment has the potential to create a good feeling in the partner, and thus improve the climate of conversation between the two. But you should make sure that the compliment is really genuine. Generally, people have good instincts and are able to distinguish fake compliments from true ones. Therefore, care should be taken to ensure that the compliment is really meant seriously and does not come across as a false compliment or mere flattery.

> You yourself, as much as anybody in the entire universe, deserve your love and affection.
>
> —The Buddha

Complimenting your partner's strengths may initially flatter and strengthen their feelings towards you, but it could also backfire when your compliments are recognized as false. This will plant the seed of mistrust in the mind of your partner, which, in turn, can lead to an unhappy end of the relationship.

Example: Grant was upset with his girlfriend Leyla. At the beginning of their relationship, he had received so many 'likes' from her on his Facebook timeline that he integrated her into his closed, exclusive group of 'very best friends'. However, after he had granted her access to this group, Leyla suddenly started ignoring his postings. Grant felt that she had just 'ego-stroken' him to get access his group of best friends. He decided to befriend her. Leyla resented this. They had an argument that brought the relationship to an end after only a short time.

OTHER SIGNS OF AN UNHEALTHY RELATIONSHIP

NO AFFECTION AND INTIMACY

Lack of physical affection and intimacy can be a warning signal that something is wrong in your relationship. Here, the term intimacy is meant to refer to the close emotional and physical bonds that exist between two people.

It is understood that everyone has their own comfort level and personal views when it comes to physical intimacy.

Example: Mateo and his wife Luna have different points of view when it comes to kissing and hugging in public. Mateo feels totally comfortable doing this in public, while Luna considers it awkward and embarrassing. Mateo, who feels relaxed about it, believes that lack of public display of affection constitutes a lack of affection in the relationship, while Luna who considers intimacies in public undesirable, thinks otherwise.

Theoretically, a relationship can survive without intimacy, but it is doubtful whether the partners will be truly happy or secure this way. Without happiness and security, the basis of a relationship seems fragile. This assumption is made in consideration of the idea that love and affection are basic needs similar to sleep, food, or water. It's in a human being's nature to require love, affection, and physical intimacy to be happy. Especially for a couple, a lack of intimacy can bring problems such as loneliness, having a lower relationship satisfaction level, feeling depressed, and being less happy.

Example: Adam's wife Sofia is outgoing, fun loving, playful, and flirtatious preferably with other men than her husband. In the privacy of their home, with Adam around, Sofia shows almost no affection and behaves strangely distant and cold. Adam is in love with her but he feels increasingly uncomfortable and unwanted when Sofia is around. He needs Sofia's affection and physical intimacy, and also sees it as a way to show her his love. But Sofia isn't responding to his wishes, even after Adam tries talking to her about his frustration. Sofia brushes off his concerns brusquely by saying that she is happy and loves him, and that he should stop bothering her with baseless projections. Adam reacts angrily and starts believing that he might be happier if he would be a single again.

Physical and emotional intimacy go hand in hand. As shown in Adam and Sofia's example, it is hard to imagine how a close relationship can be maintained that is exclusively based on emotional affection without physical intimacy. Also, the other way around, it is difficult to imagine a long-standing relationship where you have a physical connection with your partner but without feeling emotional intimacy.

Therefore, the absence of physical affection and intimacy such as hugging or kissing, or, if your relationship has become totally sexless, should not be ignored and glossed over. It may signal the existence of a bigger problem, which could hide behind it. In this case, you should seek an open dialogue with your partner to avoid sleepwalking into the end of the relationship.

DISTANCING

Another warning signal is when your living together has become a boring routine with no excitement or stimulus. For instance, when there are no longer any interesting conversations, no plans for joint ventures, and no more shared interests, but only rudimentary conversations about administrative things that need to be done, such as shopping or tax reporting. Physically, you may be in one room together with your partner but in reality, you may feel alone, ignored, isolated, and bored.

You discover that you more and more frequently (day) dream about a happier future in which your current partner does not play a role anymore. Because of a lack of interaction and mutual attraction, you may feel a growing distance between the two of you, and you suffer from the fact that there are no longer moments of intimacy, complicity, and happiness.

DEGRADING BEHAVIOUR

In the long run, constant demonstration of superiority and lack of respect is no longer just a one-time mistake or trivial matter, but a lasting disappointment for the degraded partner, which works to the disadvantage of the relationship.

In a well-functioning marriage—and out of a sense of mutual trust—the partners usually reduce their respective individual defence mechanisms against attacks and criticism from the outside to a minimum. Therefore, they usually react all the more sensitively to attacks from their partners.

Among the most blatant cases of attacks are insults, belittling, ridiculing the partner, and recurring disparaging remarks as well as bringing out the partner's shortcomings in the presence of third parties. In addition, sarcastic, ironic or mocking remarks can also be very offensive, especially if the partner does not have the ability to defend himself adequately. This constant demonstration of superiority and lack of respect not just a trivial matter for the targeted person but a psychological shock that can cause great unhappiness.

STONEWALLING

Choosing to block out your partner, refusing to compromise, and being overtly honest are all negative practices that will further taint and, may even ultimately destroy, your relationship. In such a situation, the negatively affected partner will perceive your behaviour as a lack of trust, and this will ultimately lead to unhappiness in the relationship.

NAGGING

When one partner constantly confronts the other with negative statements, regularly accuses, attacks, criticizes or nags, they are not only forcing the partner on the defensive but also destroying any sense of shared happiness.

Examples:

> 'You're always forgetting something.'
> 'How can you wear this—you've bad taste.'
> 'You always come too late.'
> 'You only care for yourself.'
> 'You never do anything right.'
> 'Don't embarrass me and shut up because you don't know anything anyway.'
> 'Whenever you open your mouth, nothing meaningful comes out.'
> 'I don't like your friends; they're all losers.'

Nagging is frequently called a *marriage-killer*. It stands for continually complaining, criticism, fault-finding, demanding, nit-picking, and the like. The reason for calling it a marriage-killer is that there will be a point in time in a close relationship when both partners get tired of the vicious cycle of resentful remarks.

Example: Claire married Jordan and, according to the textbooks, she believed that she and her partner would love each other unconditionally. However, after some months after marriage, Claire realized that Jordan showed signs of behaviour that were not up to her expectations. Each morning, after he had left for work, she was annoyed to see the bathroom in a chaotic state. He never cleaned the bathtub or shower, never cleaned the sink after shaving, forgot to flush the toilet, and threw clothes on the floor. After a while of grudging tolerance, Claire found that she couldn't forgive Jordan for his negligence anymore. She talked to him about it but in vain. Therefore, Claire began something what Jordan later negatively called 'parentifying'. She behaved like his mother and started treating him like a child that doesn't know how to manage his life. As a long-term consequence of Claire's 'parentifying' behaviour, Jordan lost interest in being intimate with her. He just didn't want to have sex with someone who was nagging him like his mother and bossing him around like his dad.

There are alternative ways for partners in a relationship that can help to change the manners of a partner they don't like. In the case of nagging, the appropriate response could be appreciation. Appreciation is the opposite of disappointment and constantly pointing out the partner's faults. If you are disappointed, for instance, that your partner doesn't clean up the bathroom after using it, you should let them know that you would appreciate it if they could do their bit and contribute to the proper maintenance of the common household. It would be good if you could take a minute and explain to your partner that they should better appreciate you and your efforts at maintaining the household.

At the same time, it would be psychologically clever, to also remind them what you find positive in your relationship. You could also add that your personal stress comes from the feeling that you have a long to-do list and that could help you to get to the bottom of that list much quicker. This would very likely make you feel more joyful, relaxed, and happy—a feeling which you would like to share with them.

DISREGARD

Under normal circumstances, the most effective way for resolving relationship conflicts is dialogue between the partners. However, in some cases, partners can become so rude that they don't listen to each other anymore.

Example: Karen tries to convince her husband William to spend the next long weekend with her at the seaside. While she's talking, William does not stop using his smartphone to browse through social media. After a while, Karen asked William to switch off his smartphone and listen to her. He gets angry and chooses to ignore her blatantly. Karen feels hurt and unhappy by his insensitivity and reacts with anger. William fires back harshly, and they have a dispute which lasts long into the night. Karen's frustration is not only caused by this one event but by what seemed to have become a pattern of behaviour, which has gradually become offensive.

When just a trivial issue is able to turn a couple from lovers into enemies, one can assume that there is an underlying pattern of frustrated expectations, unhealed resentment or poor communication which caused this behaviour. In other words, smaller disputes over minor issues may actually be covering up a more serious problem in the relationship, such as growing disinterest, indifference, or even loss of love.

Whilst the partners may believe in these cases that they fight about the issue which caused the dispute, the real cause of the confrontation may lie much deeper and be an expression of a more serious problem.

In the above example, Karen would be well advised to inquire why William had changed his attitude towards her and why he doesn't respect her anymore (this would be an important message) or whether he just happens to be rude (which would just be a flaw).

ONLINE INFIDELITY

The widespread use of the internet has gradually led to a rise in online infidelity. Digital technology and designated online platforms are allowing people to flirt online and even start emotional affairs. Increased usage of the Internet has given rise to a new challenge to marriages: That of online infidelity, which is perceived to be as traumatic as actual infidelity. This article highlights the negative impact of online infidelity on marital relationship and its detrimental effect on the mental health of the offended spouse using a case vignette. The article discusses the importance of marital therapy in dealing with the factors contributing to online infidelity and in rebuilding marital trustfor unhappy partners, the temptation of online flirting and dating applications with instant connectivity and unlimited availability of new people to connect with may seem 'too good to resist'.

If one assumes that married couples have always struggled with temptations, today's accessibility presents its own challenges. Infidelity has always been commonly understood as a violation of the marital agreement, a betrayal of the partner's trust, and a threat to the marital bond. The internet has added to this definition a sexually oriented relationship with a third party, which is maintained by using electronic (digital) means.

As the institution of marriage involves emotional and sexual loyalty, sexual involvement with someone other than the partner will typically occur in secrecy and is usually kept hidden from the spouse.

Example: Ella, a thirty-one-year-old woman, was married to Cooper. Until a short time ago, Ella didn't know that her husband was heavily involved in chats of a sexual nature with his cyber chat partner on the internet. After she had caught him by accident when he was engaged in a sex chat, she was extremely hurt and asked him to discontinue this activity. She thought that she could trust Cooper's promise to stop chatting, but a few months later she discovered that, late at night, he had again begun spending hours on his computer. She was devastated with her husband's 'cheating' and perceived his actions as infidelity.

Online infidelity could potentially become as devastating as virtual infidelity in deteriorating marital relations. The partner who is active on the internet will likely spend a lot of his free time online and not share as much time with his wife as he used to do. The effects of such behaviour can lead to an increasingly distant relationship, decreasing intimacy between the partners, growing sexual dissatisfaction, and, as a result, depression, frustration, anger, and, possibly, the wish to leave. In addition, frequent online sexual encounters of one partner can cause pre-existing marital problems to surface, such as boredom, sexual dissatisfaction, or poor communication.

Many people engaging in emotional and sexual conversations using social media have a sense of false security. This reflects an illusion that everything digital is just that, an illusion, and that there are no 'real-world' consequences for sexually oriented online activities. They may feel that they can hide behind the screen and stay anonymous.

However, these people ignore the fact that not everything that takes place online will stay online. Instead, they should be aware that, even when it's only virtual, they are giving themselves to someone else and that there is no guarantee that their activity will stay confidential under all circumstances.

Of course, there are many other signs of a confrontational relationship which, individually or in combination, can threaten the relationship and result in unhappiness.

In families with children, the children play an important role in conflicts and confrontations between the parents. These conflicts have a strong potential for leading to confrontational relationships because of their fundamental and sometimes ideological character; for instance, disputes over non-religious or religious education.

In principle, two scenarios are at stake: In the first case, there are differences of opinion between the partners independent of the children, which lead to conflict between them. The partners would have these disagreements even without children, but the existence of children can either aggravate the disagreement or make them more difficult to manage. In the second case, the problems would not have arisen if the couple did not have children. These mostly concern the children or their upbringing.

CHILDREN AND HAPPINESS

PARENTHOOD CAN AFFECT HAPPINESS

Most of us still long to start families and have children of our own though we know that bringing up children is a long process and stressful and can even become a challenge to the happiness of the parents. But in some parts of the world, having children has increasingly become a matter of choice—in these cases, it is no longer considered a natural outcome of a relationship.

Whether having children is a 'good' or a 'bad' thing is decided individually by each person/partner/couple. There are no general guidelines that can answer this question, and there is no 'one-size-fits-all' solution since each case is different from the other.

> All happy families are alike; each unhappy family is unhappy in its own way.
>
> —Leo Tolstoy, Russian author

Parenthood can affect the well-being and happiness of people.

Example: Young parents Philip and Jade had a baby right after they married. Today, baby Annabelle is two years old. After a period of happiness, however, the parents' attitude towards Annabelle had changed. This change had been caused by Annabelle's behaviour. While at first, Philip and Jade euphorically called their peaceful child 'our sunshine', Annabelle recently showed a strong, fierce, and defiant behaviour. She had begun to rage angrily, was stubborn, resisted her parents, cried

frequently, was hiding in dark corners, and seemed to be unresponsive. Outside, she would tear away from her parents and try to run away. Philip, in particular, interpreted Annabelle's changed behaviour as wilful rebellion and malice, while Jade excused her daughter's behaviour as a temporary expression of an age-related phase of defiance. Both parents were exhausted in the end, suffered from Annabelle's changed behaviour as well as their resulting arguments and were unhappy.

What both parents seem to have ignored in this example is the fact that Annabelle's change in behaviour was quite typical for her age and that with the beginning of the third year and increasing linguistic abilities, the intensity of such 'defiant phases' usually become less frequent and are likely to disappear.

Many people believe that children are part of a fulfilled and happy life while others seem to associate (only) problems with children. But this example shows that one cannot categorically say one or the other. The question to be discussed is not really whether children generally make couples happy or not. Regardless of the positive moments of happiness and the negative disappointments and fears that raising children brings with it, the question is not a simple 'for' or 'against'. Instead, the question arises whether the parents are prepared for a child and how they can best ensure that, regardless of all the joys and burdens expected of children, they can be happy.

Some parents claim that children are an investment for the future. They expect that, in terms of life satisfaction, children will pay off for them one day-but only in old age. This is when children have become independent, moved out from home, and possibly got a form of social support for the ageing parents which, for them, is generally associated with less loneliness and greater happiness.

This more long-term view can help to make you immune to all developments and events that, on the long way towards the children's independence, may affect your happiness.

But we don't have to decide in our discussion whether children are detrimental to the happiness of couple, or if they increase the life satisfaction of the parents. This is because the equation 'children mean happiness' depends on so many different factors that a general statement about it cannot be made.

Happiness with children depends on the individual, the couple, their circumstances, education, accumulated experience, and on culture of the area in which they reside. This becomes clear by comparing the extremes.

Examples:

- Risma was married to Nafal. The couple lives in a traditional wooden house in Bali. After they had married, they never had a discussion amongst themselves about having children or not. For them it was a matter of course, which was also expected from their respective families. The older people in their families saw the children not only as an emotional enrichment to their lives but also as a kind of 'social security'.
- Dario and Loa lived in Germany. Already before they had married, they decided not to have children. They considered children as a kind of 'luxury' which, according to them, they couldn't afford because both of them had to work hard to ensure a certain standard of living in a high-cost country. When Dario's widowed mother got older and needed daily care, they bought a room for her in a nearby senior-care home. At weekends or public holidays, they visited the old lady until she passed away.

HAPPY WITH CHILDREN

Your freedom to decide whether to have children or to remain alone with your partner has some important consequences for your pursuit of happiness.

It has already been mentioned that raising children does not only mean happiness for the parents, but that they are also expected to make sacrifices. For instance, it is normal for parents to put their children first, sacrifice their sleep so the child can sleep, spend more time with the child, and put their own social life on hold, save up for the child's future instead of spending big on themselves.

At the same time, even when you have children, you do not want to live for sacrifice only, but you want to live happily. Therefore, regardless of whether you have made a decision for or against having children, your first priority must always be the preservation of happiness.

With this in mind, the issue is how a couple can stay happy together and remain just as loving to each other after children have entered their lives.

> Parents and children are a lifelong bond, a bond that cannot be cut. Even if one tears down the bridges, the rubble remains lying for a lifetime.
>
> —Unknown

One of the important points that parents should agree on before birth is to de-link their happiness from the child's and make the child's happiness their first priority. This is because children suffer with parents who are unhappy with each other. Therefore, parents with children should avoid conflicts as much as possible, never carry out their conflicts in front of the children, and never let the children feel guilty for their conflicts.

EARLY AGREEMENT ON PRINCIPLES

Many conflicts between the parents could be avoided, if, before the children are born, they would discuss in all openness and honesty some basic principles on which their children should be raised and agree on them. One possible way could be to agree, in good time before the birth, on principles of the child education (e.g., 'strict' versus 'permissive'), work sharing (e.g., who does what in the household), and responsibilities (e.g., who will take care of pre-primary education).

The timing of this discussion between the parents is important. It must take place before the birth of the child. At this time, the child cannot witness parental arguments, thus eliminating possible harmful influences on the child's fragile psyche. The parents should know that already in babyhood the child notices by the raised, aggressive voices of the arguing parents that something is 'wrong' in its environment and therefore will give off signs of unhappiness, such as loud crying or increased kicking.

The partners would be well advised, not to ignore, swallow, or tolerate any possible differences which may arise between them and which have the potential for conflict between them.

Example: Natalia was increasingly annoyed by the fact that even after the birth of her daughter Tina, her husband Colin expected her to do all the housework and shopping for the family. When she asked Colin to help her, he got upset every time. He tried to make clear to her that every day, he was doing his share for the family's upkeep by earning the money on the assembly line. Now, Natalia was upset about herself that two years ago, in their discussions on whether or not to have children, she had not reached an agreement with Colin in advance about how they would share the burden of daily work fairly after the birth of the child. Now, it was too late because, in the interest of the child, she avoided any open dispute with her husband.

There is an important reason for having discussions about the basic principles of living together as a family at an early stage, before the first child is even born. If discussed at that time, possible fundamental disagreements will leave the partners free to decide against having children and in favour of their happiness as a couple.

They know that happiness in the relationship is at the very top of their priority list. If they feel that this happiness could be put at risk by having children, they should reconsider. Part of this reconsideration should be the understanding that compromises with respect to happiness are difficult, if not impossible. Unlike happiness, matters arising from the birth of children such as sharing workload are not only of secondary importance, but also much easier to compromise on.

However, the scope for such compromises is more limited after the birth of the child. It either forces the partners to jeopardize their happiness (e.g., as a result of continuous arguing) or the uncomfortable feeling of annoyance by one partner who had to give in 'for the sake of peace'.

In addition, and as mentioned when discussing confrontational relationships, the disharmony stemming from such inter-parental controversies also have the potential of unsettling the children.

Example: Marina and George, who have no children, went to a party with their best friends Katrina and Bill, who were new parents. Marina and George stayed at the party until dawn and amused themselves intensively. For Katrina and Bill, on the other hand, it was 'just another party', as they had to go home much earlier than the other guests because the next morning, their child would be on the mat as early as 6 a.m. When Marina talked to her friend Katrina the next day, she expressed pity that the child prevented Katrina from enjoying a 'wild' party to the end. She recommended Katrina not to let her life get destroyed by her child. In the first moment, Katrina did not know exactly what to be more upset about: The fact that her best friend hadn't understood what superior happiness the child meant to her, or that she had missed a 'wild' party.

In the example, Marina's misconception is that she seems to believe that children can impair the parents' private life and have a negative impact on their happiness. By doing this, she seems to ignore the fact that children add new aspects to their parents' life, which can be equally enriching and more sustainable than missed experiences.

Another important reason for having a discussion at an early stage is not only the agreement on some important principles of family life, but also all other factors that can make life in a largely self-determined partnership different from life in a partly externally determined family (largely dominated by the child's needs). Due to their changing environment, challenges, and experiences after birth, the partners' perspective on life in general, and the partnership, specifically, can change, the quality of the relationship can decline, and, in some extreme cases, the partners can even become strangers to each other.

As a result of these changes, couples may begin to realize that their partner is hardly recognizable anymore and is suddenly so different—or, that they consciously or subconsciously overlooked their partner's flaws or didn't want to see them in their enthusiasm.

Example: After their marriage and after having three children, practical things like home ownership and mortgages had become much more important for Ken and Norma than their former travelling escapades. Norma who was used to standing on heels and wearing kinky dresses was now wearing flip-flops and jeans. Ken has gained a lot of weight as he is used to staying home and can no longer tuck in his shirts into his trousers. Moreover, Norma is now unable to pay attention to Ken as much as before because she has her hands full with the two kids and the baby.

Negative emotions, quarrels, reduced partnership activities, unfulfilled sexuality, unrealistic expectations, and increased stress at home can make everyday life an ultimate stress test for the relationship and turn a happy relationship into an unhappy one.

Example: Ken came home from the office. He immediately felt that the mood was explosive. 'Don't touch me,' Norma yelled as he caressed her shoulder, 'You'd better get Lilly out of the bathroom!' When Ken saw Lilly, their five-year-old daughter, she was in tears and sobbed: 'Mama is not my friend anymore.' He understood that Lilly was disappointed because her mama wasn't playing with her. Norma didn't have time to play with Lilly because Dicky, Lilly's one-year-old brother, was loudly demanding his porridge, and Bernie, the six-week-old baby was crying in the other room. Later, when all three children finally had fallen asleep, Ken and Norma were exhausted and didn't even have the drive to switch on TV. Norma apologized to Ken for having lost her temper. But Ken was upset about all the noise and the chaos which he had to experience when he arrived. 'I expect you to have the kids under control, at least when I'm in the house. You have all the time during the day to organize yourself,' he said, and added in a threatening voice, 'I don't want to experience this again.' Norma was furious about his insensitive and brutal remark. She told him how unfair he was, but he wasn't interested. 'It's your job,' he only said and switched on the TV.

One should be careful and not assume that a discussion between the partners—prior to the decision to have a child—can prevent all of these developments from happening. But such a conversation could at least assist preparing the partners to deal with behaviour changes and, in addition, can lead to agreements between the partners on how they want to deal with conflicts, should they arise. This can also help reduce the severity of possible conflicts and offer the partners a mutually agreed basis for conflict resolution or measures to mitigate the consequences of conflicts.

In a family, the pursuit of happiness will not only concern yourself and your partner or the happiness in the relationship, but will also cover the happiness of the child/children. This additional responsibility results in principle requirements for the education of the child/children, which should also be discussed in advance.

THE CHILDREN'S HAPPY CHILDHOOD

> The most beautiful gift of parents is a happy childhood.
>
> —Unknown

As said previously, parents should understand and agree that the happiness of their children should be the overarching principle for their upbringing. In addition, their education must be aimed at and suitable for preparing the children for life in such a way that once they have gained their independence, they will have a real chance of finding their own happiness.

Memories of a happy childhood and a carefree and joyful upbringing have a beneficial effect on the well-being and inner balance of adults. Among the many factors that make for a happy childhood are unconditional love, security, authenticity of the parents, the provision of role models for orientation, time spent with the parents, and parents acting as attentive listeners and providing the children the feeling of being taken seriously.

Most parents want to offer their children a happy childhood. For many, this is a declared educational goal, especially in those cases where parents have high expectations of themselves (which are likely to be projected on to their children).

THE IMPORTANCE OF PLAYING

As pointed out—and especially in those cases where parents are ambitious themselves—many later conflicts can be avoided, if the parents can agree on some basic principles regarding the education of their children. This is best done *before* the children are born and when they are not restricted in their freedom of action due to the pressure of prevailing circumstances.

Ambitious parents who have high expectations should understand that there is no such thing as a perfect upbringing. There are always risks that mistakes will be made. In addition, parents should consider that constant projections on children about what is 'good' for them could be in reality a reflection of themselves, rather than a helpful nudge that will ready the young ones for an independent, free life.

However, even if mistakes are made, neither will the world collapse nor the children be seriously harmed. Flaws and errors in education will not immediately make children unhappy in the long term or turn them into 'failed children'. Beyond their parental upbringing, children are subject to many other influences (e.g., from teachers, friends, classmates, and media consumption), which can help to balance, reduce or even neutralize possible educational mistakes.

Different from what they intended, perfectionist parents who always want to do everything right when bringing up children, might make their children unhappy. Especially those parents who do their utmost to provide their children with all imaginable opportunities for growing and making them 'different from others' seem to overlook, that their children might miss their essential childhood happiness when they are forced to learn taking violin, hockey or tennis lessons instead of playing with their friends. The possible end result could well be that neither the ambitious parents nor the children will be happy.

Example: Inga was the only daughter of a couple which was very impressed by the (financial) successes of some internationally renowned tennis champions. At a young age already, Inga excelled as a good tennis player and her teacher singled her out as a talent. Therefore, her parents decided to invest all their savings into Inga's professional tennis career. Their ambitious goal was to make Inga an international tennis star. From there on, Inga became subject to a rigorous and demanding training schedule which didn't leave her any free time. But although Inga was talented, she didn't succeed in matching her parents' and her teacher's high expectations. In particular, Inga's parents were extremely frustrated and repeatedly blamed her for 'wasting' the family's entire savings. In response to her failure, Inga sank deeply into feelings of guilt and self-reproach. To overcome these feelings, she began to develop an unbridled sex life, drank too much alcohol, and turned to drugs. After a short time, she was only a shadow of her previous self and had to undergo psychiatric treatment. The ambition of her parents had totally destroyed her childhood happiness.

This example shows what can happen when parents put their ambitious expectations above the child's happiness. The parents ignored the most elementary aspects of a worry-free childhood, and not only destroyed the happiness of the child but possibly also their own. By imposing a rigorous training regime on the child, they killed the child's natural spontaneity and impulsiveness, which is one of the most outstanding characteristics of children.

Moreover, they ignored that there are phases in the development of children in which they do not want to be educated, but want to just have fun.

Playing is as important for the development of a child as structured learning. Through play, children develop their own identity and personality, knowledge about their own strengths and abilities, and understand their limits. Numerous skills that are important for a successful life are the result of intensive playing experiences such as social competence, consideration, cooperation with others, negotiating rules and listening, and conflict resolution. Through playing, children 'playfully' acquire everyday life skills, i.e., the ability to understand and cope with challenges.

Example: Especially in role-playing, children prefer to deal with topics related to their everyday experiences—be it shopping, family relationships or experiences related to doctor visits.

Against this background, one of the most important tasks of parents is to create a high-quality playing environment for their children, in which a variety of learning processes are stimulated. To achieve this, sufficient time for playing needs to allocated in which the children can choose their own activities free from external constraints or expectations.

Example: A highly intelligent physicist once said that there are moments when children have to be '*stupid*' to develop a feeling for happiness.

The word 'stupid' can be replaced with the word 'creative' or 'imaginative' as, in this context, it doesn't refer to 'intelligence' but the basic requirements of reasonable child development that is not destroyed by the ambitions of irresponsibly acting, overly ambitious ego-parents. 'Stupid' activities in this sense include playing traditional games in the sand, adventure games (such as 'Cops and Robbers' or 'Cowboys and Indians'), and other pastimes that require imagination and creativity. Contemporary children who mainly play computer games developed by specialist developers may be able to use technology devices early on but they tend to be more passive, reduced in social interaction and physical activity which may have an impact on their happiness.

Another basic decision that should be discussed as early as possible concerns basic educational concepts of the children's upbringing. A good example is whether the child should be brought up in an authoritative, authoritarian, or permissive way.

In view of the intended goal for the child to grow up happy and able to create its own happiness in the future, the following observations can be made:

- Authoritative parents aim at proving their children with self-confidence. Normally, they act as a role model for the children, place importance on mutual respect between parent and child, and provide their children with a 'playing' environment as discussed previously. Their goal is to give their children a happy childhood to prepare them for happiness later in their lives as adults.
- Authoritarian parents raise children with low self-esteem. They want to be obeyed without questions and usually instruct a child to conform to rules and follow orders. Authoritarian education will not help the

child to develop its own independent thinking. The absence of self-esteem can also constitute a barrier for the child to becoming happy.

- Permissive parents run the risk of raising rebels with high (sometimes unjustified) self-esteem. This model of education prevents children from learning from their parents on how to adapt to social and cultural norms that govern their environment. These children will have no experience of being seriously challenged by other people and will react inappropriately or helplessly to conflict situations. They will most likely associate these negative experiences with their permissive upbringing and feel unhappy about it.

Tip: Parents who want a happy child are neither permissive nor authoritarian. They should behave like an accomplice to the child that will later honour this behaviour with deep love.

If children are respected and treated by their parents as equal accomplices instead of 'from the top down', they will learn without any special educational effort how to stick together, be loyal, and act in solidarity.

Example: The unpleasant neighbour wanted to find out who broke the window of his rundown woodshed. When he confronted the neighbouring family, nobody answered his questions—neither the father nor the mother nor the two young boys. There was no reaction, although the parents knew that the boys had been playing football in the garden. In this situation, the parents would normally now start questioning or accusing the children. That would have been the usual way to find out the truth. Instead, the boys looked up into the air with innocent expressions on their faces and their parents shrugged their shoulders. When the angry neighbour had left, the father suppressed his grin and tried to look as sternly as possible. He wanted to proceed pedagogically, because one could not let the children get away with what they had done. 'Then it was the dog, wasn't it?' he ended the interrogation. The children nodded eagerly. 'The dog, yes, it was the dog,' they confirmed. The father smiled again but made the children understand that their tacit denial was a stupid idea in this crystal-clear situation and that next time they had to take responsibility for what they had done. The boys promised it. They felt very happy about their parents' solidarity and that they had not denounced their children to the unsympathetic neighbour. The parents had behaved like their accomplices. In the evening, just before they went to sleep, the two boys assured each other how great their parents were.

Another basic educational principle that the spouses should discuss at an early stage is whether they want to let their children grow up overprotected or spoiled or, alternatively, give them the freedom for self-development.

In our view, instead of constantly overseeing every aspect of their children's life (so-called *helicopter parents*) and being overprotective, parents should focus more on their children's happiness.

Tip: Let your children explore their world while keeping a watchful eye on them from the sidelines. This will allow you to watch your children grow into their own persons as a result of this freedom.

MAKE IT A 'COOL' DECISION

Both issues discussed in this chapter are 'cool'. Firstly, the question of whether it is good or bad to have children, and secondly, how important it is for partners to discuss openly and agree at an early stage some basic principles governing family life and child upbringing.

The first question is 'cool' because it is neither following the traditional thinking that a 'child-free life is an unfulfilled life', nor signalling the willingness to concede to the will of others—for instance, the family. Instead, it shows autonomy of partners who want to be free and consider their decision as their own. In other words, they want to do their own thing even if that means going against what others expect or prescribe.

Ultimately, whatever the decision is, the couple can be proud of who they are and must not apologize for their differences in view. However, it cannot be excluded that those who claim that a 'child-free life is an unfulfilled life' haven't met their future self yet.

Second, the advice for partners to seek early agreements on certain principles concerning children's upbringing and education is 'cool' because it appreciates and respects both individuals' differences and encourages rational decision making. The decision to have children, like a law, requires 'implementing regulations' and 'procedural regulations'. That's what these suggested early parental agreements on some basic principles are all about.

> I've got a particular weakness for criminals and artists. Neither takes life as it is.
>
> —Stanley Kubrick, American film director

Not only are the two points discussed here 'cool' but also the exemplary observations made in relation to them. Applied coolness in this particular area is helpful as the intention is not to explain and be scientific but to lead and move on. The mere development of reactions to the many demands of abstract philosophies, religions, ideologies or worldviews (*weltanschauung*) alone will not be sufficient to do this. Therefore, it is advocated here that you stay as close as possible to your daily life and experience, and not be concerned with abstract philosophies. This will automatically strengthen your will for pursuing your own course, irrespective of the norms, beliefs, and expectations of others. This will be truly 'cool'.

FRIENDSHIP AND HAPPINESS

> There is no enjoying the possession of anything valuable unless one has someone to share it with.
>
> -Unknown

So far, under the umbrella of the term 'relationships', we have discussed the factors that determine the feeling of happiness of those partners who live together and permanently in partnerships which are characterized by the partners' emotions for each other and physical intimacy.

In a friendship, there are also emotions involved, such as mutual affection, trust, reliability, and 'being there for each other'. But friendships are neither binding, nor intimate in the emotional and sexual sense. Each party lives their own, independent lives, and one can only meet occasionally and still be a friend. Despite these differences, friendships can also be an important source of happiness. This is especially the case if you have a trusting relationship in which you can rely on the other, can talk openly about everything, and feel accepted with all your strengths and flaws.

BEING SOCIAL MAKES HAPPY

You can own everything you dream of, but if you are lonely and do not have people in your life to love and to share them with, you will not be happy. This follows from our core human nature as social beings, which suggests that people are not meant to live alone but with each other. From this, it follows that your pursuit for happiness must not be at the expense of your closest relationships, such as those you find in love or those you have in your family, but must also protect your friends and other important social relationships you may have.

Tip: Don't get us wrong: This is not about having as many friends as possible—neither in the real world, nor on Facebook, Instagram, or other social media. It's about the *quality* of your relationships with a handful of people whom you consider truly important.

In this context, the word 'important' doesn't mean that your selection of friends should be based on people's status such as their finances, power, influence or fame. By important, we mean that these friends are close to you because you have developed feelings of sympathy and trust with them. Close friends make contributions to your life that other people don't make, for instance understanding, sharing, openness, trust, and advice.

> Be crazy, be stupid, be silly, be weird. Be whatever, because life is too short to be anything but happy.
>
> —Unknown

TRUE FRIENDS VERSUS FAKE FRIENDS

Different from acquaintances (people who interact in superficial ways), casual friendships (people who are not emotionally close), agentic friendships (people who share a common goal and stay pragmatic), true friendship is based on authentic emotions, mutual caring, and trust. It can provide emotional well-being and thus boost your happiness.

Tip: To better understand what category of friends you have, it may be helpful if you structure your friends as part of a 'mental stocktaking'. This exercise may be an appropriate tool to create groups or lists in which you classify your friends, including those on social media.

When you do your mental stocktaking, be critical and decide which friends make you feel really good because you feel emotionally connected or share unforgettable experiences with them. The friends who regularly communicate with you, seem to care for you, and who give something valuable in return for your sympathy also belong into this category.

> Our networks are larger than the number of relationships we can maintain.
>
> —Unknown

Being critical means that you have to be honest—foremost with yourself—because there is a risk that you may fall into the vanity trap.

Prestige-oriented thinking or vanity can lead you to believe that having a large number of friends is a positive sign for how well you are integrated. But before you get overly impressed with yourself, you should use your mental stocktaking practice to find out whether you are fooling yourself and access who your true friends really are.

Example: Robert was single and experienced many moments in his life when he felt lonely. To overcome feelings of loneliness, he developed the habit of inviting guests for dinners and hosted parties at his home. Among his guests were not only friends, but also people he had found likeable and interesting when he had met them occasionally—or even once. He did this not only out of joy but also in the hope of making new friends. Although his circle of acquaintances grew rapidly in this way, Robert soon realized that he was wrong. Instead of being happy about newly added friends, he felt that his hospitality had only been taken advantage of. After his invitations, he rarely received a polite thank you, let alone a return invitation. After some consideration, Robert realized that he was wasting his time with people who were not interested in really being friends with him. His search for new friends had turned out to be a one-way street. Therefore, Robert decided to use his time better and resigned himself to the fact that there were very few people he could call real friends and that he should devote more time to them.

As shown in this example, it's unlikely that you will feel happy with fake friends because the reason why you have tolerated them so far are of only secondary importance. Such fake friendships are built on temporal, egoistic desires such as vanity or the fear of being alone. It would be better if you could shed your expectations, identify your real friends, and begin to build closer relationships with them.

As opposed to fake friends, true friends are people who are very close to you. Usually, they are prepared to listen to you, make an effort to understand your situation, strengthen your positivity, and can possibly even provide you with helpful advice. In short, you can rely on them, even in bad times.

Example: Milan was deputy managing director in his company. Until recently, he had felt comfortable in his position. This changed when his boss hired another manager with the unspoken intention of letting him compete with Milan to see who the better manager was. Milan started to fear for his job. He didn't tell his wife Amanda his new situation because he didn't want to worry her but, of course, she had noticed that something was wrong as a result of his changed behaviour at home. She asked Milan about it but he didn't open up and she didn't take it well. Amanda got particularly upset when he repeatedly refused to join her and their best friends for their regular restaurant visits. 'I'm not in the mood to see anyone,' Milan said, 'The last thing I now want to do is be around them.'

In this example, Milan's decision to retreat to himself is not well-advised and should be resisted by his wife and his friends at all cost. What Milan fails to understand is that it is these people who are close to him and whom he loves—like his wife and his close friends—who are capable of changing his mood for the better.

> Keep smiling, keep shining, knowing you can always count on me, for sure. That's what friends are for. For good times and bad times, I'll be on your side forever more: That's what friends are for.
>
> —Dionne Warwick, American pop singer

Under his friends' influence, Milan's perception of his challenges would possibly change. For example, his friends might tell him how good he is at his job and what he has achieved so far. They may also talk about the flaws of his rival such as his lack of familiarity with the company, which, very likely will make him fail in the end. As a consequence of such a conversation with his friends, Milan may realize that 'the mountain is beginning to look more like a molehill'.

Therefore, it is recommended that when you are worried, stressed or frazzled, you turn to friends and seek moral and social support. In the end, you will find that the mere fact that you can share your concerns with people you respect and who are emotionally close to you will bring you relief. You will also feel happy about the fact that you have friends who are willing to help you when you are not doing well.

For these reasons, you should take any opportunity to enhance the quality of your friendships by showing those reactions which every good friend should have—empathy, compassion, and understanding. If your friend has good news, don't hesitate to respond positively. It will make your friend feel more cared for, understood, validated, and happier. But not only will your friend feel happier, you will too. As mentioned, it was the Buddha who said that nothing makes you happier than making someone else happy.

Even if you haven't seen a particular friend in a while, you can strengthen the bonds of friendship by reminding them of past good times. This will help you get closer again.

Tip: To strengthen your relationships with true friends, you should make it one of your priorities to communicate with them and, if possible, see them more frequently, for instance by scheduling time after work or at weekends.

Joint group activities where people meet outside their usual home or work environment can provide ample opportunities to find out who is truly acting or just pretending to be a true friend. For example, an excellent opportunity for friends to get to know each other better and intensify the relationship is a group adventure holiday.

Example: Plan a group trip on a long weekend. You will already see in the planning phase who is leaving you alone to all the preparatory work and who is offering their assistance. On such a tour, there are also many ways to see with whom you can carry 'substantive', engaging conversations and not just the ordinary small talk as well as those whom you would rather leave alone. Little problems during the trip, such as a minor injury, also show very quickly who cares and is prepared to take initiatives and doesn't just think about themselves.

If the definition of a true 'good friend' is not easy, the definition of a friend' on the World Wide Web is even more complicated. Most of the confusion and uncertainty about the term 'friend' is caused by the fact that the American company Facebook has hijacked the word for itself and filled it with content different from what we were used to. Of course, you can sign up as many people as you like on social media, but that doesn't make the people you selected as true friends. All you are actually doing is signing up people that in the offline world, you would normally think of as mere acquaintances.

In the online world, in particular, on social media, friendship is expressed as a binary value. You 'click' to become a friend or 'accept' a friend, or you choose not to do so. You 'de-friend' people at your discretion or get 'unfriended'. In the world of social media, someone is either a friend or not. This very primitive distinction ignores the fact that all our friends are not the same and that there many shades of friendship.

Example: In social media networks, everyone is subsumed under the umbrella term 'friends'. This could include your lovers, siblings, uncles, best friends, schoolmates, sports team members, colleagues, accidental club acquaintances, or people you may not even know personally.

There is no doubt that your true friends can be friends you know in real life (offline) and also be on your social media networks. Remember that the social media platform you are using is just another tool for and another form of communication. In this case, it does not only mean more opportunities for your individual communication, but they also provide a very effective way of keeping old friendships going.

Online friendships can especially play an important role, where people don't live near but want to share their special interests, for instance, music, literature, antiques, arts, history, photography or gaming. They can become part of a specialized online community which can create a feeling of belonging that would be absent without this tool.

Positive features of online relationships also include the possibility for video chats which allow the users to interact with online friends. This makes it possible for the user to maintain and even intensify the friendship and help them to see whether a new online friend really is who they say they are.

The opportunities provided by social media have created a great potential for people to increase their happiness by maintaining existing friendships and creating new (online) friendships that would not be possible otherwise.

Actually, today, more and more people believe that 'seeing friends often' is no longer particularly important for maintaining friendship. They feel that writing text messages to each other or sending images, emoji or videos is sufficient.

The question is, however, whether social media can add to your happiness by creating new bonds of friendship with people you've never met, or will rarely meet. While it might seem that your social media networks are allowing you to have more 'friends' than in real life (*quantity*), it is also more likely that increasing the size of your network appears to produce no proportional increase in your capacity for meaningful true friendships (*quality*).

At a closer look, it seems easier to develop an acquaintance online than a true friendship. Although, in case of mutual interest, social media can create superficial bonds, familiarity and intimacy quickly, there are still some qualitative and emotional features missing that are typical for true friendships, such as empathy, compassion, and mutual understanding.

Having said that, online friendships are invaluable for people who live in isolated geographical areas or who are isolated for other reasons, like disabled people or the elderly. For them, online friends may well add to their happiness and thus make them as important as friends in real life or can even replace them.

But social media also has negative aspects when we look at its impact on social behaviour.

Example: When you travel on public transport, you can see how people are literally glued to their smartphones or iPads, scrolling up and down with no interruption, and ignoring everything that happens around them.

> A wealth of content creates a poverty of attention.
>
> —Herbert Simon, Nobel Laureate

The sheer amount of content made available on social networks gives rise to the fear of being missed when you can't post enough interesting content on your timeline/story and as a result, your friends don't pay enough attention to you anymore.

On the other hand, there is also the 'fear of missing out'. Under this alternative, you feel that you can't sufficiently receive or react to the messages/posts sent by your friends because you are busy or for other reasons. In this case, you fear losing contact with your friends or risk provoking their displeasure by not reacting as expected.

Example: Enzo's wife died in a tragic accident. During the period of mourning, he stopped checking his social media accounts. When after some months, he became active again, Enzo was shocked to see that Benny, one of his close friends, had 'unfriended' him. He called Benny and asked for the reason. Benny gave him the astonishing answer that he had been angry about Enzo's lack of solidarity with him because Enzo had not responded to his repeated requests to click the 'Like' button for his postings. He pointed out to Enzo that this had been very important to him because his postings concerned his new business and his investor had made the number of 'Likes' a crucial point for his financial commitment.

This disenchantment of friends' online interaction with each other, and the crippling of language associated with the required brevity of text messages (and tweets) show that online communication and thus online friendship suffer from an emotional deficit. The problem with social media friendships is that they don't provide the social, emotional or even physical experience that is important for true happiness.

Example: On social media, we are reminded of every birthday of our online friends. Behind the automatic notification, there is an unspoken compulsion to react. Before the emergence of the social media, people sent personalised and, in some cases, even originally designed birthday wishes to please the addressee. If you don't want to just send a laconic 'HBD', social media allows you today to resort to prefabricated emoji or similar graphics and hope it will please the recipient's psyche.

When you are 'socializing' online, you know you are not engaging with a real-life relationship and an authentic person, but instead, a fairly well-arranged version of your online friend who appears in a situation that is probably largely staged and controlled by them. This can be detrimental to developing true bonds between each other.

Example: Marga has been communicating online with Nanda, an older lady of about the same advanced age who loves to play Scrabble as much as she does. They communicate electronically beautifully with each other, are friendly, laugh a lot, and toast each other on Skype when they have a drink together after a good conversation. Marga and Nanda have complimented each other at various occasions on their good looks. Marga is, indeed, very impressed with how young and fresh Nanda's face looks. But one day, Nanda's doorbell rings during their Skype session. Marga sees Nanda on her screen struggling to get up from her chair, grabbing a stick, and dragging herself to the door with great physical effort and under great pain. Marga is shocked by the contrast between Nanda's youthful voice, the fresh expression on her face, and her obviously severe disability. While she had previously felt nothing but sincere admiration for Nanda, she now felt obliged to add feelings of pity and concern. This didn't change her sympathy for her online friend, but she realized that the image Nanda had projected online was not the true image of the woman she really was, but as she wanted to be seen.

What you can learn from this example is that online friends don't have the same experiences as they would have in an offline relationship in which connection and trust can be created more easily because face-to-face a friend can see the other as they really are. This means that you will always remain a little more reserved in an online friendship than in an offline friendship unless, in the course of time, you have got to know and appreciate each other personally.

No matter how sympathetic someone like Marga may have been for Nanda on a social media platform, in the end, for Nanda, it is having 'a real shoulder to cry on' that makes the difference.

This example also suggests that it would be good for your happiness if you don't rely exclusively on online friendships, but, in parallel, also develop, maintain and take care of your friendships in the real world. The keyword here is 'time'—in other words, it is the constraint of time that is of crucial importance when discussing online and offline friendships.

To maintain friendships in real life (offline), you need a certain amount of time for your commitment and the interactions with your friends following from your engagement. On the other hand, using your time for extensive social media interaction, in particular when doing it with strangers may take an important share of your time away from your offline friendships.

Example: After the elections in his country, Chuck considered social media as an opportunity to bridge the political divide that was caused by the irresponsible behaviour of politicians from both camps. He crafted what he intended to be politically balanced posts about immigration and climate change. To Chuck's surprise, it totally backfired when some of his online friends were outraged by his comments and attacked him with insulting messages, causing him to get angry. Chuck asked himself whether engaging in a response would be healthy for him and good for his friendships because an honest response would likely affect his offline relationships. Chuck gave it some thought and decided when such a polarizing conversation came up again in the future, he would rather have a face-to-face offline discussion instead of engaging in an unhealthy and extremely time-consuming back-and-forth online dialogue. When he asked his wife Barbara-Ann about the reaction, she was even more pragmatic and said to her husband, 'Write a letter to your representative, or, even better, go offline and ignore it. It's better for your health and maintaining your friendship.'

The message here is that it is easy to get lost on the internet, especially over time. The temptation to look at, read or search for one or the other is very strong. And, it is even more time-consuming if you let yourself get involved in a fruitless online discussion. The time spent on the internet doesn't always help cultivating real friendships.

In the end, the answer to the question whether social media is good or bad for your happiness is both yes and no. There are both benefits and drawbacks of having social media friends. But they will never fully take the place of friends in real life. Thus, spending (too much) time on online friendships is not recommended but, as an additional engagement, actively interacting online can be a good thing.

Tip: If you want to make real-life friends a priority over your online friends, then you should schedule enough time to (re-) connect with old friends and the new people you are interested in, make dates with them, and plan common activities such as excursions, visits, dinners, or even a weekend or a holiday together.

THE 'FAMILY OF CHOICE'

If happiness is a priority in your life, and you are free in your mind regarding relationships, you can take a cool approach and pursue your own, non-conformist course towards happiness, irrespective of traditional patterns, such as marriage. You would act cool if you could disassociate yourself from all constraints which you believe stand in your way to happiness, such as norms, beliefs, and expectations. Instead of succumbing to them, you use your intellectual independence to balance out what is given, on the one hand, and what you really want, on the other.

As discussed previously, being social can make you happy and happiness in relationships can arise from traditional sources such as lifelong marriage and close friendships, but also from new forms of social relationships like online friendships. In addition, we also discussed that in the present-day environment, marriage may not always be a guarantee for a lifelong and happy partnership.

When talking about marriage and family, there's generally an underlying assumption that as a family member, you receive from other family members and in return, owe them loyalty, protection as well as moral and material support. However, the reality is often different from this model, and people may not feel bound to or are not interested in those people they are related to by birth. There is a new trend away from traditional patterns such as marriage towards stronger relations with friends.

This trend is increasingly influencing the role model of the traditional family. Certain functions that used to be performed by the family, such as caring for the elderly, are now more often assumed by private and state institutions, and it is friends who tend to have more influence now on decisions about when, where, and who gets married than the family.

Tip: It would be helpful for your self-orientation if you ask yourself these important questions: Do you have someone in your family with whom you can talk to when you need help or ask for a favour or simply chat with because you are feeling lonely? Is there someone in your family who would come to your aid when you need it? Would someone in your family support you when you have made a bad mistake?

Example: After a serious accident Anthony was hospitalized. Before he was taken to intensive care, he managed to send messages to his brother Sean, who lived far away, and to his best friend Manfred to inform the others. When Anthony woke up from his anaesthesia, his best friend Manfred was sitting at his bedside and told him that the doctors had been fighting for his life. After Manfred had left, Anthony was wondering why his brother hadn't come to see him although his life had been at risk. Only later, he found a text message from his brother, in which he wished him a speedy recovery and apologized for his absence because of his heavy workload.

People are putting increasing importance to friendships as a source of social relations and happiness. For instance, in the past, the one place where people could relax and recover from everyday life was at home with the family. Today, it is increasingly the circle of close friends that takes on this function. In many cases, the larger family is even perceived as stressful—at times, even more stressful than the workplace.

Example: In Germany, there are people who argue that one would feel much better if one gave friendships just as much weight as one's intimate relationships and that friendships deserve greater 'cultural visibility'. Some even anticipate the end of the nuclear family, i.e., a married couple with children, which is so typical for the social middle class.

> Today, the circle of friends is the better family.
>
> —Susanne Lang, German journalist

In short, it can be said that close friends are increasingly becoming a part of what could be called the 'new extended family' or 'family of choice'.

Unlike in a biological family, where you have very little, if any, control over who belongs to it, in a family of choice you have a say in who is part of it as it refers to people you have identified as your close friends. They are normally people who stand by your side during good times and bad, feed your self-esteem instead of depleting it, enrich your life by their presence, help empower you, and generally make you happy.

If you find that you cannot expect support from your biological family or your family is not able to for some reason, then it may be time to rethink your relationships and look out for people who are like-minded to create a family of choice. The friends you are considering should have a similar lifestyle and values to yours and have an interest in becoming part of an extended family or family of choice.

This is not to be misunderstood as a decision to force friendship into a formal corset, but as a mutual assurance to be there for each other when the need arises. In fact, to some extent, the same principles that apply to your biological family, also apply to your family of choice, notably empathy, loyalty, and the willingness to help, if needed.

Example: Asta and her close friend Karen have agreed on a reciprocal babysitting arrangement. They also assured each other that they would care for their respective children in case something was to happen, such as a medical emergency in the middle of the night. After they had made their agreement, Asta confessed to her husband Jack that now she would feel much more comfortable because of the security that had been created.

'I'm so happy we have Karen,' she said, knowing that Karen would say the same to her husband.

This trend towards stronger relations with friends does not only apply to younger people but is particularly evident for old people and the growing LGBTQ community. Both groups, the elderly and people with different sexual orientation, are frequently less linked to their families and more focused on their group of like-minded friends.

Today, in many cases of old people, the task of providing appropriate care for them exceeds the capabilities of the other family members. The sharp rise in life expectancy often leads to old people suffering from illnesses that were previously unimportant, such as limited mobility, due to earlier death. Many of the symptoms of the diseases old people are experiencing require professional care and cannot be properly handled by family members. Therefore, it is increasingly becoming the rule that old people don't remain in the family until they die, but are placed in professionally managed nursing homes. Even in Asian countries, where multiple generations traditionally live under one roof and ageing family members have been cared for in the family home, lifestyle is changing. Western influence and the rising number of elderly (dementia) patients are driving the emergence of retirement and assisted living homes in the region.

It is in senior care homes where the elderly can build new connections and, in many cases, establish new close friendships that, over time, can become closer than traditional family ties.

Something similar can apply to the members of the LGBTQ community. Frequently, they enjoy large social networks, have no children, and follow an alternative lifestyle which must not fit into a traditional family structure. Also, in these cases, close friends can become more 'family' than the 'biological family'.

THE LIMITS OF FRIENDSHIPS

The question must be asked what it means for your happiness if your 'family of choice' fails you when you really need your friends?

Example: Mary-Jo and Joey have a close circle of friends with whom they have a lot of fun. They feel comfortable with their friends and often talk about them as 'our family'. Completely unexpectedly, Joey dies of a heart attack and Mary-Jo is paralysed in grief. She needs the support of her friends in this difficult time. But they react differently than expected. Their so-called friends slowly withdraw from Mary-Jo. There are no more visits, no more joint events, no more invitations, and no more phone calls. The idea of having a family that would be supportive in difficult times was only a dream.

What you can learn from this example is that despite having a 'family', a 'family of close friends' or even a 'family of choice', you should better be able to stand on your own two feet and not fully rely on anyone else. Today, people, even if they're in your inner circle of friends, are more and more about themselves. Especially if you represent to them a 'problem' and aren't 'fun' anymore. The sad news is that if you get perceived by your friends as the bearer of bad news or a 'troublemaker', you run the risk of being shunned even when you signal the need for help. Overnight, you find yourself being an 'odd man out'.

Tip: The best way to react to such an experience is to be 'cool'. Don't get involved in a discussion, don't get upset, and don't be angry or sad. Instead, look at the situation as if you were a neutral third party. You will soon realize that, in principle, your friends are still accepting you as a friend and may also continue to like you personally. In their self-centredness, what really bothers them so much is that you have become the bearer of bad messages, that your grief is disturbing their celebrated joy of life, and that they are not willing to sacrifice anything for the preservation of your friendship. If you look at this behaviour from the cool standpoint of a neutral observer, you will quickly see that, in reality, this behaviour is nothing special and not directed against you but a quite common behaviour pattern about which you mustn't get overly excited. Instead, believe in yourself and take pride in developing the willpower and the ability to solve your problem without the help of others. Seek your temporarily lost happiness not with your friends, but with yourself and within yourself. If you are successful, it will make you freer in relation to your friends, as you no longer have expectations that are likely to be disappointed.

SEXUALITY AND HAPPINESS

> Love could be the road to happiness but most times happiness leads you right to the doorsteps of love because only happy people can really love.
>
> —Unknown

People often think of the sequence—love first, followed by happiness. But this does not necessarily have to be the case. If you are happy with yourself, you can be more pleasant and good to be around. In addition, your positive charisma, i.e., your quality to attract, influence, and charm others can make you a more effective communicator and draw positive attention—or even love—to yourself.

> It is not the things that worry us, but our view of things.
>
> —Epictetus, Ancient Greek philosopher

If, on the other hand, you show all the signs of an unhappy person, it usually does not make it easier for you to open the door to a romantic relationship because typically people use outer appearance to discover other people's inner attractiveness. When expression reveal negativity or unhappiness, at least at first sight, it might not be very appealing.

It is highly individual whom people are attracted to and why. But there are some behaviours that can be considered safe when it comes to being perceived as appealing, such as being pleasant, charming, interesting, or humorous.

This positive perception can be further intensified when you have sex appeal which refers to your ability to attract in a sexual way by being interesting, exciting or even inciting sexual arousal. Often people tend to believe that in order to be sexually appealing, they need to alter their physical appearance, for instance by selecting sexy clothes or manipulating their face or body.

The individual sexual attraction and sexuality as such may make you feel good as they are commonly associated with well-being. However, as said before, well-being as such does not lead to happiness, unless other elements such as positive feelings, emotions and personal affection are added.

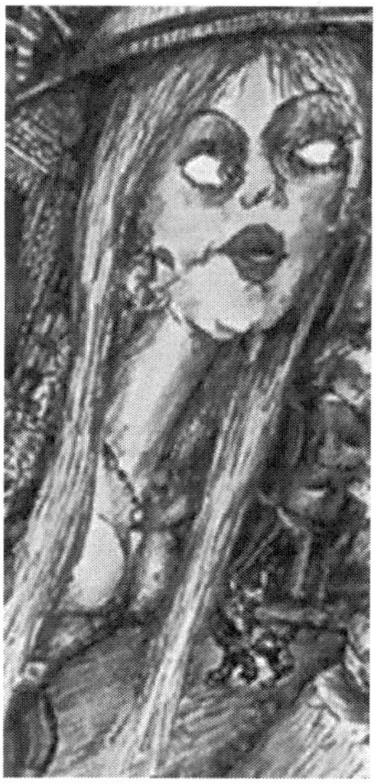

Affection in particular is a very personal thing, just like happiness itself. It can exist regardless of the nature of your relationship be it marriage, (close) friendship or other forms of relationships. Sexuality promotes the intensity of your affection for your partner. As a result, sexuality will also affect your happiness. Therefore, there is a clear interest in looking at the role of sexuality when talking about happiness.

EROS AND SEX

> Why should we take advice on sex from the pope? If he knows anything about it, he shouldn't!
>
> —George Bernard Shaw, Irish playwright, critic, polemicist, and political activist

If there is a bond between your happiness and the influence sexuality has on the affection you have for your partner and your partner has for you, you should still not make the error to put sex appeal, i.e., your physical attractiveness, in the foreground by making it a priority of your appearance. This would rather reduce than increase your chances of becoming happy long-term. Be reminded that it takes more than just sex to be happy. Of course, a sexually appealing appearance will have its desired effect on other people. And for the moment, this may satisfy your vanity and also strengthen your self-confidence, but don't forget that the interest in you shown by others will mirror your 'invitation' which, in this case, will be solely based on your sex appeal. All other important facets of your personality will remain unconsidered. This will increase the risk of misjudgements and put you into undesirable competition with other people with a similar sex appeal, a competition that carries the seeds of a short-term affair rather than a long-term relationship.

> Eros is a unique experience but it is not love itself. It bridges the gap between sexuality and love; it spans the chasm between two people.
>
> —John Pierrakos, American physician and psychiatrist

This is where Eros comes in as an important factor because Eros has the potential to enrich mere sexuality to a new, higher quality.

Note: The word Eros comes from Ancient Greek and means love. The English word 'sex' comes from Latin *sexus,* which originally meant 'division', and refers to the division between men and women.

Although used interchangeably in common speech, Eros and sexuality actually designate two different concepts.

Example: People commonly refer to 'having sex'. But you cannot say 'to have' Eros because as Eros is not 'technical' but 'spiritual'.

Sexuality is strongly related to your biological potential as it is directly influenced by the limitations of the physical body. For instance, with old age, sexuality diminishes and can even completely disappear (menopause and andropause).

In contrast, Eros is completely free of your physical body's limitations. It can manifest itself at any age, from before sexual awakening of the child until very old age.

Example: When he was over ninety years old, Picasso painted erotic motifs as he was fighting for his life. Anyone looking at his last, highly erotic works would have never guessed that they were done by a ninety-year-old, and, much less, that they were created as a wistful and rebellious act against his fate shortly before he passed away.

> Eros would be the most beautiful thing in the world, if there wouldn't be this terrible sex.
>
> —attributed to George Bernard Shaw,
> Irish playwright, critic, polemicist, and political activist

Sexuality is urgent and fast in character. It manifests itself in physical reactions, such as tension in the body. It's mainly focused on obtaining pleasure by any means which can possibly reduce the other person to a mere object (as it happens, for instance, in prostitution). Sexual needs can never be completely satisfied because the physical separation of the partners is a default. The physical merging can only take place for a short moment, and even then the partners still remain two isolated egos.

> Sex without Eros is nothing else than gymnastics without apparatus.
>
> —Saul Bellow, Canadian writer

On the other hand, and in principle, Eros stands for sensual and slow, creating a bond between people that is stronger than just (spontaneous) sexual attraction. Eros goes beyond mere sexuality because it encompasses additional elements not essential for mere sexuality, such as harmony, playfulness, positive tension, beauty, and enthusiasm.

Unlike sexuality, Eros is not accompanied by a state of exhaustion but a state of relaxation. It leads to the expansion of your consciousness that can charge you with happiness that can last longer than the period of sexual contentment.

When people are in true love with each other, they generally develop a deep natural desire for union with their partner. As pointed out, this desire can never be completely satisfied because of the partners' bodies' separateness and the mere momentary character of their physical merging. Although in their union, the partners seek completion by coming together as one, they understand that, in the end, they will remain distinct as their bodies only serve as vehicles through which the desire for union is fulfilled.

This deficit can, at least, be alleviated by Eros and thus help to create, maintain, or intensify the feeling of attraction and happiness in the relationship. Expressed in other words, Eros—no matter in which form—is the basis for your love life with your partner, provides a foundation for your sexual life and the happiness derived from it.

You may want to ask, what precisely can be perceived as erotic or what precisely might have an erotic effect on the other person. Unfortunately, this cannot be determined in a general way but varies from person to person. In addition, it can also depend on cultural differences. Every society and every societal group have ideas about what is considered desirable and erotic.

Example: While in Europe, a naked bosom is considered erotic, Chinese men of earlier centuries used to associate crippled women's feet as erotic, and US high society people may have a weakness for Barbie-style blondes.

In principle, Eros is a form of social communication that someone, consciously or unconsciously, uses to let another person or groups of people know that one is interested in sexually motivated closeness and togetherness.

For instance, erotic can be purely optical aspects such as a hairstyle or a smooth face. Also, the tone of a voice, the movement of the body, a certain scent or a style of clothing can have an erotic effect. Apart from the optical stimuli, the way a person presents themselves—stylish appearance, self-confidence, ambition, openness, or intelligence—can have erotic effects. Erotic can also be activities such as a candlelight dinner for two, sharing a plate of oysters at a beach restaurant, or a massage in a warm ambiance with soft light and relaxing music. In all these cases, Eros goes beyond mere sexuality and enhances it by positive tension, mystery, instinct, harmony, or playfulness.

Example: In the 1920s, the actress Marlene Dietrich became world-famous when she threw her head back with the expression of physical devotion. She was wearing a silver top hat and frilly underwear when she sang with a rough voice about infatuated lovers fluttering around her like moths to a flame.

Erotic behaviour combined with sexuality can help to produce positive tension and deeper bonds between partners that can give their sexuality a dimension that goes beyond the simple satisfaction of their sexual needs. The feeling of happiness that arises from sexuality enriched by Eros exceeds what is perceived as mere sexual satisfaction.

SEXUALITY IS NO SIN

The connections between sexuality and happiness and sexuality and Eros seem to be clear. On the one hand, sexuality acts as a catalyst for the affection between partners, and on the other hand, Eros acts as an enrichment which lifts sexuality out of the banal satisfaction of instincts to a higher level of longer-lasting feeling of happiness.

However, precisely in this essential area, where the natural happiness between two people should be free of ideological, religious and political considerations and restrictions, many barriers have been erected that stand in the way of becoming happy. With regards to sexuality, people in many parts of the world must (still) encounter numerous obstacles on their path to happiness as they are prevented from realizing the full potential of their sexuality's positive influence on happiness.

A good example of these obstacles is the tendency, which prevails in large parts of the world, to demonize sexuality, to associate it with something dirty and forbidden, or even repress it altogether. This contributed decisively, at least in the public perception, to attribute feelings of wrongdoing, sinning, and uncleanliness to sexuality, instead of filling the heart of people with joy and happiness.

Tip: In this context, you should remember the questionable moral idea, largely prevalent in the 19th century, that sexual intercourse should only serve the production of an offspring and be to the 'benefit of the nation' (which, provocatively put, meant the production of new soldiers). This narrow view of sexuality lacks any reference to the happiness that two people can feel when they come together in love. From the present day perspective, one must question the principles of this view to prevent happiness from becoming a victim of moral or ideological principles that seem to have been overcome long ago.

Among others, with some exceptions such as the Indian *Kama Shastra*, religious teachings take a large part of responsibility for the negative perception of sexuality. Contrary to some other world religions, the *Kama Shastra* accepts sexual energy as one of the most important and most intensive energies in the universe. Here, there is no denunciation of sexuality as immoral or 'dirty'.

It must be mentioned here that many world religions are responsibility for demonizing sexuality. A mention must also be made to the many repressions that are imposed on young children who don't yet have the ability to judge and choose themselves.

Tip: If you do not feel free sexually, you should try to find out whether, perhaps as a child, you were exposed to unusual experiences or prevented from enjoying your natural sexual awakening by indoctrination and strictly enforced taboos or other repressions.

The result of such a self-analysis may be surprising. You may come to the conclusion that the feelings of sin or guilt after a beautiful sexual encounter, which may disturb your sense of happiness and torture your conscience, may be the result of being forced into a corset of norms that goes against your natural instincts.

> Christianity gave Eros poison to drink; he did not die of it, certainly, but degenerated to Vice.
>
> —German philosopher Nietzsche in *Beyond Good and Evil*

A good example for illustrating this conflict between natural instincts, on the one hand, and imposed norms, on the other hand, is premarital sex.

As mentioned, many religions preach that sex outside of marriage is immoral. In the same vein, the response to the question of whether sex before marriage is okay if the partners love each other also remains generally negative. It is argued that such an act is still sinful since it continues to go against religious norms. That means that for the religious advocates, being in love doesn't alter the reality that the sexual act was done outside of marriage.

Example: An American woman who grew up in an evangelical church learnt that premarital sex was the unforgivable sin. She and her family cared and were deeply involved in the community in which they lived, and she never felt any reason to question what her community stood for. She believed that someone who lies can come clean, and someone who kills can repent, but if you're not a virgin on your wedding day, you can never go back and fix it.

Even if this American woman in the example had rebelled inwardly, she would have become a victim of the social pressure exerted on her to conform. As much as she may have preferred an alternative approach, for her it would have been difficult to break with the official line when her community was all for total conformity.

BE 'COOL' TO BE FREE

As discussed in the section 'Obstacles to Happiness', you are not condemned to accept barriers which may stand in your way to happiness, regardless of whether they are subjective (e.g. credulity) or objective (e.g. imposed norms). Instead, if you have the willpower, you have the opportunity to remove, through your own actions, those barriers. It has also been pointed out that the way to do this is first, to be cool when you look at yourself and the situation you are in and, second, free your mind from the constraints that bother you.

You will have better chances of success in achieving inner freedom and independence and prevailing over limiting factors in an environment governed by sociocultural norms and/or internal obstacles, if you are approaching the task in a cool way.

> Hate the sin, love the sinner.
>
> —Unknown

When you do your analysis, you may find out that you are confronted with a paradox.

Example: On the one hand, the society or religious community you belong to wants the best for you, when they impose commandments and want to dictate your behaviour (e.g., prohibiting premarital sex). On the other hand, it is this very commandment that leads to your unhappiness.

This contradiction (in itself) can be resolved if you start asking questions. You must know that everything is relative and can be questioned, including beliefs and norms under which you were raised. So, asking these questions is not a sin. On the contrary, your questions can help to clarify for yourself—independent of norms and other people's views—what you want to believe and what you allow to influence your life. This process is, indeed, a reassurance to yourself, if you use your answers as a basis for your own position.

You can call this process truly cool because you are not giving yourself up to the feeling of self-pity, self-lying, and lamenting, but, as a first step, facing your situation free from passion, looking at it from a neutral, detached point of view, and trying to understand and analyse your reality as a third party would do.

On this basis, you can then come to the second step of this cool process, i.e., the search for constructive ideas on how to solve the problem, or, in other words, which way you will choose to resolve the contradiction in the paradox, referred to above, in a non-conflictual way.

Example: Diego is madly in love with Krisana, whom he wants to marry. He feels so attracted to her that he can hardly refrain from showing his love physically. Although Krisana does not consider sex a taboo or believes that premarital sex is a sin, she does not agree to have premarital sex. She was brought up in the firm belief that a 'good' woman must preserve her 'innocence' for her husband. Diego comes from a different culture where the free physical expression of love is common. They have many discussions during which Diego revolts against her belief by referring to the strong affection they have for each other. But whatever argument Diego brings forward, she stays firm and continues to argue that she feels more comfortable preserving her 'innocence' until after marriage. The main reason for her position is that this would be the best way for her to honour herself and her partner. At a meeting with his close friends, Diego tells them about Krisana's refusal to sleep with him. They laugh about it, mocking Krisana as a 'saint' and cannot understand why Diego is tolerating her attitude. But Diego withstands their pressure and his own desire because he really loves Krisana very much. After careful consideration, Diego is able to step back from his point of view, react less passionately, and finally accept Krisana's position. Their discussions come to an end. Diego's understanding has helped the couple not be frustrated with each other but to look forward to their future. Surprisingly, Diego even began to develop a high respect for Krisana's autonomous decision to stand firm on her conviction and to wait before fully devoting herself to her partner after their wedding.

This dispassionate, almost neutral process, clears your mind. It exposes contradictions and allows you to act not in the interest of others but in the interest of yourself, your partner, and to the benefit of the relationship. it gives you the freedom in your mind that is necessary to overcome constraints.

Freedom, in this context, also means that sexual experience, fulfilment, and satisfaction should not be forced upon us by our own selfish needs and desires which may degenerate into a behaviour that has the potential to harm both partners. Instead, freedom should be understood as an expression of the playful and joyful side of our sexuality, free from feelings of guilt, resulting in happiness.

UNSATISFACTORY SEX

Joke:

I asked my wife why she married me.
Wife: 'Because you are funny.'
Me: 'I thought it was because I was good in bed?'
Wife: 'You see? You're hilarious!'

If, as concluded above, in a relationship, your affection for your partner and your happiness can be strengthened by satisfying an erotic sex life, the question arises, what kind of effects an unsatisfying sex life can have on your happiness.

Sex life in a relationship can be described as unsatisfactory when the partners' sexual relationship has (almost) fallen asleep (no sex), when the sexual encounter between the partners is perceived as unsatisfactory at least by one partner (bad sex), or when extremes occur that put a strain on the sexual relationship (e.g., excessive consumption of pornography by at least one of the partners).

NO SEX

The reasons for not having sex are manifold. The most common are lack of love; disinterest and lack of sexual arousal; psychological reasons such as stress, anxiety disorders, depression; general partner problems such as jealousy or breach of trust; physical causes that inhibit the libido, including drug addiction or age-related issues.

> Oversexed and underfucked.
>
> —Ariadne von Schirach, German author and philosopher

In addition to these, permanent flooding with sexual stimuli can also lead to a pressure to perform, fear of failure, and a permanent sexual abstinence.

Over time in a long-term relationship, intervals between sex can become longer. If this is not the result of absolute disinterest, it's not a reason for concern. Rarity or complete absence of intimate contacts may rather signal that the partners do not need constant proof to assure themselves of their love and togetherness, and they feel safe and secure in the relationship even without sex.

Example: Busan and Angelina both come from highly respected families of lawyers. For them, it was a matter of course to continue the family tradition and also study law. Although they had run into each other several times at law school, they never came into closer contact, though their families were well acquainted with each other. Neither of them had been particularly interested in social contacts. For them, their studies were of paramount interest. After their final exams, their families urged them to find a suitable partner to ensure the continuation of their family line. Since it was difficult for both of them to find someone, Angelina's father had the idea to marry his daughter to Busan. Busan's parents supported Angelina's father. When Busan and Angelina met at an arranged joint family event, they didn't find anything to discourage them from fulfilling the wishes of their families. However, to the dismay of their families, even after several years, their marriage remained childless. Instead, both partners made an unprecedented career which determined the character of their marriage. Although they lived together normally and loved each other, they seemed to be married more to their profession than to their partner. To close friends who knew that they slept in separate bedrooms, their marriage seemed more like a marriage of convenience in which there was no passion except spiritual closeness.

How long you can live in a relationship without sexuality depends, however, on the strength of the bond and the tolerance of the dissatisfied partner. It cannot be generally determined. Some people succeed at having a stable relationship without sexual activity and sometimes call it a more 'mature form of love'.

But not everyone involved in a sexless relationship agrees that it is okay to show your affection with words and tenderness alone. A lack of sex can lead to relationship problems and unhappiness for various reasons.

For instance, the absence of intimacy in marriage can become a major source of frustration, insecurity, and unhappiness, as soon as at least one of the partners suffers from the fact that their need for sex is not reciprocated and fulfilled or not understood. In this case, the lack of sexual activity can damage the affected partner's self-confidence and causes their doubts on being loved. This will inevitably lead to disharmony that can affect other, previously functioning, areas of the relationship.

Sometimes, it could also make partners want to seek sexual satisfaction in an alternative relationship. This risk is particularly high when the partners, out of fear or shame, do not frankly exchange with each other or tactically accept and/or ignore the changed conditions.

Here we provide a three-step recommendation for a dialogue aiming at a finding a *modus vivendi* (provided that the partners have agreed in principle to stay together):

- The first step is to set up an intimate dinner for two, preferably at home where there is no disturbance.
- The second step is supposed to generate a harmonious climate between the partners. This means first, to detox the atmosphere, by leaving possible anger, bitterness, or resentment aside and show love and affection. In some situations, it is possible to evoke nostalgia by remembering the past. When touching upon sensitive issues such as frustrations, the partners should not get excited, angry or emotionally upset. The worst would be if the partners start complaining or engaging in an argument, making accusations, finger-pointing or blaming each other. This would probably mean the end of the conversation.
- The third step is to make commitments. If all goes well during the conversation and the partners find an amicable agreement on how they want to continue their relationship, they should commit and celebrate the success together, even when it means little steps in the right direction.

BAD SEX

> Oh, love isn't there to make us happy. I believe it exists to show us how much we can endure.
>
> —Hermann Hesse, German poet

Sexual dissatisfaction caused by 'bad' sex seems to be one of the leading reasons for partners to separate. What 'good' and 'bad' sex mean is highly judgemental and subjective and must be left to individual judgement. Without going into further details, it is worth noting that 'good sex' is when both partners feel something and want it, and that sex resulting from ignorance, inexperience, insensitivity or coarseness can be called bad sex as it leaves the partner(s) disappointed, unsatisfied, disillusioned, humiliated, hurt, or simply disinterested.

What can be discussed in this context, however, are the effects on happiness when a partner accuses the other of 'bad sex'. Considering the importance of a satisfactory sex life for a relationship's happiness, it can be assumed that this will make the partner unhappy.

Example: Sandra came home late after a long and stressful day at work and was looking forward to a cosy evening with her boyfriend Spencer. She wanted to relax, cuddle, and feel intimate with him. Unlike Sandra, Spencer had an easy day. He had recently quit his job and decided to take some time out to think about his future. When Sandra came home, he had spent the whole day in bed enjoying his favourite hobby. He was playing a first-person shooter video game competing with millions of people online. After taking a shower, Sandra took off her clothes and laid down on the bed next to him. But he didn't even look at her. His eyes were fixed on the video game screen. After a while, when the game seemed to pause, Spencer turned to her. But Sandra got a bit scared when she saw the hungry wolf-like look in his eyes. But she forgot about it when he abruptly jumped on her and began making rough and abrupt love. Soon after, he was satisfied and turned back to his video game just as abruptly and told Sandra that his team was waiting and he had to finish the game. Sandra couldn't believe what had just happened to her. She was completely frustrated. What Spencer had done was the exact opposite of what she had expected from her partner. 'Better no sex than bad sex', she said to Spencer, took her night gown, left the room, and switched on the TV in the living room.

As discussed at the beginning of this section, sexuality has an effect on the partners' affection. Thus, bad sex can reduce the feelings of affection of the partners and affect their happiness. Therefore, the question to be discussed is how this negative impact of bad sex on happiness can be reduced or prevented.

As mentioned previously, every person (or couple) is different with their own characteristics. This also applies to sexual behaviour. In addition, it can be assumed that many couples develop different expectations of their sexual life over the years.

If the results of this process start to negatively affect the couple's happiness—for instance, because of the partners' views on what's good or bad clash—actions should be taken to protect that happiness by turning a perceived bad sexual experience into a good one. When considering possible steps towards achieving this goal, it would be helpful to understand that sexual behaviour is not only determined by the choice of sexual techniques, but mainly by the 'thoughts behind the action', or in other words, the attitude of the respective person towards sexuality, in general, and the partner, in particular.

When you enter a relationship, you normally have not completely reached the end of your sexual development. At its beginning, you are probably positively mirrored by your partner. This, of course, feels great because you get positive feedback about yourself. However, in a steady partnership, this feedback can diminish over time and mutual desire can weaken. In this situation, you may ask yourself, whether it is important for your happiness to make your own desires, to a large extent, dependent on the recognition of your partner. This question comes up especially if you think you have had sexual experiences with your partner which you perceive as 'bad'. Bad sex normally signals (sexual) problems. But instead of silently accepting or complaining, you can also use such an experience constructively to initiate a further development.

> You are only afraid if you are not in harmony with yourself. People are afraid because they have never owned up to themselves.
>
> —Hermann Hesse, German poet

A possible cool response may be that you decide to grow. To do this in a relationship, you should make yourself as independent as possible from your partner's judgement, try to stand on your own two feet and, instead of blindly conforming to your partner's ideas, be clear about who you are and what goals are important to you. This approach seems to be the only way to develop sexually, possibly rekindle passion, and avoid further bad sexual experiences.

The critical point is that this must be talked about. Many people may have bad sex, but it is likely that only few are willing to talk about it openly. Especially when it comes to sex, it is not easy to find the right time, the right place, and the right tone.

If you are prepared to deal with the problem, it would be helpful if you could overcome your own (psychological) obstacles such as fear, shame, cowardice or false pride (e.g., face-saving). If that's done, the first question that arises is 'how to start' the discussion without unnecessarily arousing, annoying, embarrassing, or humiliating your partner. The chances of success of such an open conversation depend on how honestly the partners deal with the subject, i.e., whether or not the sexual issues are being clearly addressed.

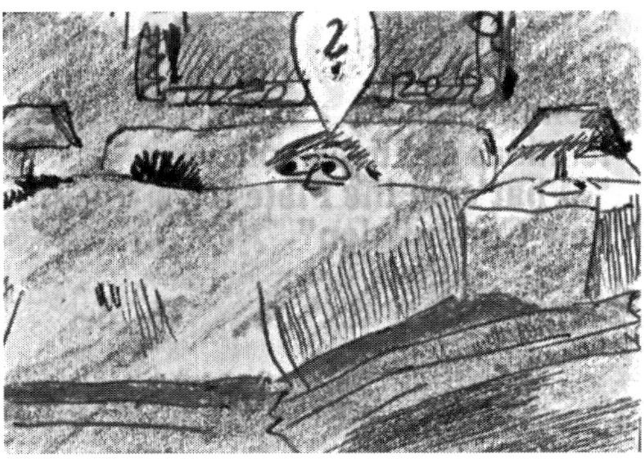

Tip: As a result of your new found, partner-independent, cool position, do not pretend that something pleases you just because it is something your partner seems to like. Tell your partner what you like and guide them carefully until they have understood.

In the event that the two partners are not successful in dealing with their differences in a face-to-face conversation, a mediation by a confidant could be a good idea.

Example: Pat experienced no progress in a dispute with her husband Jacques about the sexual frustrations she had recently experienced with him. Instead of listening to her, Jacques insisted that in order to continue talking, he first needed her apology for her alleged 'bad' behaviour. Pat overreacted and ran away from the discussion. Afterwards, when she had calmed down, Pat realized that they both seemed to have some trouble handling frustration and stress. Pat decided to talk to her closest friend Donna about it. Donna had studied psychology and was knowledgeable about solving inter-marital problems. After listening to her story, Donna told Pat that she and Jacques seemed to have deficits in emotional self-regulation. She said that it was not Jacques' behaviour but the way Pat reacted to it that mattered most. She advised Pat to stay calm next time, take a pause between her arousing feelings and her action, take the time to think things through, wait patiently, and make a plan. 'You have three options,' Donna said. 'Approach, attack, and avoidance. You selected the last option. Do you really feel like running away from a difficult situation?' Pat was a bit embarrassed because it was normally not her habit to run away from challenges. She promised Donna to follow her advice and restore her inner balance by focusing on the larger picture, rather than getting carried away by her emotions at the moment. After she had left Donna, Pat called Jacques and invited him for dinner. 'Let's talk,' she said and he agreed.

PORNOGRAPHY

> I think that we have successfully said that rape is not sex, it's violence. But what we have not successfully said is that pornography is not erotica. Porn means female slaves. Eros has an idea of love and mutual pleasure and free choice. I fear that pornography is taking over sex when in fact it's way more about domination.
>
> —Gloria Steinem, US journalist

Like no sex, unsatisfactory sex, or bad sex, pornography too can affect people's happiness in a relationship. Driven by easy internet access, pornography has become readily available these days.

Example: Oscar was in a relationship with his high school sweetheart Victoria. After graduating from high school, he got his first job on an offshore oil rig, where he worked in shifts of fifteen days off the coast and fifteen days on land. During his time alone at sea, he developed the habit of sexually satisfying himself by watching various types of porn movies, preferably featuring women with voluptuous features and curves that excited him. Back home, after one of his fifteen days' absences, Victoria was shocked by the change in his behaviour. When they had first met, he had been a passionate and sensitive lover. But after his return, he had become indifferent and machine-like towards her when they were together. His insensitive comments such as 'your boobs are too small' or 'I am not aroused' or his strange demands for doing extreme positions made her feel like a sex object to him. When this behaviour appeared to have become a pattern, she increasingly felt disgraced and miserable. 'I have always thought that sex with my lover makes me happy. But honestly, that's not what I feel', she revealed to her dearest friend.

Some people say that pornography adds another dimension to their sexual enjoyment; others warn that it can get in the way of a relationship.

At the end of the day, only you can determine whether the consumption of pornography is good or bad for you and your relationship—not other people.

If you and your partner enjoy porn and it doesn't cause any issues in your relationship, why don't you enjoy it. We know that humans come with a wide variety of desires. Pornography may have the advantage of satisfying people's curiosities, improving their self-exploration, sexual skills and knowledge, or may be another way to discover new options or increasing sexual well-being, sexual enjoyment of and interest in sexual activity.

However, there is an issue when pornography, or specifically excessive porn consumption, results in a situation where one or both partners feel increasingly dissatisfied in their relationship or sex life. This can happen if you start comparing your own ability to attract a sexual partner, sexual performance, or body to the fictional standards of porn.

There are some additional situations in which pornography can affect your relationship negatively and can lead to unhappiness. Some examples include the following:

- One of the partners is into porn and the other is totally against it.
- One of the partners is into a type of pornography the other simply can't tolerate.
- The consumption of pornography leads one partner to devalue the other.
- The excessive use of pornography by one partner leads them to develop unrealistic sexual expectations, or the desire to do things that don't interest or even disgusts the other partner.

Also, it cannot be excluded that partners in a long-term relationship interpret consumption of pornography as a sign of dissatisfaction in the relationship.

In order to prevent pornography consumption from becoming perceived as a sign of turning away, an open, honest, and cooperative discussion between the partners is required, similar to the other cases of sexual relationship problems discussed previously.

In such a conversation, the first thing to find out is whether the partner's excessive pornography consumption is basically due to an unsatisfied, disproportionate sexual hunger or whether they are specifically signalling dissatisfaction with their current situation in the relationship. If the latter is the case, an intimate conversation between the partners should provide clarity. This could also reveal that the partner's dissatisfaction is limited to the sexual sphere or whether his discomfort is due to a fundamental disturbance in the relationship for which the sexual dissatisfaction is only an indication.

In each of these cases, the partner's reaction will have to be different, whereby it is also essential here whether the partners principally agree that their relationship should continue. This question should be asked and answered at the beginning of the discussion.

If the partner's excessive porn consumption is a signal of turning away, then the conflict is no longer about sexuality and the happiness derived from it, but about the relationship itself.

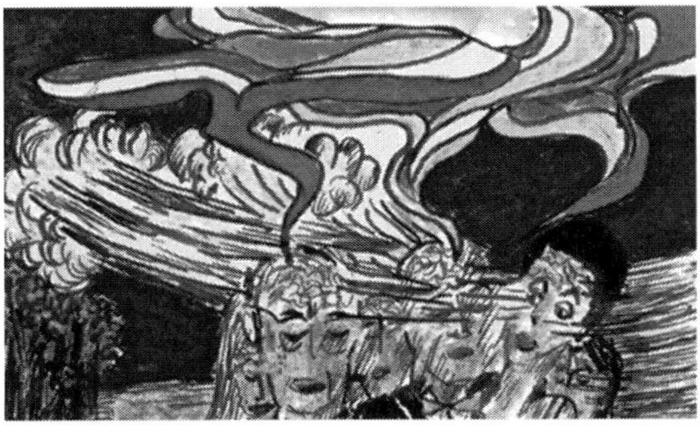

If the partner's dissatisfaction is limited to the sexual area, both partners should openly reveal their wishes and ideas, even those they have kept to themselves until now, and agree on a common path. In this case, the less demanding partner has to decide whether they want to submit to their partner's wishes, or whether there is perhaps another way to satisfy them.

In any case, a compromise will have to be reached in which both partners will have to approach each other. Should the partners find such a compromise, they should make sure that what they freely agreed upon is also compatible with their own personal wishes and feelings. Their agreement will be worthless from the start if one partner is feeling pressured and decides against their feelings, is forced or coerced into doing something and, if they are honest with themselves, do not want or cannot do what the other partner demands of them without feeling raped.

3

HAPPINESS AT WORK

THE WORK–PRIVATE SPHERE INTER-RELATIONSHIP

> Doing what you like is freedom. Liking what you do is happiness.
>
> —Unknown

During your professional life, you usually have little free time at your disposal because most of it is devoted to your job and work-related activities.

Therefore, your personal happiness depends not only on fulfilment and satisfaction in your private life, but also to a large extent on your satisfaction at the workplace.

If you are unhappy in your professional life, it is very likely that your private and social life will be affected. This is because the professional and private spheres are closely connected.

Example: You argued with your spouse all night long. Afterwards, you had a short and restless sleep because the controversy excited you so much. As a consequence, the next day, you find it difficult to concentrate on your work at your workplace. As a result, your manager criticizes your work as inadequate. You also react disproportionately irritably to the usual remarks of your colleagues. The evening after this 'terrible' day, you return home exhausted and angry with yourself and take your frustrations out on your wife and kids. Especially the children suffer from what they call 'bad mood' because they don't understand what they have done to deserve it.

Example: You feel uncomfortable at your workplace because you cannot stand your dominant boss. In addition, you feel contempt for the conformist behaviour of your colleagues who do everything to please the superior. One day, you realize that your dissatisfaction at work has started to affect your private life. Your spouse complains about your frequent mood changes and the children suffer from your lack of patience and your more frequent aggressive reactions. Your spouse is unhappy with you and the children are reacting with increasing anxiety.

> They say no man is an island.
>
> —Unknown

It is often advised that you should keep your professional and private life separate. This may sound very well in theory but it is hard to put into practice. Joy and euphoria, on the one hand, and frustration and anger, on the other hand, do not know the difference between different spheres of life, just as the Covid virus does not distinguish between Chinese and Americans. Emotions and feelings always affect the person as a whole.

The close interrelation between the private and the work spheres leads to the question, what you can do to prevent the happiness you feel in your private life from being affected by negative events in your professional sphere. Or, vice versa, how to prevent anger in the family from negatively affecting your career.

ATTITUDES

No question better demonstrates the separation and interrelation between professional and private life spheres than the question: Do you *work to live* or do you *live to work*?

In the past, it was often said that people lived only to work. Personal happiness played no or only a minor role in this context, since work was for survival and not to increase the feeling of personal well-being.

Today, however, work is widely used to do much more than just ensure survival. Many people define themselves through their job and some even work more than they live their (out-of-the-workplace) lives. For them, work is an act of self-realization, which, in turn, contributes to their personal happiness.

The work performance, the salary, or the tasks assigned to them give meaning to their lives and a feeling of achievement and happiness. Those people who define themselves in this way through their work 'live to work' as work contributes to their momentary well-being and more long-lasting personal happiness.

> Choose a profession you love, and you will never have to work another day in your life.
>
> —Attributed to the ancient Chinese philosopher Confucius

Many companies have realized this trend and have consequently created the new position of 'Chief Happiness Officer (CHO)' or employ 'happiness consultants' to ensure greater employee enjoyment at the workplace.

However, for many people, their work continues to be meaningless and 'just a job', such as assembly line workers, print paper feeders, box packers, garbage collectors, or lift operators. They tend to describe their professional activity as 'monotonous' and 'boring'. Their professional occupations are merely serving a means for securing their existence, and they do not have the privilege of being able to draw any special satisfaction from their work.

However, this view may not be 100 per cent correct. One has to also consider that the work done by people who are 'just doing a job' enables them to live a decent life by their own efforts. This prevents them from becoming welfare recipients or recipients of alms, which could make them lose their self-respect and self-esteem.

Example: Adam works as a garbage man. When he was a kid, his parents told him to work hard in school: 'Otherwise you'll end up as a garbage collector.' Garbage man or street sweeper—that was pretty much the last profession on the social ladder back then when Adam was a kid. Dirty and disgusting—in short, a job nobody wanted to do. Today, it's different. Adam sees himself and his colleagues as one of the most important assets of what is now called 'waste management'; they see themselves as service providers and as Adam's lord mayor recently referred to it: 'the business card of his community'. Consequently, Adam is happy in his position. He knows that his work cannot be replaced by any machine, vehicle or barrel technology. Therefore, his motivation and self-confidence are based on the conviction to make an important contribution to the exemplary cleanliness of his commune and compliance with environmental protection and recycling standards.

This example shows that even an activity that is widely perceived as offering no or very little inner meaning can offer people an opportunity to experience a sense of achievement and happiness.

> May your work be in keeping with your purpose.
>
> —Leonardo da Vinci, Italian artist

FENDING OFF MUTUAL INFLUENCING

The division of spheres and exercise of unrelated different functions has become part of everyday life for many people in many countries today (for instance, home/family and job/career).

The demands of everyday life, family and work require distinctive competences in dealing with stresses and in dealing with people (e.g. work colleagues, superiors, employees, life partners or children) with special consideration of the strong mutual influence of the work and family domains. Reconciling work and family is a daily balancing act for many people who are concerned about their happiness.

Example: During a party, you get a call from your boss. Instead of the whimsical colloquialism you use with your friends, you immediately change your behaviour when you hear that it is your boss on the line. You take on the role of a subordinate employee and use a more formal way of speaking.

Example: You are a chief accountant in a real estate company and a single mother. In the office, you have to be painstakingly precise with numbers, and show tolerance, forbearance and understanding in raising your children.

Whilst filling out different roles doesn't seem to be the problem, the issue is how you can find the strength to keep troubles where they were created and where they belong, i.e., at the workplace or at home, resp., despite all the legitimate feelings and emotions you may have.

There is no universal way to completely isolate professional and private life and avoid that negative emotions can spill over from one area of life (e.g., work) to another (e.g., family, relationship) and possibly accumulate with other emotions. If this 'work-to-family spill-over' (in the reciprocal direction: 'family-to-work spillover') affects your life it will be an indication that you are not successful in separating the roles you are playing in your different domains. In this case, the 'work mood' influences the family role performance, or the family-related mood within the family influences the work mood. This can negatively affect your feelings of happiness in one or both domains.

This inability can be positively influenced by a control process. This control process requires flexibility and organizational effort as it is aiming at balancing your work and family commitments and effectively containing the 'spillover' effect.

The starting point for such a control process lies in the recognition that all people exercise different roles in their lives which, although very different, must be reconciled with each other, e.g., mother at home and saleswoman in a fashion boutique.

There are some options which you may want to consider:

Tip: For instance, you can make efforts to balance dissatisfactions in one area (e.g., family) by investing in another area (e.g., work). This can be achieved by reallocating attention, time and commitment from an unsatisfying area to a potentially more satisfying area.

Tip: Another option is to separate work and family to prevent these areas from influencing each other. This demarcation can be achieved by separating them in time and place, and by having diametrically different functions of these areas.

Tip: There are many methods of coping with or consciously managing stress which can be customized for your specific situation. For instance, you can extend traditional stress trainings by including stress prevention, time management, and social skills training. This can include the creation of 'protective buffers' through which you will be relieved of negative emotions and discussions by not bringing up certain topics or learning to suppress anger. In addition, your regulative ability for balancing and positive communication behaviour can be trained.

Tip: Under another option, you can manage the drain of human resources such as attention, time and energy from one domain to another.

Tip: A last option mentioned here is your successive alignment between work and family through a third variable that behaves like a 'common cause'. This alignment aims at bringing about similarities between your work and your family. 'Common causes' in this sense could be personality traits, behavioural patterns, social, and cultural forces which could be equally applied to specific work or family related problems.

These or other options or a combination of options can actively help you to control to what extent you will allow the 'spillover' to influence your life and affect your happiness.

SELF-DISCIPLINE

This is not only a question of self-discipline, but also a question of fairness. This is because it does not do justice to the uninvolved persons if you let them feel your negative feelings and emotions (e.g., anger). They have nothing to do with it and cannot influence them.

Example: What does the domestic dispute with your pubescent child have to do with work, and what does the dispute with your colleague have to do with life at home?

A lack of self-discipline is essentially nourished by impatience and distraction that diverts you from your current focus. In order to increase your self-discipline, you need a clearly defined goal (i.e. the question 'why') that is guiding your behaviour, and the willingness to take responsibility for your actions (i.e. no excuses, blaming others, or shifting of responsibility).

It is often claimed that a successful self-disciplined separation of roles, as suggested here, can make it more likely that emotions accumulate and build-up in the person concerned. By this logic, at a point in time when the person feels that they can't bear the built-up pressure anymore, this may result in an uncontrolled outburst.

The concern is that such an outburst may cause more harm than an 'export' of negative feelings to the other sphere of life. This concern is probably justified because such outbursts will very likely be out of proportion and can cause irritations that will in all likelihood also be out of proportion. They can also lead to further undesirable consequences such as more general disputes. But most importantly, they don't contribute to the solution of the underlying problem.

To prevent this from happening, one can think of a number of methods to help to draw boundaries between the different spheres of life. These will help separate the roles and prevent an 'export' of bad feelings from one sphere of life to the other. Consider the following:

- If you can't switch off your bad feelings, try to turn the tables on the positive and answer these questions: 'What makes my work life worth living?' Or, 'What do I love about my family and how do I protect them from outside harm?'
- You could further ask yourself the question to what extent you have contributed to the spillover; for example, turbulent behaviour, pessimism, or an exaggerated tendency towards perfectionism.
- Do not hide the fact that you are angry or upset if something negative happened in the other sphere of life. For instance, don't hide from your spouse that you are facing conflicts in the office. Also, let your boss and your closest colleagues know that you have to solve a problem at home.

This openness will create understanding and prevent unnecessary and unfounded irritations with people who are not involved.

Distractions, such as hobbies and sports, are a good balance to everyday annoyances. Activities that you typically do alone are not necessarily helpful. In most cases, it is better to undertake joint activities with like-minded people for more effective distraction.

In your effort to separate your roles, it can also be helpful to use the way home as a lock between your work and your private life.

Example: Heinz was a manager in an automotive supplier company that was just fighting against a hostile takeover by a Chinese state corporation. Heinz's working day had been very intense and stressful. At the end of his working day, Heinz did not want that his wife Deirdre would see him as a stressed, angry, and irritable man. Instead, he wanted to be perceived by her as a good, relaxed partner ready to meet her needs for comforting love. Therefore, Heinz decided to listen to aggressive rock music in the car. On his way home, animated by the wild rhythm of the music, he was speeding, blowing his horn, overtaking aggressively, screaming, and pounding on the steering wheel. When Heinz arrived home, his hands were trembling, but he realized that his method had worked. His pent-up emotions had disappeared as a result of his aggressive driving style. Deirdre saw the sweat running down his face and said: 'Oh, darling, I can see that you had a hard day at the office. Let me spoil you.' Heinz took her in his arms, smiled, kissed her, and asked what she had prepared for dinner.

What can also help switch off your bad feelings is distraction through symbols. For instance, you could make a short stop on the way home to a children's playground. Nothing is more relaxing than watching children play as they are symbols of innocence, openness, carefreeness, and the future. Another option is to look for a garbage container on the way, in which you symbolically leave behind your 'thought garbage' when you drive by. Even the reverential observation of the beauty of a beautiful, old tree can help you realize that the everyday problems you carry around with you may not deserve the attention and energy you bestow on them.

STRESS AT WORK AND HAPPINESS

THE STRESS–HAPPINESS CONNECTION

Today, almost everyone complains about stress, and it seems to have become a zeitgeist phenomenon.

Explanation: As mentioned above, zeitgeist (literally, time spirit') originates from German language and can be defined as the spirit or mood of a particular period of history.

> Working hard for something we don't care about is called stress: Working hard for something we love is called passion.
>
> —Simon Sinek, British author

Even the best efforts to increase your satisfaction in your daily work life can fail due to daily stress. Perceived daily stress can also get in the way of your happiness at work because it consumes energy that you could use more meaningfully; for instance, keeping an eye on the overall picture, strategic thoughts, continuous improvements, or creative thinking.

When we talk about perceived stress, we are not only talking about big stress factors like high workload, deadline pressures, or tasks that seem impossible to solve. It is recommended that you do not overlook the many small and seemingly unimportant stress factors as they can also take up a large part of your time and attention at work. Although each one is only slightly stressful, they can accumulate and have a negative effect on your happiness at work.

Stressful situations and unnecessary frustration can even be caused if you are getting tangled in trivialities. For instance, it can add to your stress if you have to tolerate unnecessary or unsolicited interruptions and disturbances. These can become annoying, especially when there is not enough time anyway. Other seemingly trivial factors that can cause additional stress include a bad mood in the team, unlimited email flooding, difficulties concerning compatibility of the job and family, such as requests from the manager to be available at any time and access to private phones during weekends and holidays. This can become especially annoying if it is unreasonable; for instance, if you don't hold a key position in the company.

Example: Mike is a young, bright employee in a well-known advertising agency. For some months, the good climate in the agency has changed for the worse after a new director joined the team. He was soon nicknamed 'Nut'. His management style was close to unbearable for everyone at the agency, including Mike. 'Nut' was a nit-picker, he took care of every little thing, no matter how unimportant, and made everything seem complicated. Although Mike wanted to concentrate on his assignments, 'Nut' kept on intervening, commented even on nitty gritty details, and refused to concede Mike even the smallest degree of autonomy. Mike got particularly annoyed when 'Nut' called him during his friend's birthday party on a Saturday, just to tell him that he found an error in one of Mike's draft exposes. When Mike wanted to defend what he had written, 'Nut' interrupted and said that this would have time until Monday. 'Nut's' interventionist management style of telling Mike exactly what-to-do and when-to-do created an extremely stressful work environment, which absorbed a lot of Mike's energy and killed his self-motivation and creativity. Unlike in the past, when Mike had enjoyed his job, he now came home after work and felt completely stressed, i.e. physically and psychologically exhausted, although his overall work burden had not increased.

As shown in the example, perceived stress at work is not only making you unhealthier, but it can make you disengaged, demotivated, and even cynical. This negative attitude can affect your working environment.

Example: Your colleagues notice that your former lively interest and commitment to your job is lost. You give clear signals that you are no longer happy at your job. Some of your negative comments at work may even start to poison the working atmosphere.

As discussed in this section, negative stress factors from the professional sphere can easily spill over into your private life and negatively influence your happiness.

In fact, stress and happiness are connected. This is because psychological or physical stress is a reaction to a situation, which you consciously or unconsciously perceive as an assumed or real danger that is negatively affecting your well-being. From this, it follows that the zeitgeist phenomenon of stress is directly related to decreases in happiness. In other words, the lesser the stress, the more your chances at happiness. This leads us to the question what you can realistically do as part of your pursuit of happiness to relieve yourself from stress.

PRINCIPLE SOURCES OF STRESS

Before we discuss possible ways to avoid, reduce, or eliminate stress, we should take a quick look at the possible principle sources of perceived stress at work. On the one hand, there is stress imposed from outside sources (e.g., by industry trends or the work place environment) and, on the other hand, there is self-imposed stress (e.g., excessive personal career ambitions).

In both situations, the individual attitude of a person at work (whether employee or freelancer) is an important variable when assessing a person's happiness and importance of perceived stress. Positive attitude and optimism are particularly important because people who are positive may be better able to cope with stressful situations because of their constructive behavioural responses to stressors than those with negative attitudes.

Those with a positive bent of mind only consider major external developments beyond their influence or control as stress. Some examples for these mega-trends include the consequences of climate change, restrictions caused by the Covid pandemic, globalization leading to the relocation of local jobs to other countries, or technological change leading to job losses.

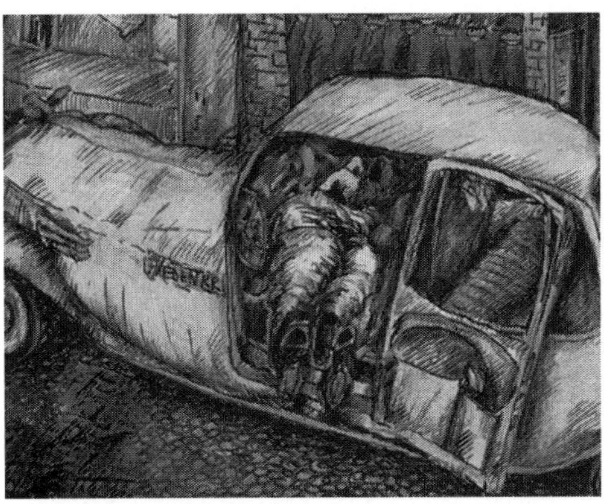

Example: The radical changes in the automotive industry from fuel-driven cars to e-drive have a great social impact. For the affected individuals, these developments lead to a fear of job loss and resultant stress. They know that the switch to electro mobility will result in the loss of several hundred thousand jobs per automobile-producing country by 2030. In the production of the drivetrain alone, i.e., engines and transmissions, tens of thousands of jobs will be lost per country. The individual employees who know about these developments feel helpless and stressed because they can neither stop nor influence this trend.

The more people are worried about trends that affect them negatively—and those they cannot control—the more actively they try to promote and control their own personal happiness. This can manifest itself in the increased desire to travel, take holidays in foreign countries, have a comfortable home, and take as many opportunities as possible to be entertained and to party.

In addition to mega-trends, there are also general internal developments in companies, which cause stress for individual employees. Similar to external mega-trends, there is no way for the affected individual to control or influence these developments.

Example: In reaction to an increasingly competitive world, the main focus of many companies is no longer long-term success (which manifests itself by a long-term strategy and vision) but the pursuit of a short-term profit orientation (expressed by the importance of quarterly results and shareholder value). This has led to the lamentable effect that many companies have put organized success (e.g., achieving the goals of the company's business plan) above personal success (i.e., the motivation and commitment of their employees).

This short-term orientation has led to additional stress for management and employees. The work burden for many employees has increased as a result of shorter deadlines and additional reporting requirements, and long-term, strategic thinkers were stressed either by getting involved in short-term activities or side-lined altogether.

Example: Tony was a very gifted engineer in the automotive industry. He had already filed numerous patents. In his industry, he was known and respected as a long-term thinker. In the early 1990s, he presented his ideas about radically new propulsion systems for vehicles and alternative clean fuels to his company's R&D board. The members of the board arrogantly dismissed his ideas as 'day-dreaming' and continued their strategy to improve existing technologies instead of considering new ones. Tony was unhappy about the board's views. He lost interest in his work and found it increasingly stressful to work for his company because he didn't believe in their short-term orientation. A year after his unsuccessful presentation, Tony left the company in frustration to become a consultant. He hoped that as a freelancer, he could get relief from his daily stress and become happy again at his job. On his way out, he forecast to his colleagues that innovation in the ultra-conservative automotive industry will not come from them but from a garage shop in Silicon Valley. More than twenty years later, a brand new Silicon Valley company called Tesla was worth more than Toyota, Disney, and Coke put together.

Note: After twenty years, in 2019, top American managers organized in the Business Roundtable have signed a statement, abolishing shareholder value (e.g., profit maximization) as a priority business objective due to the changing zeitgeist. At the Business Roundtable, it was declared, 'Americans deserve an economy that enables all people to succeed with hard work and creativity and to lead a fulfilling and dignified life.'

This US-Business Roundtable's revised position signalled a return to principles that moved people and their happiness at the workplace once again to the centre of corporate management. It is interesting to note that this reversal in position happened roughly in parallel to the introduction of the institution of chief happiness officers.

An additional external stress factor that is frequently causing unhappiness among employees is the pressure to be constantly 'available' for queries or requests by their superiors and colleagues. Often, employees stressed by constant availability and lack of break are at risk of burnout. Employee job burnout has always been a phenomenon that employers have had to face, but due to globalization (e.g., working in different time zones), competitive and cost-cutting pressures (e.g., rationalizations and staff cuts) present-day employees are more overworked, dissatisfied, frustrated, and unhappy than before.

Example: Maggie loved her job in the toy industry and her workplace. She was highly motivated to perform. Her superior and colleagues were delighted and impressed with her dedication and professionalism. She worked long hours to ensure that her team's work was outstanding. Over the last six months, she worked on a business plan for a brand new product. Her superior and

members of her team supported her in this effort. But there was a moment, when Maggie realized that their support went too far. Her days at the office were characterized by many meetings, face-to-face discussions, video conferences, and calls. In addition, she had to manage an enormous flood of emails. This pressure didn't stop at night or at weekends when she was supposed to relax and reboot. Instead, her superior and team members constantly contacted her on phone and through text messages and emails. The week after her successful new product presentation, Maggie suffered from severe burnout symptoms resulting from her months-long stress and the depletion of her resources over time. She felt physically and emotionally exhausted. She was depressed and couldn't sleep. Her superior instructed her to take time off work and Maggie missed the official presentation of her new product. She needed a long recovery before she could reach her earlier performance and well-being levels.

To provide employees with a feeling of appreciation, satisfaction, and being taken care of at the workplace, it is very important for a company's management to not ignore or inadequately support employees who run the risk of being exposed to a burnout. Company managers should have their employees' best interests in mind. They should understand that employees who are satisfied with their jobs are happier at work and far less likely to experience burnout. While every employee may have different ideas about job satisfaction, it seems obvious that stress will not contribute to it. One way is to let employees improve their work–life balance and respect their free time as a means to recover from daily workplace stress, so that they can return properly regenerated. This will help to increase employees' engagement at work, improve their job satisfaction and, following from this, their happiness at work.

In addition to these external sources for stress, there are also self-imposed stress factors that can affect happiness. Luckily, self-imposed stress is easier to deal with than external stress.

Example: Tanja, a young trainee, was extremely ambitious and worked very hard. Malcolm, her boss, noticed that Tanja was working more hours per day than he did. He knew that Tanja was doing it not only to prove to him but also to herself that she was capable of managing a high workload.

It was her ambition to become the best trainee Malcolm ever had and to get hired for a permanent position. Although Malcom appreciated Tanja's commitment, he was concerned about her private life. He knew that Tanja had a boyfriend who wanted to marry her, and he worried that Tanja's dedication to her job may displease him one day and lead to problems in her private sphere. This, Malcom thought, was undesirable, because problems in Tanja's private sphere would easily spill over into the work sphere. Malcom, therefore, decided to prevent this from happening and talked to Tanja about it. He suggested that she work more efficiently, for instance, by learning how to read faster. Tanja was open to Malcom's comments and improved quickly. After a short while, she did the same volume of work but in a much shorter time. She had more time available for her private life and was happy about it.

In this example, it is demonstrated that it is possible for you to relieve yourself from self-imposed stress. Different from external pressures, which usually are beyond your influence, self-imposed stresses can be removed or contained once you realize what you are doing wrong and by showing a strong will and the right attitude to get rid of the stressful situations.

PROBLEM-ORIENTED COPING

When faced with stress, you should not feel like a victim and submit to the stress situation, but try to manage or cope with it. In general, there are two forms of coping with stressful situations: problem-oriented coping and emotion-oriented coping. You can either decide to use one or both methods.

In problem-oriented coping, you attempt to manage or alter the problem that is causing you to experience stress, i.e., you focus on the source of the stress. You would preferably choose this method when you perceive the stress factors as controllable. This method is similar to the ones we usually use in everyday problem-solving—identifying the problem, considering possible solutions, weighing the pros and cons of these solutions, and then selecting an alternative.

Example: A book author delivers her 350-page manuscript to her publisher. Three months later, the publisher returns the manuscript to the author with the request to send the corrected version back within four days or earlier. The manuscript is peppered with hundreds of comments, questions, suggestions for improvement and rewording wishes of the editor. The author is stressing over the 350-page manuscript due in four days recognizing the hopelessness of the situation. She knows that she will never be able to make it in such a short time. As a first reaction, she watched an exciting movie to take her mind off it. Then she discussed the problem with the publisher and they both agreed on an extended deadline. If she would have taken a problem-oriented approach by trying to accomplish her task in four days, she would only have experienced frustration and even more stress.

In contrast, emotion-oriented coping consists of efforts to change or reduce the negative emotions associated with stress, i.e., the focus is on the symptoms resulting from stress. This method you would use when you are faced with stress factors that you believe you are not able to change. Under this alternative, your options include avoiding, downplaying, or distancing yourself from the problem. Other options are to start comparing yourself favourably with others who are worse off.

Example: As part of a corporate restructuring decision, Tom and fifteen of his colleagues were laid off. Referring to his colleagues, Tom said to his wife: 'I'm just thirty, so I'm not as bad off as they are because they will have difficulty in finding new jobs as they are all above fifty.'

Or, seeking something positive in a negative event, as in Tom's alternative approach.

Example: At night, Tom said to his wife: 'You know what I like about being fired? I can sleep as long as I want and finally, I have enough time to play with the children.'

Or, where the stress situation is reappraised by reinterpreting the problem which is causing the stress:

Example: To fight the Covid virus, the government has imposed a curfew and closed all bars and restaurants. Nobody is allowed to leave home between 6 p.m. and 5 a.m. Brian, who is running a late-night bar, thinks, *I'm not really upset about the lockdown. This will give me a chance to redecorate my bar and make it more appealing, which should have been done long ago. Once this ordeal is over, my bar will stick out from others and attract a new crowd.*

Especially in situations that you cannot control and for which you have no way to escape from, you may feel powerless. As an alternative to letting yourself go down that dead-end road, you should depart from the typical reaction of feeling frustrated and unhappy about your situation. Instead, you should take an open, dynamic, pragmatic, and constructive cool view with the goal of regaining control and freeing your life from the stress affecting your happiness.

As a first step, remind yourself of your strengths and achievements, be proud of them and your life story so far, and, as a second step, take this as a basis to plan targeted and determined action. The plan should be based on one of the two (or a combination of both) concepts of coping with stress discussed here—problem-oriented or emotion-oriented coping mechanism.

> True happiness is . . . to enjoy the present, without anxious dependence upon the future.
>
> —Seneca, Ancient Roman philosopher

TARGETED AND DETERMINED ACTION

Continuing the example from the automotive industry and the helpless reaction of workers to mega-trends affecting the industry, a targeted and determined action as the result of a dispassionate, cool self-analysis can be an option here. Let us look at Dick's story.

Example: Dick has been working in the automotive industry for fifteen years. He learned from the media that his industry was facing mass layoffs.

These were caused by a massive structural change in the industry. The reason for this change was the anticipated transformation from the previous production of traditional combustion engines to alternative forms of propulsion systems such as the electric motor. The production of alternative motors requires significantly fewer employees. In response to the reports, Dick decided to make a completely different decision than most of his colleagues. While they spent a lot of their time and energy following their unions' calls to take to the streets and to rally calling for solidarity and protesting against layoffs, he started to attend training courses in the new fields of digital and electrical engineering and automation. Dick knew that in the future, there would be both: massive job cuts and shortage of skilled workers. Unlike his colleagues, he was not complaining about these trends and protesting, but accepting the new challenges by opting for further training and qualification to become a better skilled worker. When his colleagues asked Dick why he didn't participate in the unions' rallies, he said the unions' protests wouldn't change the trends but confirm the workers' victim role. 'I don't want to be a victim,' he said defiantly, 'I want to be in charge of what is concerning me.'

The example illustrates that Dick's autonomous decision, his positively inspired mindset, and future-oriented move will probably help him better manage the stress caused by a likely job loss than the lamenting of many of his colleagues.

Instead of worrying, complaining, and protesting, Dick stayed cool and analysed his situation pragmatically. He didn't indulge in doomsday scenarios but rather created an idea that would help him best deal with the anticipated change. When facing the stress of being jobless, Dick decided against becoming a victim that would submit to the factors causing the stress (i.e., the revolutionary new developments in his industry). On the contrary, he made an attempt to manage or cope with it. His idea for coping with the stress was based on a combination of problem- and emotion-oriented methods. Unlike his rallying colleagues, he decided to perceive the anticipated industrial restructuring (i.e., the source of the stress) not as a threat but as an opportunity to qualify himself for a future job. At the same time, he coped with the symptoms resulting from stress by avoiding rallying, complaining, and lamenting. Instead, Dick distanced himself by maintaining his optimism and engaging himself in future-oriented constructive activities, i.e., training and retraining.

If you find yourself in a similar situation, then you should ask yourself the same questions as Dick did:

- What is it what you want to achieve?
- How do you want to progress?
- What precisely you need to do to make it happen?

In addition to the targeted and determined actions, which are directly aimed at eliminating the stressful circumstances, there are numerous other means by which you can manage stress. They are less targeted but more general in nature and can also help reduce the negative effects of stress, though in a more indirect way.

RID YOURSELF OF TASKS

There are always tasks that you put off because they are annoying or you feel uncomfortable with doing them, or simply because they seem unimportant. But at some point, these tasks become important—maybe the deadline is approaching or numerous unfinished tasks have piled up causing you stress.

Example: A long-postponed appointment with someone in the organization you don't like, a repeatedly postponed phone call to someone whom you owe an apology, the completion of complicated forms, and other small tasks which you have put at the bottom of your pile of papers. But the moment you remove an annoying task from your to-do list, you are relieved. It will help to reduce some of your stress.

Example: You can also get some relief from stress when you raise your activity level. The activities you can think of here do not necessarily have to be physical exercise though they are extremely effective stress relievers, especially when they involve socializing.

Building and maintaining relationships with others help you to establish a network of close, caring individuals who can provide social support. Other people can be very comforting to you when you are faced with stress and they can be extremely helpful in your attempts to manage stress. Social support can take many forms, including advice, guidance, encouragement, and emotional comfort.

Other activity options that can work as stress relievers are unforgettable events such as a romantic tête-à-tête dinner in a good restaurant, a shared vacation, a special birthday celebration, a night-long conversation, a cruise, or an adventure trip.

Example: Another option to manage stress is to slow down. For instance, imagine you interrupt your stress life for a short break and ask yourself a simple question: 'Why do I do this to myself?' Maybe you will realize in that moment that there's no real need to rush through your life as you seem to be doing. And, maybe you will come up with a second question: 'What would it change in the world, if I would approach it more calmly and with less haste and stress?' The answer to these questions may help you to slow down. You could start to slow down, for instance, by scheduling less things on your agenda and leave more space between activities for reflection and planning.

Example: There are a number of activities that will help you to slow down, reduce your stress, and free up your mind such as reading, walking, meditation, yoga, and doodling. In case you have to attend a lot of meetings at your job, then you know how boring meetings can be! Boring meetings can also be stressful, especially when it is an obligation for you to attend though you have a lot of more important things to do. To get some relief from your stress, you can start doodling. It is very relaxing because it combines activity and relaxation. The doodles can later be used to amuse yourself, your family and friends, or even get exhibited. Some of these drawings actually illustrate this book!

Many people who are invited to practice stress-relieving activities like slowing down or planning for an unforgettable event excuse themselves by claiming they are 'too busy'. This excuse is just another way of saying that they don't know about the harmful effects of stress on their health, their happiness, and the happiness of those close to them or ignore it and don't care because other things seem more important to them.

THE 'I-SHOULD' TRAP

THE ROLE OF UNSPOKEN NORMS

In the preceding section, we discussed stress situations at work, whose influence on the state of happiness could, in principle, be limited in time. However, for people who suffer from permanent psychological stress, the stress situation and the methods to cope with it can be quite different. Stress can be called permanent when people feel that they are under constant pressure to adopt certain behaviours or to meet certain norms that are forced upon them or which they have imposed upon themselves.

Example: In his spare time, a young lawyer named Albert painted strange pictures reminiscent of the wild fantasies of Hieronymus Bosch. He didn't mind exhibiting his paintings in the rooms of the local bar association, even though he knew that the members were ultra-conservative. During the opening of the exhibition, an elderly lawyer colleague approached Albert and indignantly asked him if he was using heroin. The message from his older colleague was clear: you don't do that and you don't show that if you want to be one of us. It was the first but not the last time that Albert felt the social pressure that was to be exerted on him.

In their workplace, people are often subjected to formal or unspoken behaviour patterns and norms that they are expected to meet without contradiction.

Example: Unspoken dress codes, office pecking orders, unspoken obligations, unspoken permanent threats, unspoken value decisions, unwritten social rules, and political correctness.

Unspoken norms are normative concepts that are assumed to be binding within a group of people. They dictate which behaviour is acceptable and which is not. Sometimes people do not even realize that they subordinate themselves to these norms unconsciously.

Example: In his private life, Theodore is a hobby DJ in a nightclub in his neighbourhood. But in his professional life, he is an accountant in a big consultancy. Theodore wanted to change his job for better salary and wrote some applications. When he was invited by the personnel manager of an insurance company for an interview, he didn't know the prevailing dress code of his potential new employer. But he had no doubt that it would be fine to wear an inconspicuous grey suit with a tie that was just as inconspicuous and discreetly patterned. When Theodore entered the insurance company's headquarters, he saw that he was right in his assumption. All employees he could see were wearing the same grey suits and discreetly patterned ties.

Some companies have flexible corporate culture and others prefer a strict corporate culture. Moreover, different corporate cultures can also prevail within a company in different departments, which can put a great deal of strain on cooperation. Most employees conform to these standards even if they are not in line with their own ideas or are forced to accept them. This is due to indifference or done for pure career reasons, even if these rules compel people to hide their real personality or force them to pretend to be what they are not.

Unspoken behaviour patterns and unwritten norms can concern lifestyle, gender, marital status, outer appearance, the way you dress and talk, whom you associate with, and sometimes even your life outside work. Generally, they have no direct correlation with the individual employee's work performance. If you are stuck in such a system and an external restraining mechanism is implanted in your brain, it can have the same effect as a brainwash. The result of brainwashing includes getting involuntarily stuck in a 'should trap'.

Example: The most prevalent example for a 'should trap' is concealing differences in lifestyle or sexual orientation; for instance, homosexuality. People who are hiding their sexual orientation or other important aspects of their personality are unhappy because they cannot live openly what they are.

In case of a successful brainwash, you may start to believe that you *should* do, *should* say, or *should* think something.

Example: 'Should constraints' manifest themselves in phrases such as: 'This is not politically incorrect', 'This is not to be said or done', 'This is not common', or 'This is not our style', 'Inappropriate', 'Not worthy of your position', or simply paraphrased with the words 'should' or 'should not'.

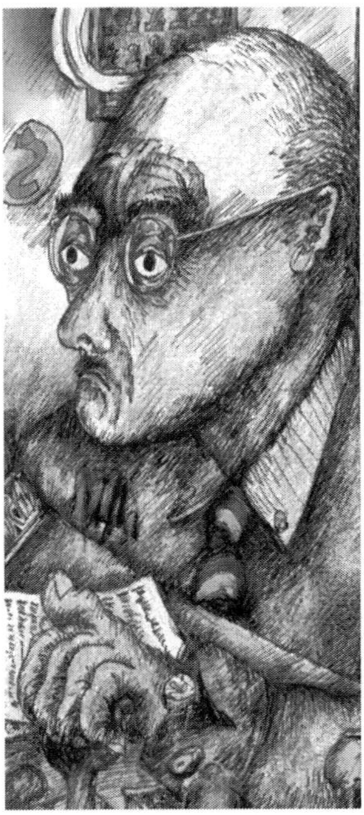

If you do not comply, you will possibly feel guilty and unhappy as you don't seem to be a member of the group that is supposed to give you a feeling of togetherness and protection. To avoid this isolation, you may start (over) conforming or pretending to be someone you're not.

This is contrary to your goal to become happier. Brainwashing plants barriers and prejudices in your mind that rob you of your independence and freedom—both prerequisites for being cool. It destroys your personality, self-respect, internal balance and, as a consequence, your happiness.

But the 'should trap' does not necessarily have to have its origin in an external influence or a brainwash. It can also come from within and be self-imposed.

Example: Dr Julia Walter, a young attorney, was hired as an associate by a well-recognized law firm. One day, a senior partner asked Julia whether she was married. Julia denied, though she planned to marry soon. Julia was ambitious and had the goal of becoming a junior partner in the firm. But she had heard from colleagues that at this law firm one should not be married or engaged if one wanted to make a career. The law firm expected full commitment from its young associate lawyers, including constant late work and unpaid work on Sundays and holidays. Julia was fearing for her career chances and decided not to tell the truth.

What Julia, however, overlooked was that professional success, her career, and the money she could earn were not the only parts of her life that made her happy.

Success at work may go hand in hand with happiness, but it should not be overlooked that success and money are not emotional, but materialistic components that only help to create a short-term feeling of happiness.

If you decide to make success and the money connected with it your first priority, then you run the risk that one of the most important emotional components of your personality, i.e. your personal happiness, will no longer play a sufficiently significant role in your life.

In continuation of the above:

Example: Julia remained true to herself, her ambition, and the unwritten rules of her law firm. Although she married as planned, she did not let this stop her from working overtime, weekends, and holidays. True to the firm's unspoken norms, her profession had priority over her private life. This was initially accepted by her husband Brian because he wanted to support her career aspirations. However, when Julia's first successes came about and nothing changed in her work behaviour, Brian began to doubt his relationship with her. After even discussions could not change Julia's mind and his attacks didn't show any effect ('You are married to your job, not me!'), Brian started looking for a girlfriend. One year later, he filed for divorce. Ironically, the separation had a negative effect on Julia's successful career. Only when Brian had left her for good, did Julia feel that something was amiss. Julia's unhappiness about this led to her working even harder. One day she was hospitalized with serious burnout syndromes. The doctors recommended to lead a more balanced life.

A good example of how unwritten rules develop can be seen in the way Julia responded to her private unhappiness. What began as simple thoughts ('I cannot ask my colleagues for help. They will think I'm incompetent at managing my life.' 'Even if I am depressed today, I must look good or they'll kick me off the list for the next senior partner.') systematically stifled her personal development. The more Julia wanted to succeed, the more she adapted to the unwritten rules. With the goal on her mind to further climb the ladder and become a senior partner in the law firm, she observed how the other senior partners in the firm behaved and emulated their behaviour.

Regardless of an organization's stated values and goals, most employees behave according to the unwritten rules that best support their ability to achieve their personal goals. Once you uncover an unwritten rule in your organization or at your workplace, you should identify whether it benefits, harms, or has no impact on you. To do so, you should ask whether the rule supports your or only the company's interest. The interests may coincide or exclude each other.

If they coincide, you can relax. You can determine whether they are neutral and can be ignored by you or further reinforce or reward them.

Example: Rick was working in a company with a strict dress code. Dark suits and decent ties were obligatory. In the past, Rick had been used to a much more flexible work environment with no unspoken dress code, which he preferred. But for him the issue wasn't important enough to make it an issue.

Your feeling of happiness at work will probably not be affected, if the issue is just a conservative dress code. In contrast, your happiness at the workplace may very likely be affected, if the owner and CEO of the company you are working for would bully employees to make a financial contribution to a specific political party's election campaign. In this case, you would work under an unspoken obligation concerning your political position.

If the unwritten rules and your personal goals exclude each other, you need to decide whether you can afford to ignore them. If they turn out to be dysfunctional, it's an issue and you need to bring it to your superior's attention.

Example: Agnesa worked as a trainee in a renowned consultancy company. After some weeks, she was shocked to see that the company had an unbelievably strong unspoken pecking order. Agnesa observed that between the different verticals and also the horizontal levels in the hierarchy, from the simple employee up to the CEO, there was a bitter permanent struggle for influence, client ownership, and budget. Even people at the same hierarchical level felt superior to their colleagues if they came from a better university or business school and used this perceived advantage to their detriment. This unhealthy company climate was further fuelled by the fact that the individual annual bonus payments were not made dependent on the company's annual business results but on the performance of each individual employee. This led to an absence of team spirit and corresponding deficiencies in the company's performance. In this environment, Agnesa felt lost and unhappy and decided not to join the company when she got a job offer after the end of her traineeship.

When thinking about your exposure to 'I-should' rules such as unspoken value decisions, it is, therefore, important to understand, which of them can be just tolerated and which could be harmful to your pursuit of happiness.

Example: An automotive supplier company introduced a dress code under which the company associates were asked to refrain from workplace expressions in support of political campaigning. The unspoken underlying reason for this dress code was to foster a politically neutral, peaceful work environment. However, some political activists amongst the employees were unhappy with the company's position and denounced the underlying reasons for the dress code as a 'threat against their right of free speech'. They claimed that they felt intimidated by the company's action because they were made to believe that they should be (not) doing something in order to comply with the company's expectations.

It is correct to say that the 'should trap' does not allow you to view your life from your own perspective, but from what you believe you 'should' be doing. At work, this could be interpreted as if your personal 'pursuit of happiness' was standing in the way of professional success. That's not true. If, what is expected of you, leaves no room for personal self-realization and thus

blocks the path to your own sense of happiness, then you have to think seriously about where your priorities truly lie and find a balanced solution.

Example: You are a very family-oriented person. You love your wife and children, and there is nothing you like better than spending time with them at the weekend. Your employer sees you as a great talent and wants to support you. He sends you to seminars and further education events and delegates more important tasks to you to test your leader abilities. You recognize the trust your employer places in you and you are grateful. However, as a consequence of your growing commitment to your job, your family is beginning to suffer from your absence. You try to explain it to your family by telling them that your career means more income, and more income means a better lifestyle. Your wife understands the logic but she also expresses her worry about the well-being and happiness of your family. The growing conflict becomes clear in your mind when, on a sunny Saturday afternoon, you play with the children in the garden, although you had promised your employer that you will be in the office to do some urgent work. Your wife is shocked when she hears you saying: 'I should actually be in the office.' On Sunday, you slip out from family life for a couple of hours to work in the office. When your employer joins you in the office and compliments you on your work, you respond guiltily: 'I should actually be with my wife and the children.' Your employer reacts without understanding. 'You should focus more on your career. Or, are you seriously prepared to jeopardize your career by playing in the sandbox with your kids? That's not serious.'

PLACING COOLNESS AND HAPPINESS AT THE CENTRE

One can assume that an employee who is unhappy with their situation cannot bring their full performance potential to their job. With this in mind, it will probably be easier for you to think about finding an acceptable balance between two the factors influencing you: On the one hand, the 'I-should' position referring to the unspoken value decision that 'the job has priority over private (family) life', and, on the other hand, your desire to be honest with yourself, do things which are meaningful to you, and be happier.

Self-suppression and over-diligent conformity won't bring out your highest productivity at work, nor will they lead to workplace happiness. This is because it prevents you from being yourself. But, on the other hand, you cannot completely ignore the prevailing unspoken obligations. Provocative non-conformity or confrontational behaviour would challenge even the most tolerant organization.

Instead, you should start placing coolness and happiness as key ingredients of sustained success at a central place of your thinking. This applies to both, the workplace and life in social environments, such as families or groups of friends. The concept of placing coolness and happiness in the centre of your thinking will allow you to understand which of the 'I-should' norms are harmless or harmful.

In this context, 'cool thinking' should be understood as a tool referring to the passionless, analytical concept you should use when dealing with your exposure to 'I-should' norms, such as unspoken obligations, unwritten social rules, unspoken value decisions, and even 'very unspoken' permanent threats.

Example: In Thai society, there are many unspoken principles that you should uphold in order to be perceived as a 'good' citizen. For instance, from an early age on, you are expected to be a 'good child' of your parents, as rebellion against any authority is perceived as 'bad'. Therefore, when you are young, you *should* listen and obey older people, when you are at school, you *should not* argue against your teacher, when you become an adult, you *should not* dispute authority, even if you have a very good point to make. It is also bad for you to criticize another person directly which makes them 'lose face', meaning make them look bad. Saying exactly what you think or doing things in your own way is not always appreciated, and you may be easily perceived as an odd man out. You are expected to avoid conflicts and cover up problems. For this, the Thai language has a well-known term: *mai-ben-lai*, meaning 'don't worry' which reflects this attitude. Peace and harmony in the society have a high value in Thailand, at least when you look at it superficially.

In this respect, cool is the tool to identify the 'I-should' norm which concerns you, to analyse its relevance for your happiness (at work), and to check its meaning for you. If you come to the conclusion that the 'I-should' norm compromises your basic human right to be happy, for instance, because you are not allowed to be who you want to be, then you should make happiness the centre of your further actions.

Happiness at work means that you can do things that make you feel happy, make you believe in yourself, make you be yourself, and are meaningful to you and make sense.

To find out whether your work makes you happy and provides you with a sense of meaning and whether there are any 'I-should' norms that are standing in the way, you should consider using ordinary artists as a model.

Different to the corporate world, ordinary artists can never be sure whether they can sell their art and generate income. There are a lot of artists who rarely succeed in selling. They have to live a hand-to-mouth existence but still seem happier than, for instance, well-paid, socially secure, and irredeemable civil servants working in public authority or well-to-do investment. The reason why artists seem to be happier may be because they generally identify themselves with their work in such a way that they can rightly claim that their work makes them happy. They can do this because for artists, their work makes sense, fulfils a purpose and is meaningful.

Example: Recently, an artist posted the following statement on Facebook, apparently talking to herself:

> Thanks to me for never giving up on art, to make all effort to make it happen. I love you art, and it is forever . . . *And my dear* . . . I think it's time for you to know that you were born to be the moon not stars. Believe me ... you are a great artist and I am proud of you. You know what I mean.
>
> —Pemapsorn 'June' Kritsadacharoenpong, Thai artist

What can be learned from the artists' point of view on their work is that any work can give the person doing it a feeling of fulfilment and happiness. This is the case when a work is designed or perceived as meaningful or making a positive contribution.

You may argue that this may be true for artists, and possibly craftsmen, doctors, researchers, company founders, and the like but not for people for whose jobs it is difficult to attribute a special meaning, a particular sense or positive contribution, such as accountants, tellers, truck drivers, policemen, auditors, sales assistants, garbage collectors, or any other subordinate simple service providers. The question is whether it is true that these people have no chance of their own happiness in their job because they do not qualify for the same.

On the contrary, it can be assumed that fulfilment and happiness can be achieved by people working in any occupational group even if it may, superficially seen, appear that there is no sense and meaningfulness in their work.

As the artist in above referenced quote rightly said: '... you were born to be the moon not stars...'— whatever work you do and whatever the importance of your specific work may be, it all makes sense and is meaningful, in particular if you see the work as part of something bigger than yourself.

Example: Conrad works as a parcel delivery guy. His job is physically hard and not well paid. The people he delivers to are not always friendly because the delivery was delayed because of heavy traffic or weather conditions, and they treated him like a servant. It is all the more astonishing for Conrad when, he receives a friendly word or perhaps even a tip or a drink at the door. In such cases, the customer was happy that the parcel was delivered. They saw that the delivery man did his best to provide him a service and was prepared to share this happiness with them. On the other hand, Conrad was happy because of the unexpected recognition he has received from his customer. He saw that his activity makes sense and that made him feel happy.

If some customers would not have made kind gestures, Conrad would just have gone on with his hectic activity. He would have been too busy to think about his job and end up exhausted at the end of each day without ever being inspired to find out about his job's meaning. In this example, something unusual happened, which disrupted Conrad's routine in a way that started him to think about what he was doing and why it was important.

PEOPLE CAUSING UNHAPPINESS

In the previous sections, we have discussed the extent to which perceived stress and social pressure ('I-should' traps) can affect your sense of happiness at work and what you can do about it. However, stress and social pressure do not come from nowhere, but are usually created by people and/or by very specific circumstances. These stressors should be discussed in some more detail.

Joke:

> Question: How do you go to work?
> Answer: Forced.
> Question: No, I mean how do you arrive there?
> Answer: Depressed!

In today's interconnected world, you're probably spending more time dealing with your colleagues than ever before.

Your constant availability via your smartphone or other electronic media makes communications possible even in the evening or on Sundays and on public holidays. Being happy or unhappy in this work environment is more than just liking what you do on the job. Beyond this, you probably want to be able to say that the hours and effort that you dedicate to your work truly contributes to how happy you are in life. Happiness at work does not mean that you have to be smiling, happy, and enthusiastic all the time. The happiness you feel at work comes from more fundamental sources. As discussed in the previous section, it is your sense of purpose and the meaningfulness of what you do that adds to your happiness at work.

In the example of the delivery man, above, it was shown that even in a service-oriented subordinate position, you can develop a sense of purpose for yourself, when your company contributes to something that you and others care about; for instance, environmental protection. The key lies in the fact that your daily work may be routine or banal, but that your work helps to secure values that give it a meaning beyond its apparent insignificance.

But even if you find your work meaningful and should be happy about it, your happiness at work can be negatively affected by other factors. The most important factor is people, especially your superiors and the colleagues you work with. It is likely that you won't look forward to a day at your workplace even if you love the work, when you find your boss unacceptable or your colleagues upsetting. Conversely, even a boring job may be more enjoyable if you like the people you're working with.

THE DISLIKED BOSS

> People don't leave bad jobs; they leave bad bosses.
>
> —Unknown

There are many reasons why you might dislike your boss. For instance, the management style does not seem appropriate to you, or there is a flagrant disregard for your work, or you have a profound mutual antipathy to each other, or you have a basic natural antipathy towards people in authority.

With regard to a possible antipathy, you should accept the

principle that there will always be three categories of people in your life: (1) People who like you, (2) people who don't like you, and (3) people who don't care about you. If you accept that as a principle, you will find it pointless trying to be the person everyone, including your boss, will like. Consequently, you have to admit that your boss too can't be everybody's favourite.

So, if you don't like your boss, you should be careful to distinguish between the professional and the more personally motivated points you may have to dislike him. Your emotionally motivated criticism should not take priority over justified criticism that relates to the purely professional part of your boss' behaviour. From this follows that when we discuss the influence of a 'disliked' boss on your performance and your happiness at work, we will focus on those points that come from the professional and not the personal–emotional sphere.

> Rest assured that your recent accomplishments at work have gone largely unnoticed.
>
> —Unknown

UNFAIRNESS

Unfair treatment at work can make you feel degraded, humiliated, unworthy, and, as a consequence, unhappy. A boss is unfair when he bullies his employees, yells and screams for no reason, makes life difficult for those around him, unfairly criticizes the work of his subordinates, sets them menial tasks, undermines their work even though they are competent at their job, and passes them over for a promotion or better opportunity because of favouritism, office politics, or nepotism.

Example: Lars, a young tax attorney, was transferred by his company's local affiliate in Sweden to headquarters in Brussels to be trained on international tax law and dividend optimization techniques. Right at the beginning of his assignment, his American boss George asked Lars to file the tax return of one of the company's American vice-presidents. George knew that Lars could not do this job because of his lack of training and experience in US tax law. But he wanted to see him fail 'to condition him' for working under his supervision. First, Lars reacted with panic and didn't know how to manage the job. But he was lucky to convince one of his US colleagues to help him. This was only the first of a string of bad experiences Lars had with George who would not fail to embarrass Lars at any occasion. As a result of this, Lars became unhappy at his job although he learnt a lot from his interesting work.

NO APPRECIATION FOR YOUR WORK

There are many examples which signal that you are unappreciated at work, such as unfair pay, being passed over for a promotion, getting blocked from growth opportunities, being ignored in the office or at meetings, or being refused the appropriate resources you need to do your job properly. Another case of disrespect is when in meetings you get talked over, interrupted, or criticized for speaking out.

Example: Alexa is a secretary in a prestigious law firm. Every day she goes to work early in the morning just to make sure everything runs smoothly, meetings are coordinated, and files are ready before her boss arrives. Her boss Henry, who is a senior partner in the firm, usually arrives relatively late to work and storms into his office without greeting Alexa as if she were invisible. Alexa feels that her efforts go unnoticed, so she tries to impress her boss by using her personal connection to fulfil his challenging requests, by always responding attentively to his calls, even on weekends, to show him that she can effectively deliver what is expected of her. But it doesn't seem to matter how hard she tries. Henry turns a blind eye, because to him she is just a secretary who is supposed to do her job to help him do his job successfully. He believes that his work as senior partner is important to the firm, not her secretarial work which does not need to be appreciated. Alexa feels more and more dissatisfied with her situation—nothing she does is good enough, and there has never been any positive feedback. She is now resolved to stop trying to please her boss, and simply does what she has to do while looking for another job.

The continuous lack of appreciation of your work makes you feel unhappy about your job. You feel unmotivated and like wasting your time.

This is also the case when your boss or colleagues repeatedly take credit for your work without even mentioning your name. For instance, when you share an idea that is dismissed when you voiced it at a meeting but then gets praised when someone else presents it, then you know that there is a problem. As a normal reaction, you would like to tell everyone who did the job in reality, but in most cases, you don't want to step on somebody's toes.

MANAGEMENT STYLE

A bad management style makes employees dissatisfied and unhappy. There are many examples of a bad management style. The boss's opinion changes constantly. They regularly throw decisions overboard and complicate everything because they can't take a decision on what's important and what's not and cannot set priorities. It is also bad management when the boss lacks the will to take decisions, when they have no social skills and cannot motivate employees. A boss is also a bad manager when they give orders in a strict tone, are unfriendly and condescending, only likes their own ideas, undermines collaborators and does not promote the strengths of the employees but makes them feel bad. Bad management style is furthermore, if a boss does not give reasons for their assessments, decisions, and orders, does not listen to people, and spreads fear due to rude behaviour.

On the contrary, a good boss will plan, organize, show leadership, motivate, takes decisions, and communicate. This prevents you from *mental resignation*, a term which is used to describe employees who are no longer motivated or committed to the company, who have no more ties to the company and only perform their duties according to the rules.

Example for general bad management style: Mateo, deputy director of the sales department of an optical instrument company, believes that he needs to know more than others, work harder, and please his bosses better to stand out as a good junior executive in his company. In his company, he is known to be a 'yes man' as he never says 'no' to his boss's requests. As much as Mateo wants to please his superior, he also cares for his own subordinates. His employees, however, particularly dislike Mateo for his ignorance and disrespect. Mateo doesn't care about team-building, doesn't seem to be interested in developing a trustful working relationship with his subordinates, and never shares important information with them. This and his selfish, self-centred and unprofessional style of management cause a high level of stress in his department. All members of his department are looking forward to the day when Mateo would be promoted to another position or would leave the company.

Example for undermining an employee: Nine months ago, Nelson joined an electronics company as a corporate strategist. He was a newcomer to this industry as he had worked in the chemical industry before. In September, his boss Michael asked him to work on the company's next year strategic plan for presentation to the company's board at the end of October. Nelson gladly welcomed this challenging assignment as he believed that this would give him an opportunity for high level exposure. He started to enthusiastically research his industry's current and future business environment, markets and trends, and used all his resources to do an outstanding job. At the same time, Nelson knew that subject to his lack of seniority in the company and the industry, he would need to dwell on his boss's long-standing experience. But Nelson got disappointed by his boss. His boss excused himself by saying that he was too busy to help Nelson, adding that even without his help, he would trust Nelson to a good job. When Nelson had completed the draft of the presentation, he reviewed it with Michael, and added some changes and suggestions Michael had made. In October, Michael asked Nelson to do the presentation in the boardroom. Nelson felt honoured. When Nelson started to make his presentation, he was excited and confident in his work. To Nelson's utmost surprise, Michael started interrupting Nelson during his presentation, asking him awkward questions, urging him to double-check some points, and questioning some of his assumptions. When Nelson started to become nervous because of his boss's unexpected interventions, Michael jumped in and presented a new set of charts with conclusions different from Nelson's and, ultimately, overruled Nelson's proposal with his own. Nelson had never been undermined like this before and was totally shocked. He was tempted to yell at Michael in front of everybody but disciplined himself and postponed his reaction to a more appropriate occasion.

NO VISION

> Purpose isn't everything, but it trumps everything else.
>
> —Roy M. Spence,
> American business writer

In case you dislike your boss for failing to set direction for your company, to define the right purpose, develop a vision and communicate it within the organization, you have a point. Nothing influences the commitment, performance, and the happiness of the employees at work more than that. One can assume that most companies meet their employees' basic needs but the vision and the right meaning meet more important deeper needs such as togetherness, a sense of belonging, pride in the company, its products or even in the whole industry sector. Employees who are inspired by their management's clear strategic direction, can better align their full resources to working towards a common goal and have a better chance of becoming happy at work.

Example: Nick works as strategic development director at the world headquarters of a leading fast-food chain. The business is going well. The company's CEO is highly satisfied with the business development and sees no reason to change the business model of the company. But Nick's job as a strategic development director is to identify new trends and help to ensure the company's future success under changing circumstances. For some time already, Nick has predicted a trend towards a more environmentally friendly packaging and more health-conscious food. He has, therefore, advocated a change in the company's business model to accommodate the anticipated changes in the marketplace. But in all discussions with his CEO, Nick had been unsuccessful. The CEO was proud of his past success, ultra-conservative, and not prepared to change the company's course. On the contrary, he vilified environmentalists and critics of the fast-food industry as alarmists and Left-wing radicals whose hysterical arguments he would never listen to. Nick had to realize that under the impact of the previous success, his CEO seemed to have lost his sense of future market developments. He was an apologist for the principle that 'everything stays the same when things are going well', and appeared unable to develop a vision for the future of the company. As a reaction to the unimaginative management of his CEO, Nick began to turn away from his boss and no longer took him seriously. He accused his boss of failing to inspire the company with a new purpose, to create new corporate values reflecting future developments, and to create the organizational conditions, for instance, to add plant-based meat alternatives to menus to align with environmental and health-conscious values.

If you consider these exemplary reasons for an employee's aversion to their boss, you will find that the answer to the question of how to restore the feeling of happiness lost at work because of the boss's behaviour is usually very similar for most situations.

OPEN DIALOGUE

> The secret to happiness is freedom, and the secret to freedom is courage.
>
> —Thucydides, Athenian historian and general, *c.* 400 BC

In principle, there is no alternative to a direct face-to-face dialogue with the disliked boss. You have to have the (civil) courage to talk to your boss about their behaviour and especially the consequences of their behaviour on the working atmosphere, your motivation and performance quality and, if applicable, on other employees.

Tip: If you are struggling with whether you should have the courage to confront your boss face-to-face for his behaviour, then you should realize the following: So far, you were probably swallowing your bad thoughts because you were fearing negative consequences for your career, which your boss has a lot of influence on. However, you should be aware that the moment you ignore that fear and speak your mind, it can be perceived by you as a liberation. You will not only be proud of your courage, but also free yourself from an inner burden and be happy that you brought your message across.

During your conversation with your boss, they will also learn that you (and perhaps other employees) no longer feel happy at work because of their leadership style. The boss should ideally react to this as they will be aware that employee happiness at work has an influence on their performance.

Tip: It is worth noting that such a conversation may be better suited one-on-one. It may seem safer in a team-setting (when more employees are affected by your boss's behaviour), but you should be aware that this may put your boss automatically on the defensive and make them less flexible.

It is also important to understand that this face-to-face conversation cannot be replaced by a written communication such as an office memorandum or letter. Firstly, writing is much less flexible in language and form. Only in a face-to-face conversation, ambiguities and possible misunderstandings can be resolved immediately. In addition, a letter is normally used to put something on record. This means that it can be interpreted by your boss as a threat that may influence his tone and possible flexibility during the conversation but also his position.

Tip: If the conversation ends in a dispute and without result, you can still say that you will summarize the points and positions discussed in a memorandum. This will be taken by your boss as an indication that the matter is not yet over for you and may lead him or her to change his behaviour.

> A man with outward courage dares to die; a man with inner courage dares to live.
>
> —Lao Tzu, ancient Chinese philosopher

The willingness of your boss to deal with your arguments depends greatly on the way in which you present them. Needless to say, a plaintive, accusatory, threatening, or aggressive tone could easily be counterproductive, as your boss's attitude will most likely harden and he will act defensively. This is not helpful and questions the success of your brave act. It would be best if you based your argument on a cooperative philosophy. This means that you are arguing in a problem-solving way and not making your boss feel like they are being charged.

Tip: Try something like: 'I'm really unclear about your expectations and I really want to do the best job I can. So, I'm wondering if we can find a way to communicate better so that I understand what you need.'

This cooperative approach puts you in a joint problem-solving position. Your starting point should be wanting to help your boss to improve. Of course, you shouldn't tell him that directly because he would most likely reject this idea, but it should set the tone of your argument.

This approach may succeed when you see it as part of your role to trigger doubts in your boss about the correctness of their behaviour and, at the same time, to show them a way to improve. In order to achieve this willingness to consider your proposal, you need a *hook* on which your conversation tactics can be hung. This *hook* can look like this:

- First, you should demonstrate to your boss that your motivation for talking to them about such a sensitive subject was not solely based on your personal individual interests.

  Tip: You should discipline yourself in such a way that you don't get perceived as arguing *pro domo*, or on your own behalf, but as if you were a neutral arbitrator representing to the boss the case of a third person or a superior interest, such as the company's well-being.

- Second, you should refer to an overriding value that your boss also feels obliged to. In this particular case, the overriding value is the company's and its shareholders' interest in the smooth running of operational processes without waste and frictional losses due to dissatisfied, poorly performing employees. Therefore, you should focus on how your boss's behaviour has affected your productivity as an employee and, possibly, the team as a whole. You can then point out that it is not only in yours but, more importantly, in the company's interest to change this for the better.

  Example: Wolf is working as a junior officer in the military in the counterintelligence unit. He is used to military hierarchy and discipline. With increasing experience in his field, he realizes how unprofessional his superior is. In reality, his superior is just a bureaucratic, work-shy paper-shuffler. He is afraid to take a stand and avoids taking any responsibility. The military system even rewards him for this because promotions are not based on performance but on seniority, conformity, relationships, and family background. One day, Wolf is confronted with a blatant case of misjudgement by his superior which, if implemented, will cause serious damage to his unit. He tries to talk to his superior about it but his senior uses his disciplinary superiority to silence him. Wolf feels unhappy because he does not know what to do. On the one hand, he feels it is his duty to bring his superior's misjudgement to the attention of the commander-in-chief. On the other hand, the hierarchical thinking in the military prevents him from making this move as it could have a negative impact on his career. When once again he can't sleep because of this, Wolf has a good idea. He decides to deprive his initiative with the commander-in-chief of any personal motivation and neutralizes his action by referring it to an 'overriding value'. In this case, the overriding value would be the oath all members of the military have sworn 'to protect and defend the welfare of the country and the head of state'. Wolf decides to use his oath as the 'hook' for his complaint to the commander-in-chief. As his superior's misjudgement will cause serious damage, he acted against the interests of the country and its head of state. This constitutes a violation of his duties. Therefore, it is no longer at Wolf's discretion rather than his duty under the oath to disclose this case to the commander-in-chief. Wolf's initiative to speak up is solely based on superordinate interests and must, therefore, be disassociated from him personally.

POSSIBLE REACTIONS

It's not impossible that the conversation with your boss might not go as planned. For instance, your boss may feel attacked and not let you speak up at all, interrupt you, yell you down, or treat you so condescendingly and humiliatingly that you lose your temper and forget to implement your concept.

The best way to not let this happen is to be prepared for it. Therefore, before seeing your boss you should play through all situations once, like in a role play or mock trial.

Explanation: A mock trial is an act or imitation trial. Attorneys preparing for a real trial use a mock trial consisting of volunteers as role players to experiment with each other. In the American TV series *Suits*, the featuring law firm does its annual mock trial by making the associates go against one another to prove their worth to the partners at the firm.

There is also a chance that your boss may just be waiting for you to make mistakes to use them against you. Therefore, keep a cool head if the situation should become heated or confrontational and stay as neutral as possible, don't get emotional but argue about facts, ideally combined with suggestions for improvement. The latter approach is supposed to be perceived as 'constructive' and, therefore, more difficult to dismiss.

Irrespective of the reaction, you can be relatively sure that in most cases, your behaviour will have impressed your boss (even when he doesn't show it) because in a similar situation most employees wouldn't dare such a bold move. Even a weak boss with little self-confidence and limited social competence, will very likely perceive your brave behaviour at least as authentic and be impressed by your affirmative and self-confident personality. They will notice, but probably not appreciate, your decision to be different and volunteer to speak out, ignoring possible negative repercussions. They will probably also notice your inner strength that allowed you 'to swim against the tide' and challenge them, though this doesn't mean that they will accept it. Instead, they will rather feel challenged by it because in all likelihood, they will never dare to be in such a situation like yours.

The difference between a 'weak' boss and a 'strong' boss lies not so much in their individual perception of your personality, but in their reaction to it. A 'strong' boss who doesn't suffer from self-doubt and assumes that he is doing everything right, is more likely to evaluate your courage and frankness positively. A 'strong' boss might even interpret your courage as a sign of leadership potential, which may qualify you for a better job.

Ask yourself honestly, how would you react to an outspoken employee? As a superior, you would probably not be happy in an illusory world not corresponding to reality in which your subordinates were hiding unpleasant truths from you, gossiping or plotting behind your back, and only pretending to support you. You would most likely prefer a situation in which your people talk openly even if it meant more controversy.

In case your boss shows the strength to see the positive aspects of your initiative, don't expect them to immediately show you their newly developed respect. Their thoughts may be influenced by pride or their feeling of not wanting to lose face in front of you. You should, therefore, be patient and hope that any possible positive effect of your initiative will only be reflected in your boss's behaviour later in the course of time.

COMPLAIN TO THE SUPERIOR OF YOUR BOSS

However, if change doesn't materialize and your boss does not change his management style and you continue to be unhappy at work, your last option is to speak with the superior of your boss. However, this can turn out to be a double-edged sword. No matter how justified your accusations may be, you will likely be accused of lack of loyalty, disrespect for the established hierarchical order, and denigration.

Example: Ben gathered courage and informed the CEO of his company in the most neutral manner possible about the blatant shortcomings of his boss, the CEO's deputy, in the day-to-day management of the business. During the first moments of their conversation, the CEO didn't seem to listen to what Ben had to say. After some seconds, he interrupted Ben to ask him whether he had already tried to talk to his boss directly.

If you answer negatively to this question, the chances that the CEO will continue to listen to you are very slim. In case of doubt, he will protect your boss and ask you to talk to him. You may get the same reaction, however, if you report that you had a conversation with your boss but it was fruitless. Also, out of loyalty to your boss and in order not to stab him in the back, the CEO's principle position will always be to assume that your boss was right and not get persuaded by you to turn against him.

This may be different, however, if, according to the principles discussed above, you can demonstrate to the CEO that your motivation to discuss your boss's shortcomings is based on an 'overriding value'—in this case, the interest of the company and not solely motivated by your personal interest. It will become even more evident to the CEO when you point out how your boss's behaviour has been affecting your happiness at work and consequently your performance.

You can also involve your colleagues, but only if you have their consent. You do this knowing that one of the primary tasks of a CEO is to keep the level of employee motivation and happiness in the workplace high because performance, productivity, and quality depend on it.

Indeed, if presented by you as suggested here, the CEO would be negligent or biased if he didn't take your initiative as a warning sign and investigate the matter further.

This situation is similar to the one of whistle-blowers, whose value is recognized and protected in some jurisdictions. If the CEO would refuse to follow up on your complaint, he would risk that other unhappy employees would be dissuaded from raising their legitimate concerns about possible risks for the company's well-functioning.

TOXIC CO-WORKERS

> Poisonous people are like black holes. They drain your mental, emotional, and physical energy leaving you like a hollow husk of your former self.
>
> —Unknown

Difficult co-workers come in all forms. In some cases, you may think a co-worker is your friend only to find out by accident that they are talking badly about you behind your back; or, you may notice that you are cut out of important information flows or get fake information to make you make erroneous judgements.

> If there were in the world today any large number of people who desired their own happiness more than they desired the unhappiness of others, we could have paradise in a few years.
>
> —Bertrand Russell, British pacifist and philosopher

In addition, self-centred colleagues or an egocentric boss characterized by a 'me-only' or 'me-first' attitude, can also add to the toxic atmosphere at work and can turn a peaceful workplace into a minefield.

Example: Selfish colleagues usually think: What's in it for *me*? They are typically servile, smiley, and nice towards the bosses, but treat their colleagues and subordinates poorly. For instance, they let you do all the work, reject your creative ideas only to steal them, and then, somewhat later, present them as their own and take all the credit for themselves.

Example: An extremely ambitious corporate lawyer was overly convinced in his abilities and leadership qualities. His goal was clear: one day, he wanted to become the CEO. He didn't shy away from clever manipulations like spreading targeted half-true information, or even initiating intrigues like letting one of his competitors run into the open knife when he encouraged him to make a homophobic joke at a party at which the CEO was also present, even though he knew that the competitor was not aware that the CEO was gay. In another case, he had gone so far that one of his targets threw in the towel and left the company.

To be around and to even work with toxic colleagues in a team can make you angry, sad, and unhappy. As in the case of a disliked boss, this can have a negative impact on the working atmosphere and affect the employees' motivation and performance.

The question is how you can deal with a toxic co-worker in order to protect or regain your happiness at work.

Never put yourself in a position of allowing things to grow to the point where you become excessively frustrated and angry. Challenge the behaviour of a difficult co-worker head-on. Once you have allowed emotions to build up over a period of time like hot water in a covered pot, you may be more likely to lash out, which will possibly cause you to become even more frustrated, angry, and unhappy (with undesirable spill-outs into your private life).

Tip: An option to stay cool in a possibly heated environment caused by toxic behaviour at work is to balance out your emotions by a continued intensive focus on your work and a distracting private life outside the unpleasant work sphere.

HEAD-TO-HEAD ENCOUNTER

The best option to make the problem go away is to confront the co-worker in question directly.

But before doing this, you should take a cool, dispassionate, objective look at yourself and check upon your own behaviour. In the past, you may have been 'toxic' yourself, even if it was just by retaliating another person's rude behaviour.

> People who live in glass houses shouldn't throw stones.
>
> —Old German proverb

This is to make sure that you can't be accused of having been 'toxic' yourself because this could easily put you in the defensive during the course of a discussion.

Tip: You better don't have this conversation with the 'toxic' co-worker when you are angry or upset. It would be much better for the climate of the conversation, if you wouldn't confront the other person when you are upset. Wait until you've cooled off, for instance, after a good night's sleep, a family day, or a quiet walk.

Another preparatory step before you confront the 'toxic' person directly would be to inquire whether the 'toxic' colleague is aware of what they are doing and what impact their behaviour has on you and the team.

This is an important step, because 'toxic' behaviour is not always based on a person's bad will. Sometimes, the interests and wishes of those involved simply do not coincide or the work style is totally different. Often, personal characteristics and perceptions can also diverge without this being meant to be 'toxic'. This can particularly happen in societies with many immigrants from different countries and different cultural backgrounds.

Example: Barak, a Greek guest worker, was shunned and excluded from the group of his German fellow workers. They teased and ridiculed him because they perceived him as notoriously unfriendly, negative, and rude. As a result of their attitude, Barak became increasingly monosyllabic and unfriendly towards his German colleagues. Small-scale hostilities ensued, as a result of which he was labelled 'toxic' and accused of poisoning the working atmosphere. It was only during a conversation with Helmuth, one of Barak's more understanding German colleagues, that Barak explained why he seemed so 'toxic' to his colleagues. The Greek head shake for 'yes' is a head shake, which for the Germans, stands for 'no'. Conversely, a nod of the head, which is considered a 'yes' in Germany, is considered a 'no' in Greece. Barak's colleagues, unaware of this cultural difference, were repeatedly annoyed by the fact that Barak rejected everything they liked and when they rejected something, he nodded his head in such a way that they understood an opposing 'yes'. Only because of Helmuth's initiative, they found out that their perception of Barak as 'toxic' was based on a mere misunderstanding.

In these cases, and as shown in the example, the problem can be due to poor communication. Bad communication or no communication can easily lead to misinterpretations and misjudgements which can quickly result in accusations and hasty comments or rejections. In such cases, the possibly embarrassing conversation or the head-on conflict with the 'toxic' colleague can be avoided by seeking better communication than controversy or by downplaying the controversy.

If non-awareness and absence of bad will can be excluded, you should take the courage to seek a direct conversation with the toxic co-worker. As in the case of the 'disliked' boss, it is not always easy to take the decision for such a conversation. With all the emotions and sensitivities that may have built up, resolving a conflict is no easy task and for most people it is quite unpleasant. Therefore, the most important rule is to remain objective. This is the only way to prevent a (renewed) escalation of the conversation.

But you should also understand that it is you who is actually doing the 'toxic' person a favour. If you wouldn't have the courage to tell the 'toxic' co-worker the truth about their behaviour and its impact on the happiness at the workplace, they would have no chance to face up to the facts and change.

Example: Very likely, self-centred persons do not want to be seen as selfish egoists. One day they have to face up to the fact that it can be detrimental to their mental well-being and their happiness if they focus exclusively on their own interest. They will learn that resulting from their behaviour, trust and respect will be destroyed and people will be driven away, even those who may have been close.

Example: Some people have a reputation for always blaming others when something doesn't work out. One day they have to face the fact that it's not going to help them feel better because by not taking responsibility, they risk losing the important sense that self-determination can give their life. If it is always someone else's fault, in the end, they will feel helpless and unable to take effective action.

During the frank conversation, the difficult colleague should be made aware of the impact their behaviour has on you, and possibly also on the atmosphere in the whole team. In addition, they should understand that their behaviour will also lead other colleagues to withdraw from them, and in the end, they will find themselves isolated ('odd-man-out') or even kicked out.

It would be helpful if you remain calm and formulate your perception of the problem without interpreting or judging anything. It would also be better if you speak about your feelings and not about what the other person seems to have done wrong.

Tip: To be successful in such a conversation, you should make sure that the 'toxic' co-worker does not perceive your remarks as criticism or accusations. You'd better consider taking a positive and constructive approach so that they can possibly take your remarks as well-intentioned collegial advice, which might save them from many frustrations in their future (professional) life.

Example for careful wording: Instead of saying, 'You never copy me in important emails affecting my job', you may want to say: 'I'm not sure if I didn't receive a copy of this important email on purpose or by mistake, but in the future it's important to me that I am included in the distribution list for messages on this subject as it concerns my area of responsibility. How can we avoid this in the future?'

During the conversation, it would be good if you are perceived as listening carefully and honestly trying to understand the other person's version.

Ideally, the colleague should walk away from that conversation as highly motivated to reflect on their behaviour. The co-worker may also be encouraged when you/your colleagues offer to improve and intensify the communication within the group, which could deal effectively with conflicts that may arise. You can also help improve the climate by expressing your joy about the constructive conversation. Whatever the outcome, give yourself and your counterpart some time to process what you have discussed and adjust to the new situation.

INVOLVING THE SUPERVISOR

If you can't solve the problem with the 'toxic' co-worker in an amicable way, you will have to involve your supervisor. You should make sure that you meet them not with the intention to complain but to solve a problem in a constructive spirit.

Tip: In a discussion with a supervisor about a colleague's behaviour, it is important to avoid being perceived as someone who argues only in their personal interest or acts like gossip. In such a situation, you should consider the use of the same tactics outlined above for discussions with disliked bosses. Your smart (tactical) reference to an 'overriding value' will neutralize your discussion and keep you clean for being accused of selfishness or oversensitivity.

Example: 'Sophie is acting like a jerk, and you have to do something about it!' This won't be nearly as effective as, 'I seem to be having some difficulty communicating effectively with Sophie. I'm not sure how to resolve the situation so I'd like your perspective and any tips you may want to give me.'

Example: In a meeting with your boss, you complain about a colleague who poisons the working atmosphere with malicious gossip. You deliberately refrain from claiming that this non-collegial behaviour hurts or upsets you. This would be *pro domo*, solely in your interest, and it may cause your superior to think that you cannot solve the problem on your own or act as a contemptible informer. But, alternatively, if you express your disapproval about the gossiping that is poisoning the working atmosphere for the whole team so that the quality of work is at risk, then your boss will understand that you are looking at the bigger picture and that you are taking into account how such behaviour could jeopardize the whole team's dynamics and productivity.

This tactic will tell your boss that there is a problem, but it will also tell them that you're taking responsibility for your own actions and want to resolve the situation and not just dump it on his desk.

If despite all efforts, the problem persists, then perhaps it's time to start looking for a new position, either within or outside the company.

NON-PERSONAL FACTORS CAUSING UNHAPPINESS

CAREER UNHAPPINESS

If you are content with your basic career path but just unhappy at the actual workplace, you can change your job or your employer relatively easily, normally without having to make significant sacrifices in your career development. Unlike being unhappy at the workplace, being unhappy over an entire career is a much bigger problem.

This can relate to your own personal professional development, which relates to achieving the professional goals you have set for yourself.

Example: When you were twenty-five years old, your goal was to be a deputy marketing director at thirty, and a marketing director at thirty-five. However, when you turned thirty-five, you were far away from a promotion into that position, because the company had decided to hire a high-profile outsider into the position you had envisaged for yourself.

But career can also refer to 'higher' goals.

Example: You always had the desire to change something in your country to the better. At the age of twenty-three, you entered politics and became a member of an environmentalist party. For many years, the party was slowly growing from its former shadowy existence alongside the mainstream parties, into a serious contender. Unexpectedly, however, a deadly virus hit the world and caused a pandemic. The mainstream parties could use their longstanding government experience to demonstrate effectiveness in managing the crisis. Environmental issues got less attention and fell back on the list of priorities. In the end, you were further away from achieving your career goal than ever.

In both examples, career happiness is not related to your short-term experience at work, but much more to long-term satisfaction with your chosen career path. This concerns the speed with which you develop over the course of your career, the sense of meaning you draw from your work in the organization, the pride you have in the organization's products or services, and the alignment of your personal values with the organization's and its (industry) sector's values.

Example: It is hard to imagine that a director of a company specializing in the production of weapons is a leading member of a party that grew out of the pacifist anti-nuclear movement of the 1960s and in whose program pacifist ideas can still be found today.

Career happiness is a result of job satisfaction and success on the career path. For instance, you can be satisfied with your job when you know that you are doing something good for other people. You are also satisfied with your job, when you are prepared to devote your whole heart to your work, and that your commitment will give you joy and work satisfaction.

Example: During the first peak of the pandemic in the spring of 2020, people were cheering healthcare workers on the frontlines of battling the virus. The sacrifices they made, their dedication, commitment, and courage were highly admired and appreciated by a broad public. This public attention added to the healthcare workers' happiness and increased their hope that this appreciation will lead to a reassessment of their pay.

In contrast, when you are deeply dissatisfied and only work half-heartedly you feel that something is missing, and you feel deeply empty and unhappy inside.

Work hard, become successful, then you'll be happy. This is a message that you may have learnt over the years from your parents, teachers, employers, and even television advertisements. After a while, this way of thinking ('When I . . . then I will be happy') has apparently become an unchallenged truth.

WHAT'S FIRST: HAPPINESS OR SUCCESS?

However, the relationship between your career success and your happiness is not as clear as suggested in the statement 'Work hard, become successful, then you'll be happy.'

Example: Sir Winston Churchill was reportedly depressed but had an exceptional successful political career as a wartime UK prime minister.

This example—and many examples of successful people whose marriages fail or who get involved in drugs or other challenges—show that a successful career must not necessarily lead to happiness.

Example: Ten years after the successful and most infamous Hollywood couple, Elizabeth Taylor and Richard Burton, married, they filed for divorce. When she met Richard Burton for the first time, Elizabeth Taylor was married to Eddie Fisher, her fourth husband, who had left his wife for Taylor, and whom Taylor then left for Burton. After their divorce, Taylor and Burton married briefly for the second time to get again divorced soon after.

It seems more likely that it is happiness that precedes and can lead to career success, and not the reverse. This does neither mean that happiness is the only factor that determines career success, nor that unhappy people cannot be successful. It should be understood that people who are happy and can have a positive effect on others find it easier to be successful in their profession.

Example: Audrey Hepburn became one of the most successful actresses of all time during her four decades of film career. She was also known for making the world a better place through her humanitarian work for impoverished children around the world. For generations, she was considered as an inspiration for film fans, as she was not only stunningly beautiful but also very talented. When she was asked what the secret of her success was, she said: 'The most important thing is to enjoy life—to be happy—that's all that matters.'

If that is so, it looks like you would like to ensure making happiness at work one of your priorities as one amongst other important prerequisites of a successful career.

Example: Randolph is working as a career bureaucrat in the ministry for the environment in his country. Randolph specializes in agriculture, health, and consumer protection and works on new legislative proposals in this field. In his private life, he works as a volunteer in an environmental protection agency dealing with the recycling of plastics. Randolph is very happy with his job in the ministry because his own environmentalist's values are matching the government's priorities for environmental protection, health, and consumer protection. Therefore, Randolph is highly motivated, and he succeeds in making his team a leading unit at the ministry. His conciliatory but resolute appearance, clear goal orientation, the ability to compromise, and his positive basic attitude, which manifests itself in his open and humorous personality, makes Randolph soon a widely popular colleague and negotiating partner. After only one year, Randolph is promoted from his position as head of unit to department head.

REASONS FOR CAREER UNHAPPINESS

If you are unhappy with your career, you better do some soul-searching to find out whether your unhappiness could possibly be related to yourself. That means that reasons for your unhappiness could be factors that affect your personal sense of happiness. For instance, you could feel undervalued in your current job; or you're working in a field that doesn't match your talents; or you feel uncomfortable working in a hierarchy, and would prefer to be your own boss.

TOO YOUNG TO CHOOSE

An important point of career unhappiness could be that you were not aware of what you were getting involved in when you made your first career choices at a young age. At that time, you very likely had neither the necessary experience, nor the relevant information to make such an important decision. By doing this, you have exposed yourself to the risk of only finding out what you really want through a painful or frustrating trial-and-error process.

Example: Under the influence of a conservative family member, Tony, who was just nineteen years old, decided to study law. As Tony had a creative mind, his alternative would have been to study art or join a communication agency as a trainee and rise to senior positions over the course of the years. But Tony was insecure and the influence of his family member was strong so he decided to study law, though with little enthusiasm. Later, during the first years of his legal career, Tony quickly realized that his profession did not attract him at all. He began to regret the decision he had made at the age of nineteen and wished he had made a different choice for a more creative profession, less dominated by dogmatic principles and controversy.

As mentioned in this example, it can happen that your career path might have been predetermined by someone else's choice and not by your true preferences. In this case, the risk is high, that though you successfully completed your studies, you still might think you had done the wrong thing and feel unhappy in your career.

Frequently, it is the parents or other people with influence on you who decide what kind of profession you should learn. This also can lead to career unhappiness, especially when the work you do has become a kind of duty rather than something you can thoroughly enjoy.

Example: Barbara had an above-average artistic talent. From an early age she had excelled in painting and drawing, and her parents thought she should go to the local Fine Arts School to become an artist. But Barbara decided differently. Discouraged by a talented artist friend who was hardly able to earn his living with the very good art he produced, Barbara decided to study something more 'practical' or 'economical' which would generate income instead of pursuing her passion. Barbara feared that, like her artist friend, she would never make it to the top. 'My talent is not big enough,' she said and worked all her professional life in offices rather than in studios. Years later, looking back, Barbara was unhappy with her decision. She applied for a place at the local art school but they let her know that she was too old to be admitted as a student.

NO TRAINING

Another reason for career unhappiness can also be that you are not able to get trainings and re-trainings. In case you feel like you could be achieving more, but there is a lack of training or skill improvement, it's time for you to enhance your personal abilities and sign up for education courses or look for seminars offered by your organization or professional training organizations. If your organization responds to your training request by telling you that they can't afford to train their employees, you should ask how they can afford it *not* to train. Career happiness can very much depend on employer-based development opportunities. They can influence how motivated employees are, how hard they work, and how long they want to stay with a company.

> An investment in education always pays the highest returns.
>
> —Benjamin Franklin, British–American polymath and one of the Founding Fathers of the US

In addition to improving employees' skills, developing and training employees has an important psychological effect. Employees who are regularly trained, tend to have better self-esteem and increased self-worth, and feel encouraged to grow. In addition, they feel empowered to take a more active role and are happier with themselves, which concerns their workplace and the career path. Consequently, this is helping improve performance and increase quality, productivity, efficiency, and creativity.

BEING TRAPPED

Some people are unhappy in their current career position, because they feel trapped or like they have 'hit the ceiling' in their organization. The trapped feeling or 'hitting the ceiling' feelings are typical for people who are unhappy because they were moved up the professional ladder rather quickly, and suddenly find themselves unmotivated because there are few new professional challenges left.

Their professional life has not only become a matter of routine but, in addition, lack of prospects for further advancement and new challenging tasks makes them feel depressed, demotivated, uninspired, and unhappy.

> I don't think I would be a writer if I had stayed in Chile. I would be trapped in the chores, in the family, in the person that people expected me to be.
>
> —Isabel Allende, Chilean writer and lifetime refugee

In case the organization has the policy to use career development plans for all employees, the employee who feels trapped and is unhappy about it can ask their boss to have a discussion about their personal career on basis of the plan (although with a plan installed, such a situation should ideally not occur).

Explanation: A career development plan is a document that lists the short-, mid-, and long-term goals that employees have pertaining to their current and future positions within the organization. It can help superiors support employees in gaining new skills and grow, while adding value to the organizations. It also guides employees to move forward in their careers.

If the organization does not use career development plans, the employee who is unhappy with his career development should propose its introduction. For instance, he could take the initiative and bring his draft plan to the meeting with his boss. His boss should be able to understand that it is in the company's interest to have such plans as it normally wants to retain its employees.

In principle, the alternative for the company is either to introduce such a plan and, by doing this, demonstrate to the employees that they care about their career goals within the organization, or rather let the employees believe they need to leave the company if they want to pursue their individual career goals.

Another option for the frustrated employee's discussion with his boss would be to propose that he will be assigned new responsibilities, take on extra responsibilities, or to move to a different position, even if this wouldn't result in a promotion.

It could be the case that your supervisor is not even aware that you are looking for a new challenge. He may have noticed that you are doing your job well, which would trigger the usual reaction that he wants to keep you there. Thus, it is you who has to take the initiative and let your supervisor know about your continued ambition.

Example: You are a PR executive and have had great success in your company. One day, and at a relatively young age, you are appointed to the board of your company. However, what initially looked like a great success for you turned out to be a disadvantage for your career. This quick promotion to the highest (board) level in the company can be a disadvantage when you are relatively young. After all, there are no more opportunities for growth left within the company because your own specialization makes it very unlikely that you will be moved horizontally into other positions at the same hierarchical level. So, you are trapped in your position even though, in theory because of your age, you have at least one or two career steps ahead of you.

In such a case, the only conceivable alternative seems to be leaving the company.

It's only out of reach when you choose to keep your feet flat on the floor.

—Lana M.H. Wilder, American writer

FRUSTRATED AMBITION

In addition to the previously discussed reasons for career unhappiness, professional ambition can also become the cause for dissatisfaction when it gets frustrated. Simply put, the driving force that pushes you forward to achieve what you want is your personal ambition. Ambition is not negative and has no negative impact on your state of happiness. On the contrary, it can help to make you happy.

However, you should be aware that ambition can turn from a desirable asset into a trap. This can happen when your ambition gets excessive.

Example: Throughout his early life, Eric, a young trainee, had been encouraged by his parents, teachers, and coaches to strive for more. So far, Eric's career was characterized by excellent grades at school and university, academic awards and an almost problem-free career start. His bosses had been impressed by his performance. However, they criticized Eric for not being a team player. He always wanted to be No. 1. Team goals were no priority for Eric unless they served his personal goals. Eric soon got the reputation that for achieving his ambitious goals, he would throw 'people under the bus'. Eric, who thought very highly of himself, was unhappy, because his career did not advance as expected. Instead of blaming himself for his failures, he started to blame others.

If Eric would be more sensitive to the impact of his attitude and actions on others, he would start to realize that he was pushing too hard, destroying relationships, and becoming isolated as a result of his egomaniac behaviour. Management is generally more interested in smooth teamwork than in ambitious loners, even if they have as many credentials as they like.

Example: Organizations can best be compared to a cogwheel system in that cogwheels work as a unified system for operating a machine. In such a system, small and large toothed wheels rotate and are interlocked with each other. If within such a system there are cogwheels that turn either too fast (e.g., smart or overly ambitious people) or too slow (e.g., unintelligent and lazy employees) than the other cogwheels, the whole cogwheel system (e.g., the company) stops working and comes to a standstill.

This example illustrates that excessive ambition can lead to a trap, especially if it's based on a winner-take-all attitude and ignoring the interest of the whole. As in a cogwheel system, the excessively ambitious person, with their selfish behaviour, brings the whole system to a grinding halt, thereby damaging the whole and ultimately themselves.

REGAINING CONTROL

If you are unhappy about your career development, you should think first about your personal capacity to exert influence over your career before you seek help from others. This can be done (discussed in more detail in the section on 'No Training'), by broadening the spectrum of possible career options through self-initiated training. This will make you more attractive to your current company or possible alternative employers.

Otherwise, you should try and retake control of your own career. An option to do this would be to spend some time to inventory your strengths and compare them with what you really want to be and what you want to achieve. To save yourself from unrealistic desires and self-assessments, you could ask close confidants to help you with this by giving you their honest opinion. But what should guide you in any case is the insight that you enjoy your work most when you do things that you like to do because you have interest, talent, and a good eye for them.

Before you become specific and choose certain activities, you should make a basic decision and choose the general character of activities you are most interested in. This decision is about the areas that best suit your abilities and wishes.

Example: Do you want to work in an area that requires creativity, or are you more a talented inventor, or more of an organizational or administrative type? Do you find it easy to do practical or technical work hands-on, or are you more of a theorist? Are you gifted in strategic thinking or more of a 'mover and doer' who puts strategies into action? Do you love helping others? Do you have a legal mind? Do you enjoy being challenged by problems and like to solve them hands-on? Do you like to travel frequently? Do you like politics? Do you mind being planned for the foreseeable future and having a full agenda or are you frightened by it because you feel threatened in your personal freedom? Can you imagine a career where you have to get up early in the morning and come back late at night every day and still feel passionate about it? Do you feel great to make your community and the world healthier, and if your work helps to protect plants, animals, and the environment in general?

If you make a decision for yourself in one of these fields, you'll automatically exclude a large number of specific job opportunities, which may save you from making wrong decisions that can make you unhappy in the course of your career.

Example: Griffin loved his girlfriend Tutu. They were both very young and liked partying and having fun with their group of like-minded friends. Griffin loved, in particular, to cook together with Tutu at home. He soon discovered that he had a special liking for baking and showed great talent which Tutu appreciated. Therefore, Griffin spontaneously agreed with great enthusiasm when Tutu suggested to him to become a professional baker. However, Griffin's initial enthusiasm quickly evaporated when he was confronted with the daily routine of a professional baker. When making his decision, Griffin had only thought about the fun of baking but had missed to inform himself about the circumstances under which a professional baker has to work. In particular, he had not been aware of the fact that bakers have to be in the bakery at three o'clock in the morning to ensure that fresh rolls are on the table for the customers' breakfast, even at weekends. Griffin soon started to resent that his friends were still partying when, for him, the working day had long since begun.

ALTERNATIVE OPTIONS

Even if your career might not be ideal and even if your job isn't what you hoped for, there's still a positive message: You might still be happy. You just need to realize that you have a job in a world where having a job is not necessarily a matter of course and that the income you derive from your activity is paying your bills.

In addition, and even if you are unhappy with your career, your current job still offers you a basis for meeting new people, networking, and provides you with a better chance to seek for alternative occupations than being home. This consideration should make you grateful for what you have and might be used to feel happy.

Example: For almost five years, James, a bright ambitious young diplomat, worked at his country's foreign ministry. He wasn't happy with his career development so far. No matter how good his performance was, it seemed to be ignored. James blamed the country's bureaucracy, nepotism, and the traditional seniority system for his frustration. He often thought about quitting the diplomatic service and starting something new where his talents would be better used. One day, however, James realized that his frustration was not caused by his slow career but by his way of looking at it. In fact, he was proud of having been given an opportunity to serve his country which he loved. After he had started taking another perspective, James realized how lucky he was to have his current job. So, instead of continuously lamenting about the lack of career growth, he decided to improve himself. He started to invest in his advanced studies, learn foreign languages, improve his network, and gain more experience. This would give him a chance to react quickly when the opportunity would arise to make a major step forward in his career.

However, if there really is no other option but to quit your job and seek your fortune elsewhere, then you should resist the temptation to constantly think about the mistakes you have made in your past and that may have brought you into the unfortunate situation of career unhappiness. In particular, you should not engage in daydreaming or blaming others; for instance, your parents for your wrong career choice.

You should understand that such an attitude will lead you to a dead end and make you depressed. It would be better if you could rather focus all of your energies on developing alternative options.

> Why join a navy if you can be a pirate?
>
> —Steve Jobs, Apple CEO

One possible way to dissuade you from backward-looking thoughts is through activities outside of work that will give you fulfilment and which you hope will give you a new, positive impetus that will carry over to your (future) workplace.

Example: In his current job, Robin primarily looks after difficult-to-raise children from problem-families. Currently, he is unhappy with his job because most of his educational achievements with the children in his class are counteracted or even destroyed by the children's parents when they return home to their parents after school. In addition to this frustration, Robin doesn't see any career opportunities in his current position. After some careful consideration, Robin decides to take on a volunteer activity in an association that looks after male immigrants who are difficult to integrate. He does this to balance himself out and if he would quit his current job, to have a meaningful occupation as a bridge before finding a new position. In his volunteer work, Robin sees the opportunity to bring in the knowledge and skills he has acquired so far from working with children. In addition, he also combines personal interests with his commitment as it offers him new opportunities to expand his qualification from helping children to adult education. In addition to feeling happy for doing something for the common good, Robin hopes to gain some own benefit, for instance, by balancing out his current career unhappiness and by adding to his professional development.

This example demonstrates that in situations where you are unhappy about your career, you should not let yourself get hung up. Instead, to fill the vacuum, you should vigorously counter your daily frustrations with other activities that are (more) meaningful. This will not only help you to overcome your career unhappiness but will also help mitigating its effects on you and distract you, so you have a chance to find your lost energy and work on your career.

Example: Jan, a Belgian national, worked as a junior executive in an American multinational company. After several years of hard work, he realized that as a non-US national, he had fewer chances to develop professionally than his American colleagues. He began to show signs of career unhappiness. Jan knew he had to do something about it. In the long term, that meant looking for a new job. In the short term, he had to find a balance in order not to fall into a role that was characterized by complaints, criticism, and pessimism. Since he had an artistic talent, he began to paint. Soon, he had made enough paintings to make exhibitions. Although not all of his art works were commercial successes, just the fact that his art was exhibited and presented was a success in itself and made Jan happy.

The perceived happiness Jan felt as a result, radiated on to his entire being so that despite his career unhappiness, he was perceived as a forward-looking, optimistic person. That helped him find a new job.

ORGANIZATIONAL UNHAPPINESS

NO PRIDE

In addition to being accepted and appreciated at work by your boss and your colleagues and being happy with your career path, there are some key factors affecting your job satisfaction and your happiness at work. One of them is your pride in the organization and its products, but beyond this, also the whole industry in which your company operates.

Example: You are employed as an accountant at a company that is a global leader in genetically engineered food. Your company's chemical engineers design fruit and vegetables using genetically modified organisms to be more nutritious, taste better, and make them more resistant to diseases. There is a lot of controversy over the risks of genetically engineered foods. For instance, some of your friends took a quite radical position on the safety of genetically modified foods. Although you were just an accountant—neither a chemical engineer nor a top manager in your company—they confronted you aggressively with their concerns. The last debate you had got heated when your friends accused you of complicity with your company and pushed you to leave the company for moral and ethical reasons. The continuous barrage of your friends wasn't without effect on you. Under the impression of their arguments, your doubts grew. You began to feel unhappy working for the company because you thought you could no longer reconcile their activity with your own clean conscience. If you were honest to yourself, you knew that you would have preferred to work in a company that was not in this particular industry.

Notwithstanding whether your company manufactures products that pollute the air, cheat consumers, advertise food for children which is unhealthy, or whether you are working as a staffer for a government which is engaging in questionable political conspiracies, the fact that something is morally, ethically, or even legally questionable can make you feel unhappy in your position. Ideally, you would like to be proud of your company and the industry it operates in, or take pride in a government which works for the benefit of the people. In this ideal situation, you would feel happy about your job as you could attribute a sense of purpose and meaning to your own activity, even if limited to a specific field.

> Without self-respect, genuine happiness is scarcely possible. And the man who is ashamed of his work can hardly achieve self-respect.
>
> —Bertrand Russell, British pacifist and philosopher

BAD WORK CULTURE

BAD CORPORATE CULTURE

A crucial question for company management is how the commitment of employees in the company can be continually promoted and maintained. Employees who, as previously discussed, feel happy in their industry sector, but above all in their company and in their individual workplace, are committed, motivated, and produce quality. Therefore, the company management must create the conditions under which the employees feel happy.

These conditions are created through the development of an employee-oriented company culture with a distinctive work quality that serves as the basis for sustained happiness of the employees.

Corporate culture is an amalgam of an organization's values, ethics, vision, behaviours, and work environment. It is what makes each company unique, and it impacts everything from public image to employee engagement and retention. For instance, corporate cultures can be characterized as conventional or risk-averse, progressive as it is for companies in transition, hierarchical (top–down) or horizontal (collaborative, team-focused) cultures, elite culture featuring highly talented people who will go beyond traditional limits, or team-oriented corporate cultures.

In an ideal world, employees share their company's ethics and vision that can positively affect a company's bottom line. Companies with good corporate culture often have high workplace morale and a highly engaged, productive staff. It is, therefore, not surprising that when searching for a new job, people take corporate culture as importantly as salary, benefits, and designation. People know that a culture that fits their style of work, their values and expectations, can help them to be happy in their job.

In contrast to a good corporate culture, a toxic corporate culture is characterized by emotional, mental, and psychological stress, frequently generated by excessive management control, such as a surplus in internal reporting requirements, morally questionable environments, lack of management integrity, the encouragement of dishonesty, unreasonable pressure to get short-term results at the expense of the long-term strategy goals, inequity, unfairness, favouritism, injustice, disrespect and belittlement, lack of empathy, appreciation, and support, any form of harassment and bullying.

Example: William, a young lawyer, fresh from university, proudly accepted a job offer from a renowned law firm. In the law firm, it was customary, that once a week, all professional and clerical staff would gather in the conference room to discuss the most interesting pending legal cases. Each lawyer was invited to present his most interesting case and was expected to briefly outline how he intended to win it. The more senior attorneys who were present would take this opportunity to attack each lawyer in a bid to denounce their legal argument. For those presenting, these sessions were always a kind of spit-routing. When it was William's turn, he found it embarrassing to be criticized in the presence of all his colleagues. But most of all, he felt particularly unhappy about getting cross-examined in front of the clerical staff, including the secretary, who admired him the most.

To improve corporate culture for making employees happy at work, many companies must better understand the potential and the power that they have to create good, happy work cultures which make people engage, commit, and stay motivated.

Example: Some companies have realized that perks such as office refrigerators with free drinks, cycle-to-work schemes, gym passes and yoga classes, and half-price cinema tickets, are not enough anymore to make employees feel happier at work. Instead, more creative ideas such as 'team plastic waste collection campaigns' or regular 'donation campaigns' for charities and aid projects, or voluntary activities to help those in need, are better perceived by employees searching for more happiness than additional perks.

Successful managers fix toxic cultures to uncover the untapped potential of the employees for the company. These leaders listen, appreciate, involve, and empower their workforce and act as supportive mentors. They know that happy employees are at the heart of every successful organization, and thus its most valuable asset.

> The mind will not learn until the heart has been touched.
>
> —S. Madigan, Canadian therapist

BAD WORKPLACE CONDITIONS

What has just been said for corporate culture also applies to the conditions at the individual workplaces.

Workplace conditions are as important for the happiness of employees as the more general corporate culture. Workplace conditions govern the daily experience of an employee. They include, for instance, the intensity and hours of daily work, working schedules including shift work schedules and length of shifts, the degree of employee autonomy at the workplace, the empowerment culture in which no employee feels undervalued and can act regardless of position (to make constructive contributions and are trusted to take accountability over the projects for which they are qualified), performance management, the quality of controls especially when controls start to become an administrative burden or needless paternalism, healthy and safe work environments, and the management of workplace conflicts.

Example: Tipsy was a young software engineer and worked for a start-up on their software development team. Tipsy was very devoted to her work, and she appreciated the freedom that the company allowed her to write a specific computer programming language autonomously. This trust in her ability had kept her passion for the job and made her happy throughout the course of her employment.

In contrast to a good workplace environment, a toxic workplace can only develop when those in charge are allowed to exercise unjust rule over the workforce and operate an outdated 'command and control' style of coercive management.

KEY FOR HAPPINESS IS COMMUNICATION

With regard to both corporate culture and workplace culture, effective professional (internal/employee) communication is required. Poor communication can become a major source of anger; it has a negative impact on job satisfaction and happiness at work.

Ironically, in our highly communicative, interconnected world, it is surprising that poor communication is still an issue for some companies.

Example: A photograph supposedly showing an internal training slide from a famous NASDAQ company started to circulate on social media. The slide noted that a well-known US-government representative's election slogan was a 'political' slogan unacceptable within the company. Because, at the same time, the slogan of a civil rights group was tolerated by the company, the US-government representative argued that the slide discriminated against his election campaign slogan. He called for a boycott against the company. This forced the company to release official statements explaining the company's policy with regards to political expression and denied that the incriminated slide was official. The company explained in its statements that its zero tolerance policy allowed workers to express support on equity issues, but not political campaigns. The company's internal communication behaviour was poor as it forced the company to explain something which should have been crystal clear from the beginning given the proven sensitivity of the issue. This poor communication put the company into a weak position.

This example shows that poor internal (employee) communication had a major impact on the employees. They are unhappy about being dragged into the limelight as working for a company that is publicly brand-marked and threatened with a boycott, but also its the consequences. For instance, the shares of their employer fell after the quality of their products were publicly diminished without proof. The employees working for this company must fear for their jobs as sales may go down as a result of the public call for boycott and negative comments.

Today, employees consider effective internal communication to be a vital part of their company experience. With the emergence of the internet, highly effective search engines and social media, people expect the right information to come to them when they need it, instead of having to look for it as in the past.

Example: Before 1990, every information was printed, filed, processed, and distributed on paper (paper copy, telex, fax). Employees who wanted to find information had to engage in a slow and painstaking manual search process.

A company practising poor internal communication will soon lose its employees' motivation and morale quickly as they become unhappy with their jobs. Managers and executives who fail to communicate in an effective way will lose trust of their employees, which drags morale down even further and reduces employee engagement and happiness at work. The end result is a business of unengaged and unhappy employees who are eager to leave the company.

Tip: When you talk about poor communication, compare it with the situation you are in when you open your work emails only to find an unpleasant, accusatory message from a colleague or your boss. Most likely you will react with anger, frustration, or be otherwise upset. In case you previously had a positive relationship, this might now be strained. This is a similar reaction to what employees feel when it comes to poor internal communication.

Poor internal communication can lead to stress with all the negative consequences on happiness at work. This is particularly the case when poor (or no) communication adds to a feeling that everything is urgent, causing you and others to feel tense and overworked. Poor communication can also cause unmet expectations and frustration, for instance, when deadlines are missed or people working on a project do not seem to know what their priorities and roles are, or when the left hand doesn't know what the right hand is doing. Usually, people react to this situation by feeling poorly about their performance. In fact, as a result of poor communication, employees may not reach their former performance standards and/or their true potential.

Good internal communication has become even more important during the Covid pandemic. The crisis is forcing many people to work from home. Fortunately, with the recent advances in information technology and digital communication, the crisis-caused rise in remote and flexible working was manageable. However, in terms of professional internal communication with employees, there are still many organizational challenges that need to be solved. In addition to important security issues, this also includes the staff's equipment with the right tools to communicate and agreement on the preferred media platforms and channels to be used.

In summary, in consideration of the importance of employee happiness at work, effective professional employee communication can no longer be an option for management but has to be a *must* as a competitive element in an increasingly competitive world.

TRENDY: CHIEF HAPPINESS OFFICER AND HAPPINESS CONSULTANT

This trend is confirmed by the decision of some cutting-edge companies who have started to realize that work and employment are an important source of personal satisfaction and employee happiness at work. In response to that challenge, they have created the new position of a Chief Happiness Officer (CHO).

Job Description: The CHO is the person in a company who is responsible for happiness levels within the organization, in particular, well-being within work teams and at the workplace.

Other companies didn't want to follow this example but hired external happiness consultants instead to do the task of the CHO.

> A consultant is someone who, when hired to find out what time it is, borrows your watch to find out.
>
> —Unknown

To better illustrate the task of a CHO or happiness consultant, these are some typical questions employees were asked as part of their individual happiness assessment: 'What positive influence does your work have on you as a person?' 'What do you want to do in your job?' 'How do you fall in love with what you do every day at work?' 'Who do you want to be?', and 'How do you want to be seen in your working environment by your boss and your colleagues?'

Whether CHO or happiness consultant, this trend to lift the issue of happiness to board level clearly shows that companies are beginning to take the happiness of their employees in the workplace seriously and take steps to promote it.

Example: This trend is particularly evident in France, where 250 mostly large companies such as the cosmetics group L'Oréal or the major bank

BNP Paribas, have joined a special CHO club within a short time. They explained their interest saying France has a lot of catching up to do in terms of corporate culture because it is still dependent on rigid hierarchies and a culture of grading and ranking that makes many people's happiness solely dependent on their boss.

WORKLOAD AND OVERTIME

> Hard work spotlights the character of people: Some turn up their sleeves, some turn up their noses, and some don't turn up at all.
>
> —Sam Ewing, American sportsman

As discussed in the section 'Organizational Happiness', corporate culture and work culture at the individual workplace are important environmental elements influencing an employee's happiness at work. It is one of the company management's key responsibilities to create workplace conditions that make employees happy. Part of the workplace conditions which govern the employees' daily experience are the intensity and hours of daily work and working schedules. If management fails to organize your working environment appropriately, it can be characterized by permanent heavy workloads and, as a consequence, severely overworked employees who face continuous habitual overtime work.

Example: Aaron worked for a small digital games company. The company was poorly managed. The two directors constantly fought each other, made conflicting decisions, frequently changed priorities, failed to assign clear responsibilities, didn't plan appropriately, and seemed not to know what they really wanted. Despite the chaotic management style, Aaron liked the company because of its interesting innovative product range and its high potential in the market. In addition, the company paid him an above-industry-average salary. For these reasons, Aaron accepted an excessively high workload, frequent frustration caused by wasted work due to one of the directors' change of mind, and many hours of unpaid overtime. However, when his girlfriend Nicole said he was more attached to his job than to her and when he realized he couldn't sleep anymore because of a continued splitting headache and relentless nervousness, he got worried. Until then, he had believed that his dedication to the company made sense but, looking at it more closely, he realized that the company exploited his dedication to his job. His two directors had never asked him about his private life or his well-being, they had never worried about his growing work burden, or the many extra hours spent in front of his screens. They simply seemed to take his constant availability for granted. The following weekend, Aaron didn't go to his workplace as usual but invited Nicole for an outdoor lunch. After the coffee, he said with a smile, 'Time for change.' It took Nicole a minute to understand what he meant but then she gave him a big kiss in response.

Long working hours, tight deadlines, and ever-increasing demands by your boss can leave you feeling severely overwhelmed, overworked, drained, and worried. If you spend every moment working or thinking about work, you will have no time for sleep, family, friends, leisure activities, entertainment, or exercise. This is when your stress can exceed your ability to cope and when it starts causing damage to your mind, your health, your work quality, your job satisfaction, and your happiness at work.

This can also be the case when the organization you are working for is known for its good corporate culture. Frequently, the high workplace morale, and the engaged, productive staff of such a company is exploited to the employees' disadvantage by increasing the work burden and letting them work overtime.

Although everyone seems to know about their impact, heavy workloads and overtime still belong to those factors that are lauded because they are believed to be indicators of a dedicated, hardworking employee.

The employee motives for accepting increasingly heavy workloads and work longer hours can be manifold; for instance, personal career ambitions, pressure to perform to meet rising management expectations, growing workload due to staff cutbacks, fear of being laid off, or management pressure to work constantly at optimum levels.

However, the perception of workload can be different. For instance, some employees can feel free from physical and mental stress even though they do a lot of overtime work. This can be the case, when the work is not imposed upon them but self-imposed, may be because they love their work.

This positive subjective perception does not change the impact, which long hours, for instance, may have on the employee's social life, their personal relationships, and family life. In a happy relationship, the spouse will usually demand attention and children need to be looked after by their parents. Therefore, it will be the employee's family that will suffer from their absences and, in the long run, likely react negatively with effects on everybody's happiness.

For these reasons, even if the employee accepts the work burden and overtime for personal reasons, they must acknowledge that nobody can reasonably work substantial overtime on a daily basis and over a long time without compromising private life—notably the family—sleep, and health. It remains a fact that in this case, private life and happiness at home is sacrificed to the job.

> You should not confuse your career with your life.
>
> —Dave Barry, American author.

Another reason why an employee may engage in overtime can be peer pressure.

Example: Vic was a corporate internal auditor working in a team of twelve other auditors for a big multinational company. She was highly motivated in her job and managed her work well although her workload was growing continuously due to the aggressive expansion of the company's business into many new foreign countries. Vic had a small family and was always happy when she could finish in time to join her husband and her daughter at home. So far, Vic had managed to do her work according to schedule and felt totally okay at close of business. But recently, the situation had changed. Vic observed that many of her colleagues had started to

constantly work overtime. Some even took work home, came back to the workplace on weekends, or, in one case, even cancelled vacation plans to finalize a job. Since she seemed to be the only auditor on the team who managed the given workload during office hours, she felt a bit embarrassed viz-à-viz her colleagues every night when she left. This went on for a longer time, and Vic's insecurity was growing. She started to feel somewhat guilty to be the only one who was leaving in time at night. Vic felt an unspoken pressure by her peers to do the same and also work longer hours though she was perfectly able to manage her workload in the given time. Finally, Vic gave in to the unspoken pressure, made a longer lunch break, placed some more private telephone calls during the day, and stayed later than required. From a pure work standpoint, it was not necessary but Vic felt more comfortable in her group. Her husband and her daughter were not happy with her decision but she calmed them down by saying that it would only be temporary.

Some people argue that it's just 'this one job' or 'this one project' that makes them work long hours and promise to return to normal when the job is done. Others tolerate the situation as long as they can, for instance to avoid the possibility of a conflict with their superior. This may turn out to be an error, as your management may get used to your higher 'output' and continue swamping you with work. There is also a risk that you will continue working overtime as overwork can become addictive.

> I've heard that hard work never killed anyone, but I say why take the chance?
>
> —Ronald Reagan, Former US president

Work addiction is rightly also called workaholism because someone has an uncontrollable need to work constantly (workaholic) and has symptoms comparable to those of an alcoholic.

Workaholism is signalled when you are spending more time working than intended, you are ignoring suggestions or requests from others to cut down on work, or you feel that your self-worth is (solely) dependent from your exposure to work. You may also use overtime work as a distraction from other issues or challenges in your personal life, such as relationship problems, depression, anxiety, hopelessness, or guilt.

Like alcoholism, work addiction can be a real problem, especially when it starts to interfere with the private life of a person. This is the case when workaholics shift most of their attention to the job and disregard their relationships, family, and friends in a way that it negatively affects them and their activities outside of work. This is when workaholics become unhappy because their work-related stress may no longer be outbalanced by an intact private life.

Example: Robin is an accountant. He lives with his wife in a small apartment on the outskirts of the city. On week days, he commutes by streetcar to his workplace which is far away. When his wife has a baby, he can't stand it anymore in the small apartment. The disorder caused by the baby, the fact that he is no longer the centre of his wife's interest, the frequent yelling, and the unfamiliar smells drive him crazy. He begins to stay longer at work and only comes home late. Sometimes, he even spends his weekends in the office. His boss welcomes Robin's extra time in the office and assigns more and more work to him, knowing that Robin has no problem with overtime. Even when the family is out of the woods, Robin does not change his habits and stays in the office longer than his colleagues. But this time, the reason for his willingness to work overtime is different: The boss has promised to make him chief accountant if he maintains his 'positive attitude' towards his work. Although Robin is actually tired of overtime and wants to return to a normal family life, it is now his ambition that drives him forward. Robin's wife has little understanding of her husband's behaviour and feels alone and unhappy. Her disgruntlement and criticism give Robin another reason for avoiding home. The result is that Robin and his family are unhappy with each other.

Company managers may appreciate employees who accept heavy work burdens and work long hours. But they may overlook the negative effects coming from this when practiced long term.

Long hours and work overload may even backfire on companies that cause or tolerate it. What companies may ignore in these cases is the fact is that high performance at work can only be expected from those employees who were able to strike a balance between their work and private lives. They must be given the opportunity to rest and rejuvenate after working hours and during holidays, for instance by engaging in family activities, seeing friends, doing leisure or hobby activities, political or charitable work.

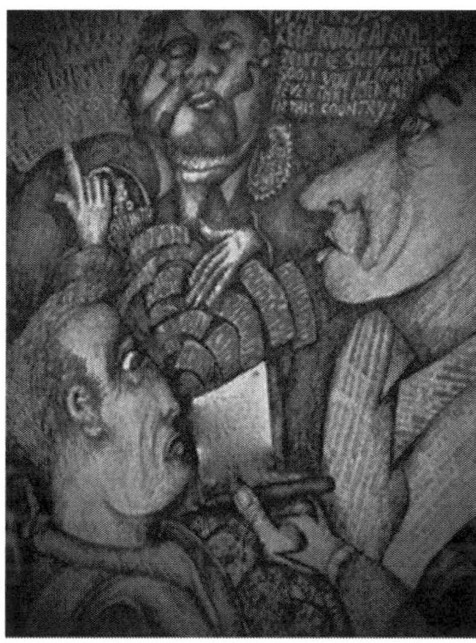

There are plenty of things overworked people can do to reduce their overall stress levels and regain their happiness.

In a situation where workload and overtime put unacceptable stress on you and begin to interfere with your work performance, health, and private life, you are not powerless, even when you are part of a hierarchical structure. Then it's time to see your boss. Your boss may be very busy himself and might not have realized the volume of your workload. Then your discussion should be used to open your boss's eyes to the unbearable situation.

It would be helpful to watch your tone in your discussion with your boss. You should not go and see him just to complain or to say a flat 'No' in response to added work, new responsibilities, or tougher deadlines. It would be better if you would propose reasonable options which could help to improve the organization, prioritization, and distribution of work.

Tip: You should use the same discussion tactics, as discussed before for 'toxic' workers, by manoeuvring the issue away from you personally and, instead, to an overriding value. This means that you transform your criticism of the circumstances leading to excessive workloads and overtime into a positive contribution to the well-being of the company. For instance, you could refer to the company's interest in highly motivated, happy employees who are more apt to produce quality than employees who are working under permanent stress and are severely overworked.

Example: Manuel was severely overworked. When he saw no end of the tunnel, he decided to see his boss.

Alternative 1: Manuel complained about the ever-increasing workload and the unfair distribution of work in the team. He added that he was close to collapsing under the excessive work burden and illustrated his misery by talking at length about his family and how much they were suffering from his stress. Then he asked his boss to do something about it. His boss listened to him and responded: The whole industry and the company is under pressure. Globalization and the market entry of some powerful foreign competitors from low-cost countries made it necessary to increase productivity dramatically. This has an effect on each individual employee. The company management was expecting all employees to contribute to helping the company survive global competition. He urged Manuel to critically review his own efficiency in order to identify and eliminate 'waste' activities and make his own work processes more efficient. At his next performance review, this would be in the centre of discussion. Manuel had not convinced his boss. He had argued in his personal interest and was dismissed.

Alternative 2: Manuel had prepared himself well for this discussion and brought some charts. He could demonstrate that the increased workload was distributed unfairly between the team members. He also showed his boss that the efficiency of the team could be improved, by taking some items off from the current list of priorities and by reducing a number of time-consuming but not essential reporting requirements. Manuel even took the courage to ask for the addition of one specialized manpower because he could demonstrate that the work of this one individual would free up three other members of the team to do alternative, more essential work. His boss listened very carefully to Manuel's proposals and they engaged in a serious discussion about each individual issue. Manuel's boss had understood that Manuel wasn't lamenting about his personal situation but making serious proposals for improvement which went beyond his personal interest. He promised to implement Manuel's ideas without delay.

Tip: However, be cautious when you talk to your boss about overtime. Your boss may show himself impressed by what you say and promise a reduction in overtime work hours. This will not make you happier unless he also addresses other, connected stress-at-work components such as the amount of work. If you don't watch it you may leave your boss's office with a promise regarding overtime, but find yourself back with the same amount or even more work to be done in less time.

Ideally, your boss should respond to your ideas, by giving you some guidance on how and what to prioritize, and what deadlines could be spaced out a bit more.

FEELING UNDERPAID

> Question: 'What is the secret to staying thin?'
> Response: 'Minimum wage.'

Many people find themselves in the predicament of being overworked and, at the same time, underpaid. Your happiness might get affected by your feeling that you are underpaid but it very much depends with whom you compare yourself, in which geographical region and how important happiness factors are for you in your current position which are not related to your pay.

Example: Donna was working in one of the leading consultancy firms as a junior consultant. Her superior gave her a lot of responsibility. He assigned a number of quite interesting client works to her and made her the leader of a team of twelve associate consultants. Initially, Donna enjoyed the job. She felt motivated and challenged and her boss gave her positive performance appraisals at her annual performance reviews. On these occasions, he told her he was happy to give her a 10 per cent salary increase because she was one of the absolute top performers and key players in the department. However, after being close to three years on the job, Donna found out through discussions with colleagues that she was still in the lower part of the salary range. Donna reacted with anger and frustration and felt that her work was appreciated but not she. Actually, she felt cheated. In addition, she was upset about some other factors which didn't please her anymore, such as some toxic colleagues, the hierarchical thinking, the frequent traveling which consumed a big chunk of her private time, and foremost, the many overtime hours. Donna wanted to check her 'market value' and started to have some interviews. To her surprise she found out very quickly that she could change employers for a job with less travel and no overtime at almost 45 per cent more salary.

If you feel underpaid for the work that you are doing, it's probably making you feel unhappy, maybe less for the money but more for the fact that your work is not appreciated (see section on 'No Appreciation for Your Work', above).

Whether you are really not rewarded fairly or you just feel overworked and unappreciated for your extra work can be found out relatively easily by personal comparisons with others in similar positions, in the same industry and in similar areas of responsibility. The best way for you to bring you up to date is to take a look at the current job market, and start sending out job applications for current job openings, or to research job-seeker platforms. The results may confirm your suspicion that you are underpaid or, alternatively surprise you by telling you that you are well paid and matching industry standards.

The question of whether employees are right to feel unhappy when they are underpaid has nothing to do with the question of whether money in general would make people happy. Money is an objective measurement and reward for performance and success. That is the reason why the topic of 'fair pay' is of great importance for people who 'sell' their services and expertise in exchange for money. The question of the amount of compensation and its 'fairness' is, therefore, directly related to satisfaction, well-being, and happiness, or vice versa, to resentment, frustration, demotivation, and unhappiness.

If money as such will not make you happier per se, it definitely will make life for you a bit easier, especially if there is some money left at the month's end to do what you like outside the job. For instance, you can give your children a better education, eat healthier food, take a more comfortable hotel when going on vacation, move to a safer and more attractive part of your city, buy a house, and afford the mortgage.

Employees who feel underpaid despite working hard are right when they get stressed and unhappy about it because they perceive the fact of being underpaid as a message that their work is not appreciated or even noticed by their superiors (see the section on No-Appreciation of Your Work, above).

However, as mentioned, it is not only money but also other happiness factors that should be taken into consideration to assess whether you have reason to be unhappy in your current position. Consider the following example.

Example: Maryanne works as a nurse in a hospital. During the current Covid-19 pandemic, she had to work literally day and night. Her commitment in terms of time, responsibility, professionalism, challenge, dedication, energy, and risk during the peak of the pandemic was out of proportion to her deplorable salary. She was not happy about it but not bitter either, because for several weeks, a Red Cross nurse had volunteered at her side to do the same job as her. In her presence, Maryanne didn't dare to complain about her low pay. Not one word of complaint had passed her lips. Only when Maryanne heard the irresponsible and unrealistic statements of some top politicians on TV, a nasty curse word escaped her mouth.

This raises the question, what the true reward of work actually is. As shown in the example, value attributed to work by society because of its meaningfulness is certainly an important reward factor in addition to money. The same applies to opportunities for fulfilment and self-realization that can also produce happiness. This refers, in particular, to normally underpaid, primarily social professions such as nurses, rescue workers, and kindergarten staff but also other types of work such as voluntary work, commitment, or educational work which usually is found outside the typical gainful employment.

Although it is the first thing your mind might go to, requesting a raise might not always be the easiest and the most appropriate solution to get a pay raise for a number of reasons. Your industry and/or your company may be in a difficult economic and financial situation, your management is in the process of implementing structural changes that affect the organization, or your current pay matches your current market value.

Example: Max is a pilot with an international airline. He checked with some colleagues from other airlines and found out that his current salary was 25 per cent under market. When he decided to go and see his boss for a raise, the airline was forced to cancel 95 per cent of its scheduled flights due to tough travel restrictions governments had imposed to contain the pandemic. Max accepted that the time to ask for a raise was no longer appropriate.

Tip: Have an open and honest discussion with your manager. Tell them how much you love working in your current company and what you do. However, don't give them an ultimatum.

Tip: Before you go to see your boss for a pay raise, you should make some preparations for a discussion. This, however, will not be easy.

Tip: Do some research by consulting with specialized websites or asking for advice from your colleagues from the same industry to figure out what your market value work is at present and under the given economic and financial circumstances.

Tip: Before you go into the meeting with your boss, you should know how well the industry your company is operating in is performing, how well your company is doing against its main competitors, and how difficult it is in your region to find your special skills.

Tip: Don't go into the discussion with your boss with only a vague idea about a possible raise. Instead, be clear about what you want and mention a specific number or percentage rate. This will make negotiations easier. But be reasonable and keep in mind the raises which are considered appropriate.

Tip: Prepare a record of your accomplishments and share them with your boss at the meeting to show him the contributions you have made and how important they were for the achievement of the company's business objectives.

Tip: Be prepared that your boss will reject a pay increase but propose alternative options. For instance, cutting back on working hours instead, or making an offer for more vacation days, or taking a financial stake in the company. Another option could be that your boss will propose an alternative position in the company where your talents could be used and you could make a more effective contribution.

If you are being underpaid and if there is no room for a raise, then it's time for you to look into alternatives.

If your only chance to get a raise is to get a new job, you have to start applying. If your job search remains unsuccessful and you can't find a more lucrative position at another company, you might come to the conclusion, that, perhaps, you don't have the right credentials to earn the pay you seek. This could motivate you to engage in training or retraining activities to make your resume more attractive, or to enable you to become a freelancer in your field of expertise.

If you do not want to change the employer, you have to engage in stress-relieving activities such as exercise, yoga, meditations, hobbies that can or put more emphasis on the alternative reward factors that have the potential to reduce the feeling of being undervalued. Or, you could add to your personal sense of purpose by engaging in activities such as volunteer work.

BOREDOM AT WORK

> I'm not faking being sick, I'm faking being well.
>
> —Unknown

Like happiness, relationships, frustration, family, friends, work, and stress, boredom too is an important life experience. In principle, there is nothing wrong about boredom (at work). It's absolutely normal to be bored or to have a slow day at work every now and then. It is no longer normal, however, if you feel continuously bored at work and feel unhappy about it. In this case, boredom can't be dismissed as normal, or as a marginal or luxury problem but becomes an issue affecting your happiness at work.

> When you're at work and wondering if getting paid is even worth the bullshit.
>
> —Unknown

Boredom doesn't always mean having nothing to do. You can find employees in companies who have a lot of work to do and they are still bored because their tasks and/or their team may have become boring for them.

Example: Corporate restructuring and new job descriptions can lead to situations when formerly challenged employees become under-challenged. There are cases where employees are deliberately put in jobs where they have nothing to do, so that they eventually quit out of boredom. In other cases, there are people who are always on the go and quickly get bored with routine work and need something new in their lives, again and again. It may also be that simply feel that your current tasks no longer suit you.

Because, at work, you want to realize your potential and make sense through your work, always pretending to have something to do—even though you are under-challenged—can become very stressful. One could say you are actually putting on a show. But it's understandable that no one likes to admit that they have little or nothing meaningful to do.

MENTALLY UNDERCHALLENGED

When you feel bored at your job, you feel unchallenged by your daily work. The reasons for this can be insufficient intellectual under-challenge and idleness at the workplace; for instance, lack of focus and purpose at the workplace that prevents you from living out or developing your talents. In this case, your motivation can get frustrated, you might lose your self-confidence and self-efficacy due to the atrophy of your strengths, get disinterested, easily exhausted, suffer from frequent fatigue, and feel stressed and dissatisfied.

> Those who do not feel emotionally tied to their company show less initiative, willingness to perform and a sense of responsibility and are more often (seemingly) ill.
>
> —Unknown

For your company, your dissatisfaction at work has consequences because your performance is likely to decline when your mental workload is too low. Boredom at work does not only affect your job performance, but in many cases will also have some impact on your private life; for example, when you return home at night without energy and in a bad mood.

> I'm very busy doing things I don't need to do to avoid doing anything I'm actually supposed to be doing.
>
> —Unknown

HUMAN NEED FOR ACTIVE LIFE

Work is often associated with stress, but on the other hand, it challenges you to do things and achieve goals that convey feelings of happiness and joy of life. Actually, work corresponds to your natural urge to lead an active life and manifests itself as a planned, goal- and need-oriented activity.

When thinking about your job and job satisfaction, you should remind yourself that your job does not only serve you to earn your living, but also shapes your personal identity and lifestyle. You give a very large part of your lifetime to your job. And when you give big chunks of your time to something that you don't want, it can be very frustrating.

Example: Nick opens a jazz bar. He spends a lot of time, money, and creativity to make it a special place. Nick put something on offer but nobody wanted to go there. He was disappointed and hurt because he felt that he had wasted a big chunk of his lifetime on something nobody was interested in.

HOW TO BEAT BOREDOM AT WORK?

Some say that every crisis is also an opportunity. You could say the same about boredom at work and ask whether there are ways to use boredom or being under-challenged to your benefit.

For instance, in view of the boredom in your job, you could be cool by stepping back and pretending that it's not you who is concerned but a third party. This will allow you to take an unbiased, quasi-neutral view of your situation and help you find solutions. This would mean that you are not avoiding the subject of boredom but embracing it with the intention to move forward and not to let you further down.

Tip: Take a weekend, or a day off, or a vacation if necessary, to really think about what you wish you were doing and achieving at work.

For instance, you could start by asking yourself why you're actually feeling bored and what it is that doesn't feel fulfilling about your current work?

Then, you continue by exploring what it would be that really would make you happy. What are your interests? Is there anything that would still appeal to you professionally in your current area of activity? Have your preferences changed in the course of time and as a result of your growing experience? Would a mentally challenging activity in your free time perhaps ensure that your boredom at work would no longer bother you so much? Do you see opportunities for change at your current job, or would it be a better idea to look for a new job within or outside your company?

SELF-MOTIVATION IS KEY

When you're bored at work, it can be easy to blame the job, colleagues, your boss or the company for your misery.

Example: Goldie complains to her husband that after an internal reorganization in her department, her job has become boring and blames her director for not utilizing all her skills.

Independent from the cause of your boredom, developing your own initiative will help you be more motivated to look out for changes without blaming or relying on others to fix things for you.

Therefore, your self-motivation is of key importance in this phase in managing your boredom at work. This means always as a first step, you should think about what you could initiate or do on your own to fight boredom at work.

Example: Baden was thirty years old when he experienced the consequences of being under challenge at his workplace. He worked in the marketing department of a cosmetic products manufacturer. After three successful years in the luxury product business, Baden was transferred to the team of the mass products business. Superficially seen, this was a promotion because the mass business was the most profitable. But in reality, Baden was checkmated by her boss Diana who was jealous of his performance.

Previously, Baden had developed new product ideas and trend reports and successfully presented them both internally and externally. Now, in his new position, at best he was allowed to draft presentations, which Diana then gave to make a name for herself. The rest of his work was pretty much standard and administrative. Baden tried to keep his spirits up by motivating himself and getting engaged in new product projects, but Diana took them all away from him when they were in their last phase of development. His new work soon started to bore the hell out of him. Baden got disinterested in his job, his motivation went down and although his mental workload was low, he felt exhausted at night after spending hours in the office surfing the internet, playing online games, and reading gossip on social media. One night, at home, he watched a documentary about the pop singer Tina Turner in which she described how, after years of humiliation and violence by her husband Ike, she left him overnight and then started over again. Baden was inspired by her story used it as a role model and found a new job.

Self-motivation is the force that you can produce from within—autonomously and without external stimulus—which drives you to do the things you want to do.

Examples:

- Barbara is a student who only completes her homework because her parents force her to do it. She is not self-motivated.
- Danny is a student who completes his homework with no prodding because he wants to learn and succeed in school. He is self-motivated.
- Jackie has a job as a teacher and dreams about writing a book in her free time. Her husband likes her idea but criticizes her for not working on her project but just talking about it. Over time, she feels pressured by him and starts working on it. But Jackie doesn't really enjoy writing because her husband controls her work, 'Without me, you would never do it.' She is not self-motivated. If Jackie's husband would not have pressured, one day, Jackie, she would have started when she felt in the right mood and would enjoy writing as she was self-motivated.

There are many ways to motivate yourself on your job:

- Try to find a mentor to learn additional skills and make yourself feeling more useful.
- Attend career-related conferences, seminars, and courses that will remind you of why you chose your profession in the first place. This might help you increase your qualification, insight, knowledge, and will qualify you for other, more interesting tasks.
- Decide to become a mentor yourself. It can be particularly rewarding and fulfilling; for example, prepare young entrants to a career in a company or at preparatory or vocational schools by providing vocational training.
- Meet like-minded people in your company and outside for sharing experiences and information.
- Support colleagues or develop a new, self-initiated project and present it to your boss for review.

In any case, you should let your boss know that you still have free resources. In addition, you should ask for a review of your career development plan with the intention to discuss more mentally challenging fields of activity for you.

Tip: In this case you should not say: 'I feel so bored at work.' It would be better if you signal that there are still free capacities and that you would like to take on new tasks. In larger companies, there are always opportunities for changing departments or units.

If, at the end, you see no chance that your current role will ever provide you with the sense of purpose you'd like and if your discussion with your boss were unsuccessful, it may be time to make time for what you love outside of work and ask yourself if you're in the right role or even in the right company or industry. In this case, the same principles apply that were discussed for mitigating career unhappiness.

STAY OR LEAVE

> I believe I used up all my sick days, so I'm calling in dead.
>
> —Unknown

Whether you are experiencing a stressful environment, career unhappiness, organizational unhappiness or you are exposed to a disliked boss, toxic co-workers, excessive workloads and overtime, or whether you are underpaid or suffer from boredom at work, in the end, you will always ask yourself the same question: stay or leave.

Quitting a professional relationship can be like ending an emotional partnership, and it is just as difficult to find the right moment to take the decision to leave.

Example: When the last thing you hear from your boss is: 'I'm glad to see you go'—consider this remark as a victory.

If the end of a working relationship is foreseeable because it shows all the features of a creeping fatal illness and your unhappiness at work has begun to intoxicate your private life, then you should end the employment as soon as you can.

Tip: When the stress of your current job is making you unhappy, you don't enjoy your life anymore, your emotions are running high or low, and you are feeling depressed, then listen to these signals, because they are telling you that your job is not healthy for you anymore.

> Happiness is quitting the job you hate.
>
> —Unknown

However, not many people who are unhappy at work, change jobs easily. Although, in principle, they are ready to do it, they are scared of the consequences of leaving, in particular when they are the sole earning member of the family or are responsibility for other people.

Before you decide to leave, you would normally review all alternative options available to you. Obviously, the first option you will consider is staying on. If you decide to stay on your job, you must ask yourself the question how you want to cope with a workplace that makes you feel unhappy.

Tip: Objectively, you may be stuck, but, subjectively, it doesn't mean you *should* feel stuck. Just accept that this job is not where you want to be, even if you can't make a change today. But begin taking steps to change things in the longer term.

One option might be to upgrade your contribution to the company. This could be achieved by improving or adding to your skills through learning. This may help you do your current job more efficiently or get fit for new opportunities such as different, more interesting jobs elsewhere.

Example: Improving your skills through learning is already an essential part of the widely spread *continuous improvement* process. Under this process, all workers and employees are permanently asked to improve the quality of what they do. This involves continuous improvements in processes (quicker, easier, less monotonous, less expensive, more effective) and products (better quality).

As a positive side-effect, the learning process as such might possibly help lifting your spirits.

Another option may be to optimize your job in such a way that you can spend more time on activities which inspire and/or relax and make you feel happy. For instance, you could decide to do your regular work more efficiently and faster, be at the office strictly only within contractual working hours, unless overtime is absolutely necessary. Otherwise, you leave the office on the dot as soon as your shift ends.

Example: Yana, a young, talented, multilingual female government official sees herself as a victim of a strictly conservative hierarchy in her agency. The rigid corset of the government's promotion system and the traditional discrimination against women in promotions to senior positions, leads to Yana's demotivation. However, Yana's personal situation as a single mother doesn't allow her to risk her position for an uncertain alternative. Ultimately, Yana decides to stay on. She books self-improvement and other courses on the internet to improve her workplace efficiency. This enables her to do her regular work more efficiently and in less time which creates sufficient space for Yana to engage in a more interesting part-time job.

An interesting option for employees who are unhappy with their current job but cannot or do not want to leave is to look for an interesting part-time job.

Tip: Depending on the prevailing legal situation, your secondary activity needs to be discussed in advance, and possibly approved by your employer. Essential for your employer's approval will be that your additional activity does not bring you into a conflict of interest. This would be the case, for instance, if the secondary occupation would affect the business interests of your primary employer.

Examples: When you work every evening of the week in a club and you would regularly reach late to work and look sleepy at work, your employer will probably take exception to such a job. Or, if you are employed as a hairdresser and you work part time in another hairdresser's shop in the neighbourhood, your employer will very likely not tolerate that you are working for a competitor.

If your motivation for engaging in a part-time job is not only additional income but your interest in doing something more meaningful, then you should carefully consider whether the part-time job in question matches your talents and interests. For instance, it would be ideal, if you could turn your hobby into a second job. In this case, despite the additional stress, your happiness is guaranteed because this is something you enjoy doing and are passionate about.

Example: There is an increasing demand for images. Over the years, you have stored thousands of quality photos. You can start marketing your own digital photo files. Or, you like restoring old furniture. So, you can start the sale of old and/or reconditioned items at antique and flea markets. Or, you are living close to a busy business district. You provide an early morning delivery service for breakfast, food, drinks to office workers in your neighbourhood. Or, you buy second-hand luxury fashion items and accessories and resell them to interested customers via an online platform created solely for this purpose. Thanks to the internet, all products and services such as these are now just a click away. So, it has never been easier or cheaper to try out your own product or business idea.

> My boss told me to be more proactive; so, I started to work on my resume.
>
> —Unknown

If all your attempts to improve your professional situation have failed, if your boss does not respond satisfactorily to your discussions, if there is no room anymore for compromise, and if the company doesn't seem to be able or willing to create the conditions in the workplace that will make you happy again, then you have to face the realities and look for an alternative.

AFTERWORD

With this book we want to make it clear that you - no matter where you live and what your background may be - have the right to be happy, just like any other human being. But unlike rights enshrined in laws, personal happiness is not enforceable. There is neither a legal basis, nor an institution to which you can turn for 'happiness'.

Instead, you have to work for your happiness yourself. Happiness does not fall from the sky by itself, neither by wish nor by chance.

But happiness is not just a romantic dream. It is very real and achievable. And it is desirable because it puts us in a state of harmony that has a positive impact on our well-being and radiates to others around us. Therefore, we can rightly say, 'Being happy is cool'.

Don't listen to those who want to make 'happiness' a social obligation ('a must'), but see happiness as a result of your free choice.

With this book, we want to give you many ideas and a concept to help you exercise your free choice. With this in mind, we have chosen an approach that, as a first step, aims to create the inner freedom that will allow you, in a second step, not only to recognize the obstacles that stand in the way of your happiness, but also to remove them.

It is definitely 'cool' when you are able to take a step back from yourself, dispassionately analyse your own position in life and take an almost neutral look at your current situation, as if you were an independent third party and not yourself. The emotional distance you'll gain from yourself as a result of this process, will enable you to develop creative ideas that will help you overcome these obstacles. The ideas you'll produce may well be unconventional or 'out-of-the-box', but that is what your new-found autonomy through this 'cool' process allows you to do.

Much of what is said in this book will seem like what is understood as 'common sense'. Frankly, we would not be bothering you with our thoughts on 'common sense' issues if it were not for an unfortunate flaw associated with 'common sense': 'Common sense' is not always 'common practice'.

Therefore, it is our intention, to inspire and motivate you on your path to happiness to make 'common sense' your 'common practice'.

In a follow-up book entitled 'HAPPYxCOOL: Unlocking Happiness', we plan to cover in detail some additional important topics that influence happiness, such as the influence that expectations, projections, judgements, attitudes, shyness, shame, the infamous face-saving concept, the escape-from-misery method, blame-the-other concepts, loneliness, consumerism, cyber-socialisation and social media can have on your state of happiness.

* * *

Made in the USA
Monee, IL
08 October 2024

67319862R00178